NUMBER 70

W9-DIT-961

Yale French Studies

Images of Power Medieval History/ Discourse/Literature

Yale French Studies

Kevin Brownlee, Stephen G. Nichols, *Special editors for this issue*

Liliane Greene, *Managing editor*

Editorial board: Peter Brooks (Chairman), Alan Astro, Ellen Burt, Lauren Doyle-McCombs, Shoshana Felman, Richard Goodkin, Leonard Koos, Christopher Miller, Charles Porter, Allan Stoekl

Staff: Peggy McCracken

Editorial office: 315 William L. Harkness Hall.

Mailing address: 2504A Yale Station, New Haven, Connecticut 06520.

Sales and subscription office:
Yale University Press, 92A Yale Station
New Haven, Connecticut 06520

Published twice annually by Yale University Press.

Designed by James J. Johnson and set in Trump Medieval Roman by The Composing Room of Michigan, Inc. Printed in the United States of America by The Vail-Ballou Press, Binghamton, N.Y.

ISSN 0044-0078
ISBN for this issue 0-300-03653-1

EDITORS' PREFACE

L'objet de la lecture critique est à la fois texte et événement. Comme
texte, matériellement identifiable, comme événement il n'est point
donné, mais choisi.

—Paul Zumthor

"To recall the past is a political act: a *recherche* that involves us with
images of peculiar power, images that may constrain us to identify with
them. . . ." Walter Benjamin wrote these lines to remind modern readers
that the past is not a closed system of dead languages but a dialectical field
of forces whose artefacts can be actively engaged through theory, interpretation, transformation, parody, subversion, whatever. The Middle
Ages offer a particularly cogent venue for applying Benjamin's thesis, for,
as Paul Zumthor noted not long ago, "The Middle Ages are both near to us
and distant; foreign, yet familiar, self *and* other. They belong to *our* history, belong to *us* in a special way because biologically and culturally we are
descended from them in a direct line."

And yet, we need to liberate our conception of the Middle Ages from a
false sense of propinquity, from the feeling, all too common among philologists of an earlier generation, that we know the languages of this period
as systems with a predictable integrity. For five centuries, from roughly
A.D. 1000 to 1500, literary discourse in Western Europe participated in
what we are coming to view as a dynamic language movement. Freed from
the misconceptions that held that modern European languages are simply
avatars of Latin and the medieval vernaculars, we can now cease to treat
the latter as though they were simply contiguous, spatially and temporally, with our own languages.

We do not need to ask these old languages, as Bernard Cerquiglini
observed so appositely, to perform the doubly futile task of revealing to us
our own language and of furnishing us with the fleeting triumph of mastering the words of the other ("ni la plénitude fugitive de dominer les mots de
l'autre"). By privileging the alterity of Old French, by looking at it as a
"ruin" testifying to a dynamic dialectical field of forces, we can, in Cerquiglini's words, authentically "rechercher les phénomènes spécifiques de
l'ancienne langue et s'attacher à leur opacité; enfin, reconnaître dans cette
langue la marque d'une écriture" ["study specific phenomena of the old
language, paying particular attention to their opaqueness; in short, recognize in this language the sign of an *écriture*."]

1

We may do this by posing a number of questions regarding the nature of medieval discourse viewed not as a closed system or as teleology but, to quote Zumthor, "as a veiled and proteiform subject" given in texts situated at the nexus of a variety of cultural forms. We may call this cultural expression "history," if we understand the term as denoting conflictual and often contradictory social movements, ideals, and aspirations, all mediated by and through language. For some, *écriture* may define itself in terms of production and exchange of texts; while for others, it will rather take the form of a specular interplay of "books reading books," or the rewriting of texts within the process of textual production itself.

All those who seek to revalorize our understanding of medieval cultural expression need urgently to explore the "images of peculiar power" which engaged medieval discourse in a paradoxical enterprise. Often misconstrued as transparently logocentric, naive or simplistic, medieval language self-consciously promulgated its condition as écriture. Yet this involved a privileged status for the word, for discourse, that cannot be confused with mimetic referentiality.

Rather, a complex problematics of linguistic authority is at issue, related to a broader medieval problematics of ideological and social authority. History and literature as discourse are *always* being questioned in the Middle Ages; they are always *at stake*. Their status is not yet a given, especially in the vernacular, but is continually being called into question by the existence of authoritative models, both classical and scriptural. But at the same time, these authoritative pretexts *authorize* as well as contest their emergent epigones. Insufficient awareness of this crucial dialogic process has led medieval discourse to be perceived as insufficiently problematic by modern standards. We have, in short, been asking the wrong questions.

The purpose of this volume is to suggest new lines of inquiry. We must ask, first of all, as do a number of the articles in this issue, whether it is only in the category of the "mimetic" that one may discern the historical, political, and economic implications of the discourse modes developed between 1000 and 1500? For the mimetic that we now perceive as inadequate is very much a construct of modernist interpretation.

Or, to pursue another line of questioning adopted by some of the contributors, how did medieval discursive systems, even in their most rigid codifications, succeed as dynamic codes by virtue of exploiting their own gaps and inadequacies? The efforts to codify rhetoric (as in the *ars dicendi*) or to thematize expressive forms (as in Guillaume de Lorris's *Roman de la rose*) paradoxically enrich medieval texts by forcing a "poetics of silence," a poetics in which lacunae signify the inability of rhetoric to achieve its ends. For, as Dragonetti observes, "dans la langue des trouvères la 'trouvaille' (*troveure*) et le 'trou' (*troueure*) offraient une certaine ressemblance, et jusque dans la lettre" ["in the language of Old French poets ("trouvères"), there is quite literally a certain resemblance between fortuitous inspiration ("la trouvaille") and empty space ("le trou")].

And finally, can one indeed re ver the inscription of paradigmatic "hypertexts" or "*architextes*" that con...olled the form taken by discourse in given works, thus generating generic transformations? In this regard, Jauss's concept of the generic "horizon of expectations" provides an essential point of departure. For we see genre functioning as a changing locus of interaction between text and reader, between literary text and social context. This phenomenon also represents a dynamic process in the Bakhtinian sense of the term, for the *architextes* are not simply abstract concepts, but emerge from and indeed signify historical processes.

To ask such questions does not presuppose an intent to promulgate a uniform theory of medieval literature. It does, however, suggest that theory can resituate us in history, while avoiding the futile nostalgia for a universal model. The theoretical perspective may be as simple and uncompromising as Bahktin's dictum that "every situation is historical." But in revealing that history, too, is proteiform, theory allows us to avoid historicism by asking hard rather than "right" questions of historical situations. And hard questions begin with the presupposition that we revisit the past, as Eco points out, not in order to "negate the already said, but to rethink it ironically."

It was to engage in just such an ironical rethinking of significant aspects of medieval and Renaissance discourse as related to history, literature, and linguistics, that the scholars here represented gathered at Dartmouth College's Minary Conference Center on Squam Lake September 23–25, 1983. Initial versions of the papers provided the basis for intense discussions that ranged from specific debate on particular texts to broader questions of theory and history. The contributions of Renaissance and seventeenth-century specialists to the discussions helped us to sense the continuities as well as the ruptures linking the medieval and early modern periods.

The benefits of such collaborative efforts cannot be measured uniquely in terms of publications, but one may safely affirm that the papers included in this issue profited from the excellence of the discussions, and from the comments of colleagues who attended the conference as observer-participants. The Dartmouth Study Group in Medieval and Early Modern Romance Literatures provided both the model for the conference and collegial support. For material assistance allowing the conference to take place, we gratefully acknowledge the Ramon and Marguerite Guthrie Fund. Professor of French at Dartmouth from 1930 to 1963, poet, and intellectual mentor for generations of Dartmouth students, Ramon Guthrie himself encountered the Middle Ages at the conjunction of modern history and literature when, as a World War I veteran living in France, he studied Old French with Alfred Jeanroy in Paris and the troubadours with Joseph Anglade in Toulouse.

Kevin Brownlee
Stephen G. Nichols

Introduction

BRIAN STOCK

History, Literature, and Medieval Textuality

There exists at present, as there has not for some decades, the possibility of serious cooperation between the fields of history and literature. This happy state of affairs has been brought about by a number of complementary forces. Among intellectual historians, positivistic assumptions, where they are not under attack, appear to be dying a natural death. Accounting for what actually happened is now recognized to be only part of the story; the other part is the record of what individuals thought was happening, and the ways in which their feelings, perceptions, and narratives of events either influenced or were influenced by the realities they faced. Among critics and teachers of literature, one finds a renewed interest in literary history, not defined, as in the period before new criticism, as a mere summary of literary, historical, or biographical information, but, under the influence of linguistics, anthropology, and semiotics, as a recognition of parallel modes of interpretation. "The historical perspective," a recent commentator notes, "enables one to recognize the transience of any interpretation, which will always be succeeded by other interpretations, and to take as object of reflection the series of interpretive acts by which traditions are constituted and meaning produced."[1]

Some of the factors contributing to this renewed awareness of the historical dimension have arisen from within historical research, like the study of *mentalité* within *Annales*, or, although it has operated more diffusely, the tradition of hermeneutics and social thought which has descended through Dilthey, Max Weber, and the critical theory of the Frankfurt School. Other causes lie outside the field of history. In general, twentieth-century historiography has had to adapt itself from a cultural climate of self-confidence to one of self-questioning. No less than philosophic

---

1. Jonathan Culler, *The Pursuit of Signs: Semiotics, Literature, Deconstruction* (Ithaca: Cornell Univ. Press, 1981), 13.

idealism, the pure history of ideas belonged to a period of social and political consensus. Today's intellectual universe is pluralistic, and as a consequence historical relativism has once again become fashionable. Yet a considerable gap exists between what intellectual historians would like to be doing and what in fact they have been trained to do. To borrow Heidegger's terms, most are instructed how to deal with "documents" rather than with "works," that is, with repositories of information rather than with structured texts. Competent to handle the factual side of historical research, and, until recently, secure in their assumptions about historical objectivity, they have paid little attention to aspects of cultural analysis such as *langue* and *parole,* synchrony and diachrony, or *histoire* and *récit.* As Hans Kellner has remarked, at present, despite an interest in the oral and the written, "language studies seem to have no clear single place in historical methodology."[2]

Other factors contributing to the potential cooperation of history and literature have arisen from recent trends in literary criticism. An important principle of structuralism, continually reiterated by Barthes, is the separation of the author, and, as a byproduct, of the author's intentions, from the textual product of writing, which, as a result, is seen to have a set of depersonalized relations with other texts. All texts, including historical texts, are thereby placed on an equal footing. One of the stated tasks of semiotics is the description of the range of meaning derivable from literary works by critics and readers in which there is no distinction between the historical and literary appreciation of signs. Again, Jauss's notion of "horizons of expectation" implies a serious programme of literary history, as, in a different way, does the study of intertextuality, which, like *Rezeptionsästhetik,* denies the autonomy of the text and suggests that signification results from the imposition of prior knowledge upon present meaning. For Marxist criticism the issues of subject versus object and of historical determination remain primary concerns. Here the problem is seen as demonstrating the relationship between a literary work and some aspect, material or formal, of its social context. One can even see in Derrida's rejection of Foucault's strong emphasis on discontinuity a return to a type of sequentialist thinking, since, for deconstruction to work properly, one must assume that the act of signifying, which contains its own contradiction, operates over time. "Tout concept," he writes, criticizing Saussure, "est en droit et essentiellement inscrit dans une chaîne ou dans un système à l'intérieur duquel il renvoie à l'autre, aux autres concepts, par le jeu systématique de différences."[3]

2. "Triangular Anxieties: The Present State of European Intellectual History," in Dominick LaCapra and Steven L. Kaplan, eds., *Modern European Intellectual History: Reappraisals and New Perspectives* (Ithaca: Cornell Univ. Press, 1982), 114.

3. "La différance," in *Marges de la philosophie* (Paris: Minuit, 1972), 11.

The study of the Middle Ages has played, and should continue to play, an important role in this development. Medievalists have made among the most lasting contributions to the study of *mentalité:* one thinks of its inventors, Bloch and Febvre, as well as Paul Alphandéry, and, more recently, Jacques Le Goff, Emmanuel Le Roy Ladurie, Jean Delumeau, and, above all, Georges Duby. On the literary side, it is worth recalling that figures as influential as E. R. Curtius, Erich Auerbach, and Mikhail Bakhtin all spent a part of their careers in medieval research.

These are direct debts; in addition, there are indirect relationships, often undiscussed, between recent trends in intellectual history and revivals of interest in medieval culture. The contemporary rethinking of anthropology, literary criticism, and the history of ideas is in fact part of a more general rebirth of the field of language and culture, involving, in France, structuralism and poststructuralism, in England, the theoretical implications of Wittgenstein and Austin, and, in Germany, to the degree that they are linguistic, the issues raised by Gadamer and Habermas. The common ground of these diverse approaches is textuality: without this point of contact, for instance, the recent debate between Foucault and Derrida makes no sense. If one is allowed to give a historical dimension to the linguistic concerns raised by such movements and authors, then the natural starting point is the period in which Europe becomes a society of texts. This is the Middle Ages. To put the matter another way: if we are to increase our understanding of how, let us say, competence and performance work in contemporary society, we must return for at least a chapter of the story to the moment in time at which texts became recognizable forces in historical development. For the student of the Middle Ages there is a certain irony in all this. Paradoxically, if he wishes to understand medieval culture, to the degree that it is possible, on its own terms, he is obliged to adopt methods which are medieval in origin, but which have only been rediscovered by recent investigations in linguistics, philosophy, anthropology, and psychoanalysis, disciplines which are unconcerned with the medieval epoch and as a rule ahistorical in nature.

Understanding how a textually oriented society came into being presupposes a more basic chronology of the growth and development of medieval literacy.[4] In general terms one can pose the problem as follows. If we take as our point of departure the admittedly arbitrary date of the year A.D.

---

4. For a broader survey of these problems, see my study, *The Implications of Literacy: Written Language and Models of Interpretation in the Eleventh and Twelfth Centuries* (Princeton: Princeton Univ. Press, 1983), esp. ch. 1. A useful review of English evidence is M. C. Clanchy, *From Memory to Written Record: England, 1066–1307* (Cambridge, Mass.: Harvard Univ. Press, 1979). Important recent studies of the literary aspects of the question include F. H. Bäuml, "Varieties and Consequences of Medieval Literacy and Illiteracy," *Speculum* 55 (1980), 237–65; B. Cerquiglini, *La parole médiévale: Discours, syntaxe, texte* (Paris: Minuit, 1981), and P. Zumthor, *Introduction à la poésie orale* (Paris: Seuil, 1983).

1000, then it is arguable that there were both oral and written traditions operating simultaneously in European culture, sometimes working together, sometimes working in separate spheres of thought and action. However, from about the second half of the eleventh century, a widespread transformation began to take place. Oral traditions did not simply decline, although that happened to some degree as the force of the written word became progressively stronger. Instead, they realigned themselves so as to be able to function in relation to a reference system based upon texts. As a consequence, about this time, a new hermeneutic environment emerged in Western Europe. Its characteristic feature was that it was at once both oral *and* written. The performative functions remained verbal and individualistic, as they had always been. But they were increasingly bound to textual forms which implied shared values, assumptions, and modes of thought.

The texts, of course, were not always written down, but they were invariably understood as if they were. Meaning, therefore, gravitated towards reference as opposed to mere sense, and what had alone been expressed in gestures, rituals, and physical symbols now became embedded in a complex set of interpretive structures involving scripts, notations, grammars, and lexica. The spoken and the written were drawn into closer interdependence than they had been at any time since the end of the ancient world. The new relationship was not transitory: it was, to borrow Braudel's phrase, a change of long duration, not only announcing the birth of the European vernacular languages, but also giving rise to a group of problems in the area of language and culture which were to have a long afterlife. Among these were the question of popular versus learned tradition, the issue of allegory, with its dual interest in inner and outer meaning, and, via such thinkers as Abelard, the division of *langue* and *parole*, together with the conventional aspects of linguistic communication which Wittgenstein in his later work called forms of life. The birth of textuality also meant the invention of producers and consumers of culture, a transformation, so to speak, of the system of exchange and communication, and, via written transcription, the idea of an abstract reading public that thenceforward acted as a referential basis for the interpretation of works of literature and philosophy, and, through intertextuality, for the interpretation of experience.

Texts, textuality, and textual culture immediately raise the issue of power in society. If a new means of communication makes its appearance, who are its patrons? If new knowledge is produced, who controls it and for what ends?

The answer to these questions is not as simple as would first appear. In general, early students of the sociology of knowledge such as Karl Mannheim preferred a macrosociological approach, in which an attempt was made to match the content of ideological systems with the economic and social background of the participants. The weaknesses of this method have often enough been demonstrated, both by the intellectual left and the right, to need no further emphasis here. The successors to the early *Soziologie des Wissens* such as Lucien Goldmann's genetic structuralism inevitably abandoned the lofty ideal of describing sociological totalities and focused instead on the more manageable dimension of social groups whose actual productions and literary relations could be empirically studied. The advent of structuralism, it is arguable, both abetted and confused this development. On the positive side, structuralism emphatically desubjectivized textual experience, a necessary prerequisite for the comparison of internal elements in texts and between texts. But, by demoting authorship, structuralism also weakened the tentatively established connections between literature and society and took the entire discussion one step away from the living context of utterance, discourse, and action. The popularity of structuralism was perhaps to some degree an outlet for the frustration many intellectuals felt over the failure of a Marxist or Weberian sociology of knowledge. Its leading proponents seemed to say: if social relations cannot be revealed through texts, then we will study the properties of texts for their own sake. In Derrida, this philosophy has virtually closed the door on social analysis and restricted itself to scholastic exercises involving what are essentially alternative types of interpretation.

The rise and fall of the sociology of knowledge posed two problems for medievalists. The older approaches, those which in fact preceded Mannheim in Marx and succeeded him in Lukács, depended upon an oversimplified view of the Middle Ages in which the peasants, the bourgeoisie, and the aristocracy were portrayed as having watertight mentalities issuing in specific literary or artistic genres. But there was an even more basic problem. In pushing the doctrine of *Weltanschauungslehre* back into the Middle Ages, students often made the assumption that "medieval society" corresponded to what we more familiarly know as "industrial society" or "American society." It is arguable that this was stretching an ideal type a little too far. There were of course medieval groups, and they were bound by ethnic, linguistic, and protonational ties. But it is questionable whether we should describe this as a society in the normal, post-Kantian sense of the term, as opposed, let us say, to a group of societies, in which implicit and explicit boundaries crisscrossed and overlapped in numerous unmodern ways. And it follows that, if there was no macrosociety, a macrosociology of knowledge cannot be much use. Accordingly, we may also think of the early sociology of knowledge as having failed in two ways. An inadequate characterization of medieval society was introduced into the modern consciousness, where it still appears in textbooks and encyclopedias. Worse, medievalists attempted for some decades to apply a methodology which was inherently inappropriate for investigating the society they had set themselves to study. With a sense of relief, a younger generation turned away from such global constructions toward more specific disciplines such as folklore, anthropology, and hermeneutics.

The present can be described as a time of experimentation. There are a number of methodologies in the field, but no single one predominates. My own approach is to investigate the relationships between individuals in groups that are actually using texts for literary and social purposes, while at the same time paying close attention to the historical context of their actions and to the wider consequences. My point of departure is Weber's notion of subjectively meaningful social action, to which I have added the contemporary concern for not confusing intersubjectivity and intertextuality. The result is the analysis of what I call "textual communities," which are in fact types of microsocieties organized around the common understanding of a text. The *problématique* can be put as follows. The rise of a more literate society in the eleventh century automatically increased the number of authors, readers, and copiers of texts everywhere in Europe, and, as a consequence, the number of persons actively engaged in the study of texts for the ultimate purpose of changing the behavior of the individual or the group. This, *in nuce,* was the rationale behind much reformist and some orthodox religious agitation, to say nothing of communal associations and guilds. Such textual communities were not entirely composed of literates. The minimum requirement was just one literate, the *interpres,* who understood a set of texts and was able to pass his message on verbally to others. By a process of absorption and reflection, the behavioral norms of the group's other members were eventually altered. The manner in which the individuals behaved toward each other and the manner in which the group looked upon those it considered to be outsiders were derived from the attitudes formed during the period of initiation and education. The unlettered or semilettered members thereby conceptualized a link between textuality and rationality which they may not have understood fully or expressed in a literate fashion. Thus, while the basis of their action was textual, it was not always recognized as such, and, as if to disguise the fact, meaningful action still required a high degree of verbalization. Individuals belonging to such communities, in my view, existed in a sort of halfway house between literacy and nonliteracy. They are typical of literacy's double function throughout early modern history as well perhaps as in contemporary oral societies experiencing western education for the first time.

Let us look briefly at an example: the Waldensians. There are two different but complementary accounts of the role of literacy in the origin of the Waldensian sect, which arose in Lyons in the 1170s. The earlier and less reliable of them is the anonymous chronicle of Laon for the years 1173 to 1178.[5] The later is a chapter in the unfinished *De Septem Donis Spiritus Sanctus* of the Dominican inquisitor, Etienne de Bourbon, who died in Lyons in 1262.[6] Etienne's version has the advantage of reflecting personal interviews with two priests who acted respectively as copyist and translator for the sect's acknowledged founder, a rich moneylender named Valdès.

The story of Waldensian origins in the Laon chronicle is considered by most historians to consist of a little fact and a lot of fiction.[7] Briefly, it recounts how Valdès, inspired by a public recital of the life of St. Alexis, gave away his money and property, left his wife and two daughters, began to perform acts of public charity, and eventually adopted a life of rigorous poverty and itinerant preaching. Like Alexis he was converted at home: there, the chronicler states, he had invited the wandering singer in order to learn more about the legendary youth who achieved salvation after undergoing exile, penance, and self-abnegation. The following morning Valdès went to the local seminary, seeking, we are told, counsel for his soul and asking of the local master of biblical studies which way of approaching God was "most sure and perfect." He was told: "If you would be perfect, go and sell all that you have."[8] Etienne de Bourbon does not repeat this anecdote, but he is more emphatic on the role played by literacy in Valdès's spiritual awakening. Valdès, he relates, although not very literate himself, nonetheless desired a deeper understanding of the text of the gospels. He

---

5. MGH SS, vol. 6, 447–49.

6. *Anecdotes historiques, légendes et apologues tirés du recueil inédit d'Etienne de Bourbon, dominicain du XIIIe siècle*, ed. A. Lecoy de la Marche (Paris: Librairie Renouard, 1887), c. 342, 290–93.

7. The most skeptical recent account is K.-V. Selge, *Die ersten Waldenser I. Untersuchung und Darstellung* (Berlin: De Gruyter, 1967), 227–42. For a critical discussion of Selge's views, see M. Lambert, *Medieval Heresy. Popular Movements from Bogomil to Hus* (London: E. Arnold, 1976), Appendix C, 352–55, with which I concur.

8. *Chronicon Laudunensis, anno* 1173, 447, 34–40:

Is quadam die dominica cum declinasset ad turbam, quam ante ioculatorem viderat congregatam, ex verbis ipsius conpungtus fuit, et eum ad domum suam deducens, intente eum audire curavit. Fuit enim locus narracionis eius, qualiter beatus Alexis in domo patris sui beato fine quievit. Facto mane, civis memoratus ad scolas theologie consilium anime sue quesiturus properavit; et de multis modis eundi ad Deum edoctus, quesivit a magistro, que via aliis omnibus cercior esset atque perfeccior. Cui magister dominicam sentenciam proposuit: "Si vis esse perfectus, vade et vende omnia que abes," etc. [On a certain Sunday when he had gone down to the crowd gathered before the jongleur, he felt remorse at his words, and leading him away to his home, took care to hear him out attentively. For there was a passage of his, how blessed Alexis reposed in a blessed death in his father's home. When morning came, the said townsman hurried to the schools of theology to seek out the counsel of his soul; and when he had been instructed concerning the many ways of going to God, he asked the teacher which way was more certain and perfect than all the others. The teacher expounded the Lord's saying to him: "If you wish to be perfect, go and sell all that you have," etc.] Translated by John Gallucci.

made contact with two priests: the one, Stephen of Anse, translated passages of the Bible, while the other, Bernard Ydros, acted as his scribe. Valdès thereby acquired vernacular transcripts of many books of the Bible, together with the *auctoritates sanctorum.* These, Etienne adds, he studied in detail, making them the basis for asceticism and inner perfection.[9]

If read together, the two accounts tell us much about the precise role of literacy in the sect's formation and organization. There are in fact three stages in the making of the final textual community:

1. Purely oral contact, either, as the Laon chronicle suggests, with a jongleur, or, as Etienne de Bourbon states, when Valdès heard the gospel (*audiens evangelia*).

2. The *scola theologie:* in the Laon version, Valdès chiefly seeks advice for his soul (*consilium anime*); in Etienne, he orders systematic translations of the Bible in the vernacular (*in romano, in vulgari*).

3. Study of vernacular texts; commitment to memory; renunciation of worldly goods and activities; and preaching by Valdès or his delegates, usually in public.

Perhaps the most remarkable agreement between the two versions arises from the fact that neither Valdès nor his followers appear to be literate in the normal medieval sense of understanding Latin. The Laon chronicle makes mention of only oral-aural contact with both vernacular and Latin literacy. Valdès, it states, wanted to hear the jongleur (*audire curavit*); he was fascinated by the *locus narracionis;* and he begged advice from the local master, seeking, it would appear, not doctrine but a *via cercior atque perfeccior.* Etienne de Bourbon presents a more nuanced view, colored perhaps by his own interest in exegesis and preaching. In his version the key sentence is: (Valdès) *audiens evangelia, cum non esset multum litteratus, curiosus intelligere quid dicerent, fecit pactum cum dictis sacerdotibus, alteri ut transferret ei in vulgari, alteri ut scriberet que ille dictaret, quod fecerunt.* Valdès, in other words, knowing little

---

9. *Anecdotes historiques,* c. 342, 291: "Quidam dives rebus in dicta urbe, dictus Waldensis, audiens evangelia, cum non esset multum litteratus, curiosus intelligere quid dicerent, fecit pactum cum dictis sacerdotibus (i.e. Bernardus Ydrus et Stephanus de Ansa), alteri ut transferret ei in vulgari, alteri ut scriberet que ille dictaret, quod fecerunt; similiter multos libros Biblie et auctoritates sanctorum multas per titulos congretatas, quas sentencias appellabant, Que cum dictus civis sepe legeret et cordetenus firmaret, proposuit servare perfectionem evangelicam ut apostoli servaverant." [A certain wealthy man in the town, who was called Valdès, upon hearing the gospel, since he was not greatly skilled in (Latin) letters but was desirous to understand what the biblical texts said, made an agreement with the priests (i.e., Bernard Ydros and Stephen of Anse), according to which the one was to translate for him into the vernacular while the other was to copy what was said. They did this both for many books of the Bible and for many of the authoritative statements of the saints, which were collected according to title and called maxims. The townsman (i.e., Valdès) read and reread these often and make them as secure as he could in his mind, since it was his wish to adhere to evangelical perfection as had the apostles.] Editors' translation.

Latin, and yet wishing to penetrate the Scripture's inner meaning, ordered translations. The desire for interpretation, and, ultimately, for a new vernacular text, was not impeded by illiteracy but actually inspired by it. The interpretive function resulted not from comprehension but from a lack of it, not from continuity but from perceived discontinuity. Linguistic disjunction brought about the production of a new text, one which, Etienne notes, Valdès read, reread, and internalized (*Que cum dictus civis sepe legeret et cordetenus firmaret . . .*). He and his followers sold their worldly goods and devoted themselves to aiding the poor. But they also formed a type of textual community of which Etienne disapproved, since, in his words, Valdès *officium apostolorum usurpavit*. Of what precisely did this consist? Quite simply this: based upon the agreed meaning of gospel passages among the members of the group—which we may call the text, as opposed to the translation, transcription, or verbalization—the Waldensians, as they may now appropriately be called, took to propagating their own message. Etienne comments with evident distaste that they preached on the city streets and in the squares, Valdès attracting both men and women to his cause through his vivid recreation of the gospel message. He dared, the Dominican commentator adds, to send persons of the lowest station to preach in nearby villages: men and women alike, illiterate and uneducated (*idiote et illiterati*), they wandered about, entered homes, preaching in the open and even in churches, everywhere inducing others to do the same.[10]

"There was a Franciscan touch," Malcolm Lambert notes, "in his religious passion, throwing money in the street, rejecting the usurious business methods that had brought him wealth,"[11] etc. The observation is accurate and seems natural in historical perspective, but it also raises a set of subsidiary issues involving intertextuality. Valdès's actions were not isolated, nor was the text of the Laon chronicle autonomous. Both formed part of a network of expectations in the Lyons preacher's immediate audience and in the minds of subsequent followers, including those who later took only an intellectual interest in the events. This is not a question of sources, that is, of positive literary or historical exemplars, although these may well exist. Rather it concerns the relationship of Valdès's conversion both as an experience and as a reflective text to a body of unconscious attitudes and assumptions in his contemporaries' minds. It is both personal and impersonal: it involves Valdès's charismatic authority, for the movement begins with his living out a text of the New Testament, as well as his audience's reaction to an already contextualized set of previous thoughts and actions. These begin as early as the wandering preachers,

10. Ibid., 291–92.
11. *Medieval Heresy*, op. cit., 68.

such as Bernard of Tiron, Robert of Arbrissel, and Norbert of Xanten, take a different direction in the frustrated Gregorians of the next generation such as Henry of Lausanne and Arnold of Brescia, and are finally reenacted against the backdrop of reformed monasticism and the rise of Catharism. In other words, there is a whole series of previously enacted situations, some recorded, others unrecorded, all forming part of the collective memory and allowing Valdès's actions to be perceived as a meaningful pattern even by those who, like Etienne de Bourbon, oppose his ultimate goals. The pattern is both explicit, dramatized by his leaving his wealth and family, and implicit, involving an already established inner code through which outer behavior can be interpreted. Indeed, it is arguable that the universe of expectations that is normally associated with intertextuality was not only, and perhaps not chiefly, found in subsequent readers, who, through the history of heresy, were easily able to reenter the semantic space in which the original events took place, but instead in Valdès's contemporaries and immediate followers who, although employing largely oral means, participated in the original textual experience. In that primal moment of interaction the discourse acquired its historical dimension: for men and women not only presumed to understand the convert's actions but without consciously thinking about it modelled their own behavior on his.

The analysis of textual communities—whether these consist of religious sects, political groups, social movements, or relations between authors and audiences—requires a combination of literary and historical techniques. Both are cognitive activities. The historical is not isolated from the literary as fact and representation. The two aspects of the textual experience are multidimensional, and the objectivity of the alleged events spills over into the alleged subjectivity of the records, perceptions, feelings, and observations. The transcribed experience also feeds back into the lived experience: from the outset, it is impossible to separate Valdès's actions from the unconscious reflection of earlier lives, texts, and models. One cannot, therefore, like Derrida, wholly neglect the world outside the text, or reduce it to aspects of internality, since the recodification of behavior by someone consciously reliving an earlier text constitutes a new text, which, like the contextualized events of Valdès's life, appears as meaningful activity before it is transcribed and passed on in written form. Nor can one always assume, as both Foucault and Derrida appear to assume, that a text will reveal itself through exegesis[12] rather than through the transformation of a series of codified textual signs into rituals, symbolic behavior, and meaningful cultural activity. Although the mediated links

12. Cf. Edward W. Said, "The Problem of Textuality: Two Exemplary Positions," *Critical Inquiry* 4 (1977–78), 674–75.

between thought and action remain difficult to explain, they cannot be wished away or dealt with by a sort of textual gnosticism. Nor, finally, is the question of power merely one of exteriorities; we are not dealing with discourse only as an impersonal, authoritarian system, which effectively supersedes social relations. Individuality, intentionality, and human will also have a place in the spectrum of assigned causes. True, as Foucault argues, "relations of power are not in a position of exteriority with respect to other types of relations,"[13] such as economic processes and ideological forms. But neither are they inevitably exterior with respect to the individual who, like the early medieval saint,[14] or, in some cases, the later heterodox reformer, concretizes the latent discourse, gives it life, and, through a living example, power, thereby creating, if only briefly, a new universe of discursive space in which the older icons, temples, and forms of worship seem, to use Nietzsche's terms, to radiate life most brilliantly at the moment of their demise.

13. *Histoire de la sexualité 1. La Volonté de savoir* (Paris: Gallimard, 1976), 123.
14. See Peter Brown, "The Saint as Exemplar in Late Antiquity," *Representations* 2 (1983), 1–25.

I. Allegories of History

STEPHEN G. NICHOLS

Fission and Fusion: Mediations of Power In Medieval History and Literature

> History is the subject of a structure whose site is not homogeneous,
> empty time, but time filled with the presence of the now.
> —Walter Benjamin[1]

I. LANGUAGE, TIME, AND POWER

Between Epic and Romance

There is a space between the discourse of epic and that of romance, a gap
semantically marked by the ambiguously conjunctive sign, "and," used to
link the terms by historians and critics as diverse as W. P. Ker, Andreas
Heusler, Georg Lukács, and Mikhail Bakhtin. We have long held that epic
and romance predicate a tension between the real space and time of medieval culture which they choose *not* to represent and the concerns of philosophical anthropology which they *do* portray. The two genres, at the very
least, share an attitude whereby preoccupations essential to the culture
appear filtered through an idealized space and time that privileges the
"there and then" over the "here and now," or so it would seem.

In recent years, we have progressively recognized how literal and un-
satisfactory a reading of the texts this dichotomy provides. In particular, it
obscures the historical situation of medieval literature where discourse
constitutes a complex structure filled with what Benjamin calls "the presence of the now." And the "now" in epic and romance cannot be seen in
purely temporal terms, but as a combination of cultural time and space, as
works such as Marcia Colish's *The Mirror of Language* and Brian Stock's
The Implications of Literacy make clear.[2]

1. Walter Benjamin, *Illuminations*, ed. Hannah Arendt (London: Fontana/Collins,
1979).
2. Marcia Colish, *The Mirror of Language: A Study in Medieval Theory of Knowledge*,
revised edition (Lincoln: Univ. of Nebraska Press, 1983); Brian Stock, *The Implications of
Literacy: Written Language and Models of Interpretation in the Eleventh and Twelfth Centuries* (Princeton: Princeton Univ. Press, 1983).

We have come to see that the literary language of epic and romance constitutes a force field of cultural expression that mediates a variety of intellectual and political positions, often confused and contradictory, engaging a broad spectrum of a medieval European society in the grip of powerful forces of change and transition. At the heart of texts in either genre, we easily locate centrifugal elements that threaten to divide the fabric of the culture, opposed by centripetal movements that seek to revalorize and fuse the sense of wholeness, of unity in the sociopolitical enterprise. In the case of epic, however, the implications for the contemporary medieval context are masked by an insistent focus on another time, while romance grounds itself in another time *and* space.

There exists, however, a literature inscribed in the space *between* epic and romance, that acknowledges the presence of both genres, and yet which focuses squarely on the problematic space-time of its own present. I mean the rather curious texts that record the preaching of crusades as exemplified by Giraldus Cambrensis's *Itinerarium Kambriae*, (*The Journey Through Wales*), and Geoffroy de Villhardouin's *Conqueste de Constantinople.*[3]

"The Presence of the Now"

We tend not to think of the preaching of crusades as a canonical genre in medieval literature, perhaps not even as a genre at all. And yet, from Urban II's call to the first crusade, given at Clermont-Ferrand in 1095, the preaching of crusades might usefully be viewed as a form of cultural expression translated into the realm of practical power. If epics of religious conquest and expansion such as *The Song of Roland* or the William cycle provided a historical metanarrative of Christian triumph and hegemony in past times, crusade preaching translated the same metanarrative onto the contemporary historical scene.

In so doing, the prelates who preached crusades affirmed their belief in the ability of rhetoric to impinge upon actuality. By this shift, they radically altered the relationship of the Christian metanarrative of history to real time and space: what had been a metaphoric, and therefore idealized relationship of history to belief in the epics, became literalized and contingent in crusade preaching. Instead of recounting triumphs of the faith comfortably shrouded in a mythic past, crusade rhetoric set goals for the ability of the Christian metanarrative to alter the present and the future.

---

3. Gerald of Wales, *Itinerarium Kambriae. Giraldi Cambrensis Opera*, 6, ed. James F. Dimock (London: Rolls Series, 1868), *The Journey Through Wales and The Description of Wales*, trans. Lewis Thorpe (London: Penguin, 1984); Geoffroi de Villehardouin, *La Conqueste de Constantinople*, ed. Albert Pauphilet (Paris: Gallimard, Pléiade, 1952), 97–202. All references will be given in the text.

While this move clearly testifies to the vigor of twelfth-century Europe's logocentric aspirations, it also underscores the vulnerability of its postulates, since it is the crusade documents themselves that tell us how much at variance with historical reality that metanarrative was.

Precisely because they critique a historical present characterized by fissionary forces of linguistic and social heterogeneity, accounts of the preaching of crusades offer important contemporary testimony to the pragmatics of language as a mediator of the conflict between idealized cultural norms and perceptions of practical reality. Not only do such accounts constitute a fertile ground for studying the mediation of language and power, but they provide signal testimony, in this formative period of medieval literary history, to the consciousness of the conflicting forces of cultural expression that threatened to destroy the concept of a harmonious language model. The threat was real for a culture dependent on a language model that, like Christ or the king, had "its feet on earth and its head in heaven."[4] For the language model mediated the transcendent world order, on which, at least in theory, the medieval social order depended. And it did so hierarchically by predicating a multiplicity of *voces* at the terrestial level, dominated and harmonized by the One transcendant Voice, *Vox:*

> pax omnium rerum tranquillitas ordinis. Ordo est parium dispariumque rerum sua cuique loca tribuens dispositio.
>
> the peace of all things is the tranquillity of order—and order is the arrangement of things equal and unequal in the pattern which assigns to each its proper position. [St. Augustine, *De civitate Dei,* 19, 13][5]

Monotheism and Monophony

The concept of language order as a model of social structure implicated in the crusade accounts was originally proposed for the Christian community by St. Augustine in *De Civitate Dei*. Over forty years ago, in an interesting linking of the concept of world harmony and modern criticism, Leo Spitzer pointed out the role of monophonic language as a mediator between the ideals of harmony and social concord in *Classical and Christian Ideas of World Harmony.*

4. St. Augustine had coined a term for the geminate character of Christ which Ernst Kantorowicz applied to the concept of the medieval kingship: "pedes in terra, caput in caelo." The term equally well describes the linguistic model on which both concepts depend. Ernst H. Kantorowicz, *The King's Two Bodies: A Study in Medieval Political Theology* (Princeton: Princeton Univ. Press, 1957), 71–73.

5. Saint Augustine, *The City of God Against the Pagans,* ed. E. M. Sanford and W. M. Green (Cambridge: Harvard Univ. Press, 1965), vol. 5, Loeb Classical Library, 415; *The City of God Against the Pagans,* ed. W. C. Greene (Cambridge: Harvard Univ. Press, 1969), vol. 6, Loeb Classical Library, 416. References will be given in the text.

If we now read the definition of peace, in the form of a decalogue, as given by Augustine in *De civitate Dei*, 18, 13 (*sic*), we see that, starting from the order and peace within the body ("pax itaque corporis est ordinata *temperatura* partium"), he goes over to the order and peace in the soul (here called *consensio*), and from there to the peace and order between body and soul; then we proceed to the peace of men among each other (called *concordia*): peace in the house and in the state, as well as the *ordinatissima et concordissima* peace of the souls enjoying God in the *civitatis caelestis*. The whole table is summarized by the final statement "pax omnium rerum tranquillitas ordinis" ("the peace of all things is a tranquillity of order"). [71][6]

Now the accounts of crusade preaching, prefacing texts like Fulcher of Chartres's *History of the Expedition to Jerusalem, 1095–1127*, or Gerald of Wales's *The Journey Through Wales*, an account of the preaching of the Third Crusade in 1188, or Villehardouin's report of the preaching of the Fourth Crusade in 1199, clearly invoke the equation of power and monophonic language as a manifestation of participation in divine order. Geoffroi de Villehardouin tells us as much in the opening paragraphs of his *Conquête de Constantinople* in describing the efficacy of Foulques de Neuilly who preached the Fourth Crusade:

Et cil Folques dont je vos di comença à parler de Dieu par France et par les autres terres entor; et sachiez que Nostre Sires fist maints miracles por lui. Sachiez que la renomée de cel saint home ala tant qu'ele vint à l'apostole de Rome, Innocent; et l'apostoles envoia en France et manda au prodome que il preschast des croiz par s'autorité. . . .

And this Foulques de Neuilly of whom I speak began to preach about God in France and in other nearby lands; and you should know that Our Lord wrought many miracles for him. Know also that the fame of this holy man spread till it reached Pope Innocent in Rome; and the Pope sent [a message] to France ordering the good man to preach the crusade on the pope's own authority. . . . [*La Conquête de Constantinople*, 1, 97]

Such passages testify to the continued belief in the power of language to mediate disharmony by transforming the Babel-like discord of multiple language registers into the concord thought to arise from the monovocal model that was after all appropriate for *mono*-theism.[7]

---

6. The quotation represents only a part of Spitzer's notion, all of which bears on the problem discussed here. See Leo Spitzer, *Classical and Christian Ideas of World Harmony*, ed. Anna Ganville Hatcher, foreword, René Wellek (Baltimore: The Johns Hopkins Univ. Press, 1963), chapter 3. The quoted text erroneously cites *De civ. Dei*, "18, 13" as its source. Spitzer was referring to *De civ. Dei*, 19, 13.

7. On the equation by Augustine (and others) between mono-theism and the unitary model for artistic expression, see Spitzer, 29ff. For example, "The cithera of Augustine is a monochord, i.e., an instrument with one string—everything tends towards mono-theism" 30.

When Gerald of Wales, for example, talks about the disparate sociolinguistic registers manifest in the world around him, he does not deplore the variety of ideolects within the society, for the concept of diversity *per se* within the social order accords with the oxymoron, *concordia discors*, on which the unity of the religious state depended. As Augustine pointed out in 17, 14 of *De civitate Dei*, the chapter *De studio David in dispositione mysterioque psalmorum* [On Davids's mystical purpose in his arrangement of the psalms]: rational and proportionate symphony of diverse sounds conveys the unity of a well-ordered city knit together by harmonious variety. [*de Civ. Dei*, 17, xiv.][8]

Gerald's comments, in the Preface to the *Itinerarium Kambriae* on the variety of ideolects and pursuits accord with Augustine:

> Unde et quoniam dispares mores disparia studia sequuntur, armata militia tirones exultant, togata vero causarum patroni delectantur: alii cumulandis divitiis anxie suspirant, et summum bonum opulentiam putant; hi Galienum approbant, illi Justinianum applectuntur. . . .

> Conditioned as they are by their different social backgrounds, men will devote themselves to pursuits of the most varied kinds. Young soldiers delight in waging arms and waging war; lawyers take pleasure in putting on their gowns and and arguing cases; others strive anxiously to accumulate riches and see wealth as the supreme good. Some study Galen, others give all their time to Justinian. [Giraldus, *Itinerarium Kambriae*, "Praefatio Prima," 3–4; translation, Thorpe, 63]

What bothers Gerald in this diversity is a historical problem: the asymmetry between the variety of discourse in his own time and the absence of a superior harmonizing voice rising above the babel to impose the controlling metaphor of harmony. It is not a matter of merely finding people who write well, although that capacity constitutes a necessary foundation for translating logocentric ideals into the language of pragmatic affairs: "Men who really speak or write well, using languages in an elegant way, as for example, it is heard in many cases argued so eloquently in law in the vast body of our jurisprudence, stand out as worthy of the highest praise." [*Itin. Kam.*, "Praefatio Prima," 6; Thorpe, 66]

Like Augustine, Gerald conceives of the act of writing and reception as part of a continuum involving intellect and affect: affect to motivate the ego's involvement with the text-as-object, and intellect to mediate the rational faculties:

> Auctores siquidem elegantium verborum, non auditores tantum, repertores non recitores, dixerim laude dignissimos. Curiam autem, et Log-

---

8. Spitzer points out that, "in the *cum*-prefix Augustine sees more than the 'togetherness' of the manifold (as does Ambrose); he sees rather the convergence, the *Ubereinstimmung* in one proposed aim: *cum*- is to him, grammatically speaking, perfective (cf. the nuance of Latin *conficere=perficere*); *consonare, concinere* mean 'to arrive at harmony, unity'" 30.

icam, tam in alliciendo, quam in vix deserendo persimiles invenies. Dialecticae tamen notitiam, tanquam aliarum omnium tam scientiarum quam artium acumen, cum moderamine morae inculpatae, certum est esse perutilem: curiam vero, nisi blandis solum palponibus et ambitiosis, non necessarium.

For myself I would have said that those who can string sentences together in a pleasing way are much to be admired, not the listeners ('auditores') merely, not those who have occasion to repeat what is written by others ('recitores') but the actual writers ('repertores'). You will find that the language of royal courts and that of the schools have many points in common, designed as they both are first to attract your attention and then to hold it. There is no doubt at all that a skill in dialectics is of the greatest use, a shrewd assembling and appreciation, as it were, of all the other arts and sciences, but only when employed with the control and moderation that become perfect by practice. In itself courtly language is not all that necessary, except for suave syncophants and men of great ambition. [*Itin. Kam.* "Praefatio Prima," 6; Thorpe, 66]

But these practical observations on the mediation of writing and reception require vertical integration with the transcendent logocentric ideal. Diversity must be harmonized to achieve the "rational and proportionate symphony of diverse sound" that attests the perfective process connoted by the term, "*compactam*" of Augustine's proposition and that leads to the unity of social order ("compactam bene ordinatae civitatis insinuat unitatem").

That dimension can only be provided by the David figure, the paradigmatic *poeta,* in the sense Dante understood the term (see Brownlee.)[9] For it is the "poeta"—by which Gerald understands both "poet" and "historian"—who harmonizes the dialectical diversity of practical ideolects with the monologic language of divine purpose. Without this accord, language loses the power of mediation ascribed to it by Christian neo-Platonism.

Sed inter tot hominum species, ubi divini poetae; ubi nobiles morum assertores; ubi linguae Latinae moderatores? Quis hodie scriptis, sive poeticis seu historicis, literatam adornat eloquentiam? Quis, inquam, nostri temporis, vel mores astruit, vel inclite gesta perpetuis literarum vinculis aeternitati ascribit?

Among so many different sorts and conditions of men, where are the divine poets? Where are the worthy souls who preach morality? Where are the masters of the Latin tongue? Who nowadays in his writings,

9. Kevin Brownlee, "Why the Angels Speak Italian: Dante as Vernacular *Poeta* in *Paradiso* XXV," *Poetics Today* 5, 3 (1984), "Medieval and Renaissance Representations: New Reflections," 597–610.

whether they be poetry or history, can hope to add new luster to the art of letters? Who in our time, I ask, is building up a system of ethics, or, held firm forever in the works he writes, recording for eternity deeds which are nobly done? [*Itin. Kam.* "*Praefatio Prima*," 4; Thorpe, 64]

Medieval Polyphony and Dialogism

For Gerald, language mediates action at two levels: the practical and the ethical. But the two dimensions are not equal in importance and therefore in efficacy. Intentionality controls ultimate meaning, but intentionality, as Augustine tirelessly reiterates, is hierarchical. Intelligence alone cannot determine transcendent purpose, as Gerald caustically observes: "We can wonder at the logicians, who, when they have made some small progress, are so delighted with their studies that we watch them pass their later years in the mazy labyrinths of dialectics with as much joy as if they were bearing down upon the rocks where once the old Sirens sang." [*Itin. Kam.*, "Praefatio Prima," 4; Thorpe, 64]

If we consider the growing sophistication of polyphony in this period, we can better understand one of the controlling metaphors of literature authorizing its attempted mediation in the sociopolitical arena. We may also better perceive the dialectical relationship between authorial and textual intentionality. Only then can we effectively employ the methodology that Bakhtin's concepts of heteroglossia (polyphony) and chronotope, monologism and dialogism, have made available to us.

When Augustine spoke of music as a metaphor for politics, he undoubtedly referred to a monophonic model, as Spitzer noted. This paradigm fit the case so long as the emphasis fell upon monotheism as the state religion: one leader and one political entity under one God, a concept readily transferable to the Christian Roman Empire. As Peter Brown observes:

> The catholicism of Augustine . . . reflects the attitude of a group confident of its powers to absorb the world without losing its identity. This identity existed independently of the quality of the human agents of the Church: it rested on 'objective' promises of God, working out magnificently in history, and on the 'objective' efficacy of its sacraments. This Church was hungry for souls: let it eat, indiscriminately if needs be. *It is a group no longer committed to defend itself against society; but rather, poised, ready to fulfil what it considered its historic mission, to dominate, to absorb, to lead a whole Empire. 'Ask me and I shall give the uttermost parts of the earth as Thy possession.'* (Ps. 2, 7–8).[10]

10. Peter Brown, *Augustine of Hippo: A Biography* (Berkeley: Univ. of California Press, 1969), 214.

Augustine's equation of the Logos and the empire permeates Roman-esque aesthetics, as I have shown elsewhere.[11] Indeed, Rodolphus Glaber inscribes it programatically in his *Historiae* early in the eleventh century. But even though Glaber affirms that he has devoted his account

> ad illud totius quondam orbis imperium principale, scilicet Romanum

> to that Roman empire which was formally that of the entire world,[12]

we see an important difference between him and Augustine. It is not so much Rodolphus's awareness that the real power and territory of the Roman Empire has diminished. Nor is it the preoccupation Rodolphus exhibits with the continual incursions made by non-Christians against Christian lands, on the one hand, and the rise of heresy within the Christian community, on the other that distinguishes the evolution of his monophonic vision from Augustine's. It is rather his emphasis, especially in Book 3, on the pluralism of power in the Christian community.

What seems to haunt Rodolphus is the image of discord among the diverse and rightful rulers of Christendom. The vulnerability of a sociopolitical fabric invested in the persons of kings of more or less equal power and rank informs the language and structure of his work to the point where even the title, *Historiae,* must be stated in the plural. Interestingly, the implicit image advanced to counter the vulnerability of pluralism derives from that of the David figure, the king as a kind of political *poeta* capable of a political pragmatics of harmony.

Rodolphus emblematizes his concept of harmony in diversity in an account of a "summit meeting," held in August 1023, between Robert the Pious of France and emperor Henry II of Germany in which each king in different ways acts out a single saying from Scripture. The two monarchs travelled to the Meuse River, then the frontier between their territories. The followers on either side urged that king and emperor meet in boats in the middle of the river so that neither would be in the position of lowering himself to cross to the land of the other:

> pluresque ex ambabus partibus mussitarent indecens esse, ut quis illorum, tantorum scilicet regum, semet humilians, quasi in alterius transiret auxilium, hoc etiam fore potissimum, ut in fluminis medio navibus portarentur simul locuturi;

> . . . and many [of the courtiers] on both sides murmured that it ill suited two such powerful princes that one of them should lower himself to cross

11. Stephen G. Nichols, "Romanesque Imitation or Imitating the Romans," *Mimesis: From Mirror to Method, Augustine to Descartes,* ed. John D. Lyons and Stephen G. Nichols (Hanover: Univ. Press of New England, 1982); *Romanesque Signs: Early Medieval Narrative and Iconography* (New Haven: Yale Univ. Press, 1983).

12. Rodolphus Glaber, *Historiarum Sui Temporis Libri Quinque.* J.-P. Migne, *Patrologia Latina* (Paris: Migne, 1853), vol. 142, 616 B.

the river to put himself at the disposal of the other, and that the best thing would be for both to be carried to the middle of the river in boats for the meeting.[13]

The account thus creates a classic confrontation between *superbia* and *humilitas, superbia* being the linguistic marker for terrestrial power, the power of the Caesars. Rodolphus illustrates its importance for the follower class of courtiers by making it *their* reflexive response to the situation. The monarchs, however, figure in his *Historiae* as the David figures, exemplars of a transcendent harmonizing discourse intended to integrate vertically the disparate secular events in a narrative of transfiguration whereby contemporary history will reveal divine intentionality.

Stressing the wisdom of the monarchs, Rodolphus portrays them as independently guided by a single inspiration: a verse from Ecclesiasticus 3, 20: "Quanto magnus es, humilia te in omnibus" ["However great you are, humble yourself in all things."] The emperor, as the greater of the two lords, first crosses the river to meet with King Robert who reciprocates by the same action in the opposite direction the next day. They banquet at a common table, and then Robert offers Henry sumputous gifts of gold, silver, precious stones, and more than a hundred magnificently equipped horses along with suits of armor and chain mail. Henry, however, accepts only a gospel book encrusted with jewels and a reliquary containing a tooth of Saint Vincent.

Ecclesiasticus, the book of the Church (not adopted by the Synagogue), is not a chance reference in this context, for it explicitly gives as its project the mediation of scriptural wisdom and worldly power: "Many and wonderful are the gifts we have been granted by means of the Law and the Prophets. . . . But it is not enough merely for those who read the scriptures to be learned in them; students should also be able to be of use to people outside by what they say and write." [*In Ecclesiasticum Iesu Filii Sirach Prologus,* 1–6].

In Rodolphus's account, the dictum provides the harmonizing Word that vertically integrates the gestural language of the two kings in a paradigmatic demonstration of princely power based on the *humilitas* of understanding. The discordant notes of *superbia* sounded by the courtiers are less harmonized by this paradigm, than silenced. Rodolphus certainly evokes the elements for a polyphonic narrative, but strives to maintain the monophonic model of Augustine and Boethius by a hierarchical imposition of monody: the true Word of wisdom effacing the lesser language of worldly power.

He achieves his goal by writing history out of the project. Rodolphus's

13. Ibid., 3, 2; *MPL,* 142, 649 A.

anecdote remains just that: a moment of time frozen out of the flux of contemporary politics. Rodolphus ventures up to but not beyond the immediate past-present. A century and a half later, Gerald of Wales will abandon Rodolphus's caution to push the frontiers of narrative space-time into the realm of the present and the future-present by writing about a referential reality still in flux. Gerald, quite simply, set out to play the David figure by attempting to harmonize the discordant themes of contemporary history in terms of medieval polyphony. In so doing, he gave us an early (and almost certainly unintentional) example of the dialogic consciousness.

II. GERALD OF WALES: EPIC PAST, ROMANCE PRESENT, CRUSADE FUTURE

The Strong Voice of History

Gerald's account of the preaching of the Third Crusade in Wales illustrates brilliantly a thesis of Bakhtin's to the effect that critical history confronts and makes manifest the conflictual contexts of historical discourse.[14] Gerald begins his account with a dramatic—and complex—evocation of space and time: at the beginning of Lent, 1188, Baldwin, the Archbishop of Canterbury, crossed the border from England into Wales with a large retinue of English and Welsh prelates that included Gerald himself. The purpose of the journey was to preach the Crusade in Wales:

> Baldwinus, in salutiferae crucis obsequium ab Anglia in Walliam tendens, apud Herifordiae fines Kambriam intravit.

> Baldwin, in the service of the Cross, from whence cometh our salvation, marching from England into Wales, entered Kambria [across] the borders at Herefordshire. [*Itin. Kam.*, 1, 1, 13; Thorpe, 74]

Although Archbishop Baldwin figures prominently at the head of the work and the journey, Gerald himself firmly establishes his own rhetorical authority over the work as a strong first-person actor and speaker. Within two paragraphs of the opening, Gerald upstages the Archbishop by thrusting himself bodily into our field of vision:

---

14. "The strategy Bakhtin proposes to break with [monologic] tradition is to focus on and emphasize the dialogic characteristics of all language: that is, the traces of the historical dialogue of conflicting languages at the basis of any language system. His goal is to desacralize the dead, alien word and all other words, to undermine the integrity and self-sufficiency of formal, linguistic-semiotic systems by historicizing them from 'within' and thus bringing life to them." David Carroll, "The Alterity of Discourse: Form, History, and the Question of the Political in M. M. Bakhtin," *Diacritics*, Summer 1983, 70.

In Radnor Baldwin was met by Rhys ap Gruffydd, Prince of South Wales, and by other nobles from those parts. The Archbishop delivered a public sermon on the taking of the Cross, and this was explained to the Welsh by an interpreter. I myself, who have written these words, was the first to stand up. I threw myself at the holy man's feet and devoutly took the sign of the Cross. It was the urgent admonition given sometime before by the King which inspired me to give this example to others. . . . I acted of my own free will, after anxiously talking the matter over time and time again, in view of the insult being done at this moment to the Cross of Christ. In so doing I gave strong encouragement to the others and added an incentive to what they had just been told. [*Itin. Kam.*, 1, 1, 13–14; Thorpe, 75]

Gerald weaves himself into the interior and exterior of the text here, figuring himself as grammatical and rhetorical subject, author and actor, exemplum and gloss. The stamp of a strong subjectivity could hardly be more pronounced, nor could one expect to find a less subtle example of monophonic discourse. And yet, the passage is only partially typical, indeed almost atypical of Gerald's relationship to his text.

Much of the text uses a third-person self-representation of Gerald at moments when he appears as master trope, the David figure, an embodiment of the rhetoric and wisdom linking the Christian metanarrative to history. The division into a subjective and objective persona multiplies the voices and speaking modes Gerald can assume within the work; they run the gamut from minor anecdote to his manipulation of the form of *Itinerarium* itself.[15]

The objective self-presentation of Gerald's David persona extends to the very form and language of the work. We see this as soon as we ask why Gerald chooses to cast the account of the crusade preaching as a pil-

15. The third-person self-presentation lends portentousness to otherwise seemingly insignificant anecdotes. In the following example, the third-person persona permits Gerald to put himself forward as an authority on patristics: a seer in terms of his ability to interpret visions; and, like a prophet, a voice for whom history came true: "About the same time a certain priest called Hugh, who served the chapel of Saint Nicholas in Brecon Castle, dreamed that he saw a venerable old man standing beside him. "Take this message," said the venerable old man, "to your master William de Broase, who has had the effrontery to keep for his own use the property granted long ago to the chapel of Saint Nicholas for charitable purposes. 'What is not surrendered to Christ is removed by taxation. What you refuse to a priest you will hand over to a godless soldier'." This happened once, twice and a third time. In the end the chaplain travelled to Llanddew to see the local Archdeacon, who was none other than the author of this book. He described the vision to the Archdeacon and repeated the message. . . . The Archdeacon immediately recognized it as a quotation from Saint Augustine. He showed the chaplain where it was to be found in his writings and explained what it meant. Saint Augustine was criticizing those who refused to pay tithes and rents and other church dues. What he threatened in this passage certainly happened very soon to the person in question." [*It. Kam.* 1, 2, 21; (Thorpe, 81–82).]

grimage, an *Itinerarium*. By the late twelfth century, the *Itinerarium* stood for a literary form with almost a millenial association with the Holy Land, from the fourth-century *Itinerarium Egeriae* to eleventh-century accounts of Charlemagne's putative pilgrimages to Palestine.[16] In every sense, the *Itinerarium*, in a context where the Holy Land is an issue, represents a pretext for crusade as a declaration of prior Christian rights in Palestine.

Gerald's title, *Itinerarium Kambriae*, thus projects an ideology onto the form of the work and the space-time in which it takes place. From the outset, Wales shares with Palestine an aura of sacred time and space, although the reasons do not become fully apparent until later.

Monologic Authority, Dialogic Context

The pilgrimage form casts the author, usually, as a primary observer and interpreter of the sacred space-time through which the travelers pass. We have already seen that Gerald deploys both his objective and subjective persona in the first chapter; he does the same for the work itself when he literalizes the narrative form by making the beginning of the account the actual beginning of the journey. Simultaneously, he situates Wales itself both subjectively and objectively within the narrative and outside of it by evoking an extradiegetic historical context that provides a universal panorama of the sacred and political hierarchy of the known world: "In the year of the Incarnation of the Lord 1188, Urban III was Pope, Frederick King of the Germans and Holy Roman Emperor, and Isaac Emperor of Constantinople. Philippe, son of Louis, was then reigning in France, Henry II in England, William in Sicily, Béla in Hungary and Guy in Palestine." [*Itin. Kam.* 1, 1, 13; Thorpe, 74]

Another extradiegetic element introduces the image of conflictual simultaneity, or discord, in human time that threatens this picture of an ordered universe:

> anno scilicet quo Saladinus, tam Egyptiorum quam Damascenorum princeps, occulto Dei judicio sed numquam injusto, publico belli certamine victoria potitus, Ierosolimorum regnum obtinuit. . . .

> In this very same year God in his judgement which is never unjust but sometimes difficult to understand, permitted Saladin, the leader of the Egyptians and of the men of Damascus, to win a victory in pitched battle and so seize the kingdom of Jerusalem. [*Itin. Kam.*, 1, 1, 13; Thorpe, 74]

The invasion of the Kingdom of Jerusalem provides the diegetic rationale for Gerald's account; it also transforms the nature of the introduc-

16. For a discussion of the *Itinerarium*, the Holy Land, and the epic, see Stephen G. Nichols, "The Interaction of Life and Literature in the *Peregrinationes ad Loca Sancta* and the *Chanson de Geste*," *Speculum* 44 (1969), 23–33, and "From Passion to Pietà: Modes of Death in the Legend of Roland," *Aspects of Literary Scholarship*, ed. Joseph Strelka (Bern: Peter Lang, 1984), 1041–73.

tory paragraph from a seemingly factual historical *mise au point* to something much less innocuous. Ideologically, Gerald's evocation of the universal political panorama, inscribed in a sacred time-frame of Salvation History ("occulto Dei judicio," "in salutiferae crucis obsequium") makes an equation between political normativity and language normativity: his Latin prose obeys the same rules as the ideal political order necessary for world harmony.

Note, however, that the disruption of this harmonious picture arises from the speaker of an alien word: Saladin, a Saracen, who defeats the forces of the Latin world and seizes the *Latin* kingdom of Jerusalem. Saladin does not represent a sacred alien word, e.g., Greek or Hebrew, but a cognitively dissonant language seeking to control the physical and ideological space in the Holy Land that gave meaning to the authoritative sacred languages of Judeo-Christianity.

This invasion of the space of Latin politicolinguistic authority creates a negative space of dissonance in the picture just painted above, since one of the kings, Guy of Palestine, has been suppressed. In fact, the information about Saladin shows that the preceding panorama of western rulers is a normative picture of a monologic world, the way it would be if there were no solecisms, no rule violations.[17]

To displace Saladin utlimately requires warfare, but first the monologic authority, the universal normativity of *Latin* Christendom must be reaffirmed. Crusade preaching is not just a device for recruiting armed forces, then, but a socioreligious act reasserting the power of monologic discourse. It is shamanistic in part, and so represented by Gerald and by Geoffroi de Villehardouin.

In chapters 18 and 19 of his autobiography, *De rebus a se gestis*,[18]

---

17. "In Bakhtin's work, monologic discourse . . . is an extension of authority. The philologist, the philosopher, and the priest serve one and the same function; their power comes from their self-proclaimed proximity to the 'truth of the word'":

> The first philologists and first linguists were always and everywhere priests. History knows no nation whose sacred writings or oral tradition were not to some degree in a language foreign and incomprehensible to the profane. To decipher the mysteries of sacred words was the task meant to be carried out by the priest-philologists. It was on these grounds that the ancient philosophy of language was engendered: the Vedic teaching about the word, the Logos of the ancient Greek thinkers, and the biblical philosophy of the word. . . . The Vedic priest and the contemporary philologist-linguist are spellbound and held captive in their thinking by one and the same phenomenon—the phenomenon of the alien, foreign-language word. [Mikhail Bakhtin, *Marxism and the Philosophy of Language* (New York: Seminar Press, 1973), 74.]

Quoted by Carroll, op. cit., 69–70.

18. Gerald of Wales, *De rebus a se gestis*, ed. J. S. Brewer (London: Rolls Series, 1981), vol. 1. *The Autobiography of Giraldus Cambrensis* (*De rebus a se gestis*), ed. and trans. H. E. Butler (London: Jonathan Cape, 1937). References are given in the text.

Gerald gives several examples of the mystical powers of Saint Bernard's preaching of the second crusade in Germany and his own preaching in Wales. Moreover, the power of the word is in direct proportion to its proximity to the sacred, alien word, Latin and its romance derivative, French, when articulated by a spellbinding priest figure. Translations, into the non-Latinate vernaculars of Welsh and German, simply do not have the same effect, and we might also note that the role of the translator is deprecated. The charismatic oratory of a Bernard or a Gerald simply cannot be mediated.

Let's listen as Gerald expounds this point:

> Praeterea pro re miranda multi ducebant et obstupebant, cum archidiaconus *lingua tantum Gallica loqueretur et Latina, quod non minus vulgares qui neutram linguam noverant,* quam caeteri ad verbum ipsius flebant innumeri, et ad crucis signaculum plures quam ducenti concurrebant. Simile contigit in Alemannia de beato Bernardo; *qui verbum Domini Teutonicis faciens lingua Gallica, quam penitus ignorabant,* tantam eis devotionem incussit et compunctionem, ut et ab oculis eorum lacrimarum affluentiam, et ad cuncta quae suadebat vel facienda vel credenda facillime cordium eorum duritiam emolliret; *cum tamen ad interpretis sermonem eis lingua sua fideliter exponentis nihil omnino moti fuissent.* . . . Unde et finito sermone, cum archidiaconus, qui stando locutus fuerat, se in sessione reciperet, vir quidam hospitalaris qui prope consederat, dixit ei verbum istud: "Vere Spiritus Sanctus hodie manifeste locutus est ore vestro."

> Moreover, many were amazed that, though the archdeacon spoke only in *French and Latin, the common people who knew neither tongue* wept in untold numbers no less than the rest and more than two hundred ran all together to receive the sign of the Cross. The like also befell in Germany in the case of the blessed Bernard who, *speaking to the Germans in the French tongue of which they were totally ignorant,* filled them with such devotion and compunction, that he called forth floods of tears from their eyes and with the greatest ease softened the hardness of their hearts so they did and believed all that he told them; *and yet when an interpreter faithfully set forth to them in their own tongue everything that he said, they were not at all moved thereat.* . . . Wherefore at the sermon's close, when the Archdeacon [i.e. Gerald] sat down again, a certain Hospitaller who sat near him said to him, 'In truth, the Holy Spirit has manifestly spoken by your mouth this day.' [*De rebus,* 2, 18, 76; Butler, 101]

Let us note also, the care with which Gerald reports the identification of the *Welsh* people with the *authentic* presentation of the Latin word. The Archbishop of Canterbury, who preaches regularly makes only one notable convert, Gerald himself at the beginning of the *Itinerarium,* and then Gerald tells us that he did so "at the urgent admonition of the King" to set an example to others. Elsewhere, Gerald specifically points up the Archbishop's failure to move the Welsh, most of the latter's converts coming from the English occupation forces. An urgent political agenda cleverly worked into the fabric of the *Itinerarium* motivates this failure of the Archbishop's as we shall see shortly.

The Epic Model

First, however, let's look again at the opening paragraphs. The incursion of a strong Saracen leader into Christian territory and more specifically the seizing of Christian religious monuments by Saracens constitutes a topos for the exordium of the literary genre consecrated to the Church militant, that is, the *Historia* and its vernacular counterpart, the *chanson de geste*. Think of the beginning of the *Historia Karoli Magni et Rotolandi*, or of the *Chanson de Guillaume;* the beginning of the main part of the *Couronnement Louis;* or the implicaions of the *Chanson de Roland*. By 1188, we even are in the period of the first reworkings of the *chanson de croisade*.

There can be little doubt that the narrative model for important aspects of Gerald's introduction to the *Itinerarium Kambriae* comes from the epic tradition. The literature of the Church militant coincided with the rise of heresy in the eleventh century in Europe, and religiopolitical expansion of the Latin West in the Near East. It provided a model by which monologic discourse or logocentric rhetoric could be transformed into an assertion of political power justified by sacred authority. In the *historiae* and *chansons de geste* this authority always postulated an opposition between Christian sacred Word and alien word as the pretext for a reconquest of space usurped by the illegitimate Other. In this equation, the anteriority of Christian "rights" to the usurped space formed an important element of justification for the Church militant.

So, for example, we find the "historical anecdote" according to which Harun al-Rashid, Saracen calif, sent the keys to the Holy Sepulcre in Jerusalem to Charlemagne in 800 along with a promise to place himself under Charlemagne's protection. Both the *Historia Karoli Magni et Rhotolandi* and the *Chanson de Roland* portray Charlemagne's Spanish campaign as a reconquest of Spain from the Saracen usurpers. A more subtle form of the same theme occurs in *Li coronemenz Loois* where the Saracen king, Galafre, shows his ignorance of the difference between the Old Law and the New (but not his ignorance of the *Aeneid!*) by claiming Rome as his rightful heritage on the grounds that his ancestors, Romulus and Julius Caesar, built "the walls, the bridges, and the defenses" of pagan Rome.

> Respont li reis: "Tu n'iés mie bien sages; Ci sui venuz en mon dreit eritage, Que estora mes ancestre et mes aves Et Romulus et Julius Cesaires, Qui fist ces murs et cez ponz et cez barres. Se je par force puis ces

pilers abatre, Quant qu'a Deu monte tornerai a damage, Les clers quil servent a duel et a hontage."[19]

Gerald's use of the epic model reminds us that justification of sacred warfare necessarily played a greater role in epic than narrative description of combat. While the epic portrayed fighting, far more space was devoted to discourse, much of it in the form of affirming the authoritative Word either by priest figures such as Archbishop Turpin, or by warrior-priest personae such as Roland, Guillaume, Vivien, and others. These same warrior-priests also functioned as real or potential martyr figures as part of their transformation from secular soldier to sacralized *miles Christi*.

In this light, it is significant that the very first reported discourse Gerald cites in the opening chapter of the *Itinerarium* actualizes the warrior-martyr motivation within the context of the crusade preaching campaign.

> In ipso vero discessu Resi, cum super his quae audierat suos conveniret, juvenis quidam egregius de familia ipsius, cui nomen Griffinus, qui et postea crucem suscepit, respondisse memoratur; "Quis," inquam, "animi virilis peregrinationis hujus iter abhorreat, cum inter universa quae excogitari poterunt ejus incommoda, nihil incommodius cuiquam, nihil deterius accidere possit quam redire?"

> Only a short time before the day which he had chosen for his departure, as (Prince) Rhys stood chatting with his men about the sermon which he had heard, a young man called Gruffydd, a distinguished member of his own family who afterwards took the Cross himself, is reported to have said to him: "What man of spirit can hesitate for a moment to undertake this journey when, among the many hazards involved, none could be more unfortunate, none could cause greater distress, *than the prospect of coming back alive?*" [*Itin. Kam.*, 1, 1, 15; Thorpe, 76]

But we don't have to conjecture that Gerald conceived his account of the crusade preaching pilgrimage to Wales as a prologue to an eventual *historia* of the crusade. In the *De rebus a se gestis*, Gerald reports that as the Archbishop and his retinue were crossing the borders from Wales into England on their return, the talk turned inevitably to the coming pilgrimage to Jerusalem.

> then some of his clerks . . . asked him who could worthily cope with the glorious story of the recovery by our princes of the land of Palestine, and the defeat of Saladin and the Saracens at their hands. And the Archbishop replied that he had made good provision for that and had one ready who could handle the story exceedingly well. And when they pressed him further and asked who it was, he turned to Giraldus who was riding at his

---

19. *Li Coronemenz Loois. Chanson de Geste du xiie siècle,* ed. Ernest Langlois (Paris: 2nd ed., revised, Champion, 1925), vv. 462–69.

side, saying, 'This is he who shall tell of it *in prose*, [qui prosaice trac-
tabit], while my nephew Joseph shall record it in verse; I will attach him
to the Archdeacon that he may serve him and be ever by his side.' [*de
rebus*, 2, 20, 79; Butler, 104]

The equation between monologic normativity and political power
could hardly be more strikingly stated. The success of the preaching campaign stands as a guarantor of the success of the military crusade. At least
for these twelfth-century prelates, immured in their logocentric postulates, the strategy that counts is not military but discursive. They are their
own best converts to the authoritative rhetoric they preach. And the anecdote certainly testifies to the mediating power accorded the genres of epic
and *historia*.

The Romance Model

Ironically, this is one epic that will never be written, and certainly not by
Gerald who was obliged for political reasons to abandon the Crusade and
return to England.[20] While not wishing to dismiss the historical explanation for Gerald's dissociation from the Crusade, I would like to suggest that
within the text of the *Itinerarium* itself, we may discern a powerful discordance vis-à-vis the epic pretext. This dissonance resolves itself into a
countertheme of political and religious fission underlying the dominant
motif of logocentric harmony.

Woven into the account of the crusade preaching, and as though called
up by it, Gerald introduces a political agenda predicated not on epic and the
historia of the Church Militant, but upon romance and another kind of
historia, the *Historia Regum Britanniae* of Geoffrey of Monmouth. Gerald
has no love for Geoffrey, of whom he consistently speaks with disparage-
ment, but he does espouse the image of Wales portrayed as an independent
country and of Saint David's as a Metropolitan See independent of Canterbury and answerable directly to Rome.

We cannot read very far into the first chapter of the *Itinerarium* without encountering evidence of Wales as a territory occupied by an alien
power speaking an alien tongue. The canons of Saint David's, jealous of the
rights of their own church, object to the Archbishop of Canterbury's proposed progress through Wales and official visit to St. David's cathedral. We
are repeatedly told of transgressions by the English occupying forces
against the Welsh natives. Indeed, within a relatively short space, the

20. Archbishop Baldwin did keep his vow and died fighting before Acre in 1190. On the
advice of the Archbishop, however, Gerald, having set out on the crusade, was sent back to
Britain where he would presumably "have been of more political use to Richard I than in the
Near East" (Thorpe, 16). For Gerald's own similar view of the reasons for abandoning the
Crusade, see *De rebus*, 2, 21–22, 80–81, 84–85.

reader begins to equate the incursion of Saladin into Palestine with the usurpation of Wales by the English.

The Welsh, Gerald shows, are not entirely without responsibility for their subject status. He exposes the adroitness of the English in exploiting the fissionary tendencies in the fabric of Welsh society. But, just as cleverly, Gerald uses the Old Testament Prophetic Book of Daniel to equate the Welsh with the Jews in captivity and Wales to Palestine. Thus in Chapter 5 of Book 1 of the *Itinerarium Kambriae,* he draws an analogy between the vision of a Welsh mystic and that of Belshazzar in Daniel 5, 25–30. He then comments:

> His autem in finibus, *nostrisque diebus,* caeco dominandi ambitu, *rupto consanguinitatis et consobrinorum foedere,* fides quam enormiter in perfidiam evanuerit, diffuso per Gaulliam pravitatis exemplo, Kambria non ignorat.

> Wales knows only too well how, in this same neighborhood *and in our own times,* through a blind lust for conquest *and through a rupture of all the ties of common blood and family connection,* evil example has spread far and wide throughout the land, and good faith has disappeared, to be replaced by shameful perfidy. [*Itin. Kam.* 1, 5, 61; Thorpe, 121]

While such glossing certainly is not alien to romance, Gerald usually prefers a subtler technique for making his points.

Inscribed within the *Itinerarium* as a muted register of protest to the progress of the English retinue, Gerald interpolates an anecdotal register of opposition in a key quite different from that used for the accounts of crusade preaching. To recount these anecdotes, he detaches himself from the standpoint of either group, the better to let the Welsh express their outrage and frustration, and to portray the astonished, bemused, or indignant reaction of the English.

It is at such moments that we recognize the double-edge to the title, *Itinerarium Kambriae:* Wales, like Gerald himself, is both subject and object. It has an independent voice, as well as the voice the English make it speak, an identity unsuspected by them and as incomprehensible to their pragmatic worldview as the Welsh language they fail to master. After crossing the border, the English progress over an increasingly mythologized space—a space full of omens and portents of the kind we associate with the defamiliarized other worlds of Romance. And as they penetrate into a land made hostile, a land that refuses to conform to Augustine's corporeal metaphor for harmony within the Christian *domus* and state, the romance register reveals the crusade expedition for what it is: a display of alien force that is anything but a manifestation of *concordia,* either social or linguistic.

This force represents a new pragmatics of power that Gerald shows to be incompatible with traditional linguistic and literary models. The new view of power has no recognizable referent, either metaphysical or generic. It does not depend upon the concept of "Just warfare," as does the epic, nor does it promise identification with a transcendent image, the "miles Christi," to those who practice it. Shorn of idealism, it cannot be accommodated within a neoplatonic concept of world harmony, and thus has no transcendent linguistic rationale. If one were to make any linguistic analogy, it would have to be to such rule violations as the neologism, the barbarism, or the pleonasm. In fact, the pragmatics of power is a vernacular creation, with no Latin equivalence except as reported speech act.

Interestingly, Gerald introduces this ungoverned language of power as a confrontation between an idealized, mystical past, and a nonreferential present. He portrays it quite dramatically, in fact, as a confrontation between past and present . . . as a refusal of the present to be bound by the dictates of the past. Two rather striking incidents illustrate these points, both involving King Henry, a fact suggesting a growing equation between arbitrary power and the notion of kingship at this time.

In the first chapter of Book 2, Gerald tells us of an incident that occurred near St. David's cathedral when King Henry was returning from his conquest of Ireland (an expedition Gerald took part in and recorded in another work). A Welsh woman threw herself in front of the King to request his intervention to right a wrong she felt she had suffered. Her request was translated to the King, but he did not choose to act on it. Geoffrey reports that she then cried out:

> "Vindica nos hodie, Lechlavar; vindica genus et gentem de homine hoc." . . . *Accedens igitur ad lapidem rex, quia forte illius vaticinii mentionem audierat, ad pedem lapidis paulisper gradum sistens, et eundem acriter intuens, incunctante tamen passu audacter pertransiit, Verso itaque vultu ad lapidem respiciens, in vatem invectus, verbum hoc indignanter emisit; "Merlino mendaci quis de cetero fidem habeat?"*

> "Revenge us today, Llech Lafar! Revenge the whole Welsh people on this man!" . . . She was held back and then driven away by those who understood the Welsh language. As she went she shouted even more loudly and violently. She repeated the well-known fiction and prophecy of Merlin, so often heard, that a king of England, who had just conquered Ireland, would be wounded in that country by a man with a red hand, and then, on his return from St. David's would die as he walked over Llech Lafar. This was the name of the stone which served as a bridge over the River Alun, the stream which marks the boundary of the cemetary on the north side of the cathedral. The stone was made of very beautiful marble . . . in Welsh the name Llech Lafar means the Talking Stone. . . . *It so happened that the King knew all about the prophecy. When he reached the stone he*

*stopped and eyed it closely. Then, without further hesitation, he walked
boldly over it. As soon as he was across he turned round, glared at the
stone and with no small indignation made this trenchant remark about
the soothsayer: "Merlin is a liar, who will trust him now?"* [*Itin. Kam.*, 2,
1, 108–09; Thorpe, 167–78]

The second anecdote is also picturesque, but even more telling. Two
of King Henry's English agents in Wales put an old Welsh prophecy to a
test. The prophecy held that only the rightful ruler of Wales could command the birds on a certain lake to burst into song. The English nobles
make the attempt and fail, but then they ask Prince Gruffydd to try. After
praying to God, Gruffydd commands the birds to sing, and they obediently
burst into song. The Englishmen hurried back to the King's court to report
the divine portent.

The king responds:

"non adeo est admirandum. Quia licet gentibus illis per vires nostras
magnas injuriam et violentiam irrogemus, nihilominus tamen in terris
eisdem jus hereditarium habere noscuntur."

"I am not the slightest bit surprised. It is we who hold the power and so
we are free to commit acts of violence and injustice against these people,
and yet we know full well that it is they who are the rightful heirs to the
land." [*Itin. Kam.*, 1, 2, 35; Thorpe, 95]

The English King's reported speech places us squarely in the "presence of the now," succinctly articulated as a pragmatics of fission. In one
epigram, Henry exposes the precarious idealism of crusade preaching at
this moment in history. For what Henry says of Wales, Saladin could say of
Palestine; and Villehardouin does say of Constantinople.

Villehardouin dialogizes the transcendent rhetoric of crusade preaching in a different manner from Gerald. Instead of using the romance model
to oppose the epic, he introduces a language of economic exchange. The
Doge of Venice speaks like an accountant when he outlines the material
aid the Venetians will give to the crusaders, and when the host assembles
in Venice without sufficient cash to pay for the ships provided by the
Venetians, the crusader councils talk not about the issues raised by Foulques de Neuilly when he preached the crusade, but about the economic
realities of the situation. The same language of economic and political
pragmatics dominates his account of and justification for the conquest of
Constantinople. Even though Villehardouin consistently tries to cast his
account in terms derived from the epic model, the register of pragmatic
politics consistently undercuts the transcendent appeals. Most telling of
all, however, is Villehardouin's inability to achieve an epic closure to the
Conqueste. He ends on a kind of pastiche of the death of an epic hero, but
the lament only underlines the fissionary rhetoric that marks the *Con-*

queste from start to finish. The sign of this fissionary rhetoric, as the last sentence of the work reminds us, is "the presence of the now."

> Halas! com doloreus domage ci ot à l'empereur Henri et à tos les Latins de la terre de Romenie, de tel homme perdre par tel mesaventure, un des meilleurs barons et des plus larges, et des meillors chevaliers qui fust el remanant dou monde. *Et ceste mesaventure avint en l'an de l'incarnation Jesu-Christ mil deus cens et sept anz.* [*La Conqueste de Constantinople*, ch. 116, 202]

> Alas, how grievous a loss the Emperor Henry and all the Latin people of Romania suffered in losing such a man by this accident. For he was one of the best barons and one of the most generous as well as among the greatest knights left in the world. This misfortune occurred in the year of our lord 1207.

But rather than closing on so bald an assertion of the politics of presence, we should perhaps conclude by citing the case of the tailless dogs of anglesey. A dog, Gerald tells us, had lost its tail by accident, then sired a race of tailless epigones. An accident had thus become a historical continuity, and a natural phenomenon. Gerald's tailless dog might be said to symbolize the irruption of the barbarous into the normative and his epigones the legitimation process by which European society accommodated such solecisms . . . at the price of changing the norms.

In the narratological framework of the *Itinerarium Kambriae*, the canine mutant may be taken as a sign of fascination with the natural world as a matrix for change and as the ground for a new contextual perspective in which social fission and the pragmatics of power radically alter the nature of ideology. I suggest that this lesson was not lost on those who used the master tropes of history in subsequent generations to initiate such new literary genres as vernacular historiography, prose romances, and the continuations of the romance epic.

EUGENE VANCE

Chrétien's *Yvain* and the Ideologies of Change and Exchange

During the last few years, a tendency has arisen among certain medievalists to conceive the morphology of feudal society in terms of three "estates," "orders," or "functions" expressed by the actions of prayer, combat, and productive labor. These are performed, respectively, by the *oratores*, or the clergy, the *bellatores*, and the *laboratores:* the latter included not only serfs, but certain other social groups as well,[1] for instance, those tied to commerce and other more technological activities.

In patristic and scholastic thought, the term *ordo* implied a notion of cosmic hierarchy, and the triordinal schema underlay what we may call a "discursive" hierarchy in medieval culture as well, one that in effect consigned the lowest of the *laboratores*, as an order or class, to official silence. We may see symptoms of this willing neglect in Andreas Capellanus's *De amore*, which was written for the aristocrats of Champagne at a time of intense mercantile initiative.[2] Andreas says that the servile *agricultores*, or *rustici*, are simply incapable of the art of love because their destiny is merely to labor and copulate like beasts; hence, they are incapable even of speaking of love. If a female serf attracts us, Andreas says (1. xi), we should avoid praising her altogether and possess her directly by force.

The discursive status of the twelfth-century merchant interests me in particular, because, on the one hand, here was an unofficial function that was all too often inscribed with contempt and anathema into the official discourses of those whose mandates were to pray and to defend, while on the other, it is undeniable that the *mercator* and his interests became a

---

1. Georges Duby, *Les Trois ordres, ou l'imaginaire du féodalisme* (Paris: Gallimard, 1978).

2. Andreas Cappelanus, *De amore libri tres*, ed. Salvatore Battaglia under the title *Tratato d'amore* (Rome: Perrella, 1947). See also André le Chapelain, *Traité de l'amour courtois*, French. trans. By Claude Buridant (Paris: Klincksieck, 1974).

force that invaded the discourses of all three orders of the feudal hierarchy of late twelfth-century northern France as a sublanguage that we are now only beginning to grasp. As Lukács puts it, "the history of (feudal) estates shows very clearly that what in origin had been a 'natural' economic existence cast into stable forms begins gradually to disintegrate as a result of subterranean, 'unconscious' economic development."[3]

It is precisely the problem, both theoretical and historical, of apprehending these ubiquitous, yet subtle, discursive inflections that interests me in this essay, and in what follows I shall attempt to explore what I believe to be a new and far-reaching ideology of exchange expressed in Chrétien's *Yvain*, a poem whose discourse is centered, one may safely propose, on the order of the *bellatores*. However, for reasons that will become clear later, I shall first evoke two indirect consequences of mercantilism discernible in the theological discourse of the *oratores* in the closing decades of the twelfth century in northern France—that is, in Chrétien's own culture.

TOWARDS A THEOLOGY OF HORIZONTAL EXCHANGE

Although, earlier in the century, a mystic such as Hugh of St. Victor could acknowledge both the reality of, and the necessity for, commerce in the body politic (as he does in his *Didascalicon*, about which I shall speak later), Hugh's real interests as an *orator* in matters of change and exchange involve above all *spiritual* transactions between the soul and God, that is, mystical transactions upward (or downward) in a hierarchy of being. In his treatise, *Soliloquium de arrha animae* [*Soliloquy on the Earnest Money of the Soul*], Hugh exhorts the human soul to love the material beauties of the world, not for themselves, but rather as a kind of pledge-money by which the soul is mysteriously purchased by God as betrothed.[4]

One will recognize here a vertical projection, into the metaphysical realm, of a relatively simple model of exchange founded on gift-giving, barter and marriage doweries, one where money only measures the value of objects to be given or exchanged. Indeed, Hugh's idea about the "economy" of salvation reflects a long tradition of vertical thought about the Eucharist as a *purchase* of man's sins and about the saint's relic as *pignus*, that is, pledge-money or down payment. One will find an interesting visual expression of the valorization of the vertical over the horizontal econo-

---

3. George Lukács, *History and Class Consciousness. Studies in Marxist Dialectics*, trans. Rodney Livingstone (Cambridge, Mass: M.I.T. Press, 1971), 57.

4. Hugh of St. Victor, *Soliloquium de arrha animae*, ed. M. K. Müller (Bonn: A. Marcus and E. Weber, 1913). *Soliloquy on the Earnest Money of the Soul*, trans. Kevin Herbert (Milwaukee: Marquette Univ. Press, 1965).

mies on the Romanesque façade of Toulouse, where a statue of St. Peter, above which two angels hold coins with crosses on them, stands in opposition to a much smaller figure of a licentious woman holding near her bosom an *unmarked* coin.[5] Later in the century, the platonist Alain de Lille, writing as Chrétien's exact contemporary, elaborated a cluster of ideas rather more propitious to an ideology of horizontal change and exchange transpiring in and through physical nature, and not in an axis of vertical ascendance.[6] Alain says (*Prosa* 4) that Nature has been appointed as God's substitute in assuring that the creation succeeds itself horizontally in time within an economy of natural forms. Motivated by legitimate desire, the proliferation of forms in her womb is carefully regulated, as in the minting of coins. At a time when the clergy and high nobles of northern France were seeking ways to tame a warfaring order of less noble *bellatores* in order to promulgate a more prosperous, commercial peace, Alain's doctrine of change and succession through carefully regulated love was surely welcome.

Moreover, it was in this very same climate of promoting an economy of desire and exchange in the material world that a new, supernatural concept of purgatory emerged. As Jacques Le Goff has recently shown,[7] a major mutation occurred in Western theology when Christian thinkers in northern France—and specifically in Champagne—enunciated, between 1170 and 1200, a forceful new concept of purgatory, conceived as a specific "third place" midway between the opposite poles of heaven and hell. Here the souls of sinners were believed to spend specific durations of time purging themselves of sins committed while on earth (229). The carefully quantified labor of penitence (the very notion of labor implied punishment in the Middle Ages) was thought to culminate in the just reward of salvation. This spiritual economy allowed even for the vicarious purchase of one man's purgation in the world beyond by the charitable works and prayers of a third party acting here and now in his behalf. Le Goff is cautious about the contribution of socioeconomic developments in northern France to the theological concept of purgatory. However, it seems to me inevitable that the rapid transformation, in the twelfth century, of a barter economy into a profit-motivated monetary economy centered on travelling professional middlemen who bought in order to sell, instigating thereby a kind of protocapitalism, led to a new conception of God as a God of just prices (as opposed, for example, to the more feudal God of gift-giving and judicial duels evident in the *Roland*) and to a new spiritual topology

5. I am grateful to my colleague, Thomas Lyman, for his discussions of this façade with me.

6. Alain de Lille, *De planctu naturae*, ed. N. M. Häring, *Studi Medievali*, terza serie 19 (1978), 797–879. English trans. James J. Sheridan, *The Plaint of Nature* (Toronto: Pontifical Insitute of Mediaeval Studies, 1980).

7. Jacques le Goff, *La Naissance du purgatoire* (Paris: Gallimard, 1981).

specifying a "place" where values of time, space and service could be precisely measured and exchanged. It is well known that, thanks to the economic initiative of Henri le Libéral, Count of Champagne (whose energetic wife, Marie, daughter of Eleanor of Aquitaine, was Chrétien's patroness), the *foires* of Troyes and of five other designated fair-towns in Champagne made Champagne into nothing less than the commercial center of northern Europe.[8] Precisely as this great nobleman and his successors were inaugurating, within the new urban spaces of their territory, a specific time and place for commerce, as well as a new justice (the provost had one seat within the fair limits, another in the town),[9] devoted solely to the conduct of trade by professional merchants travelling from Flanders and Italy, so too the Cistercians, quite literally down the road, were hatching their new theological concept of purgatory where a soteriological economy was now thought to transpire.

Let us consider a second theological concept that underwent a radical reinterpretation during the rise of commerce: marriage. Marriage is both a personal relationship and a social one, to the extent that, on the occasion of marriage, powers and possessions are exchanged, even now, within the social group. It should come as no surprise that concepts of the marital relationship were also sensitive to new values emerging primarily from mercantile circles. As opposed to exchange (whether of money or of goods) transacted in a feudal structure, which generally involves unequal partners in a hierarchy and whose terms are fixed by custom, true commercial exchange demands both the legal *freedom* of partners to negotiate a contract and *equality* as they do so. As the scholastics knew, mutual consent is the basis of true commercial exchange.[10] As for marriage, previous to the midtwelfth century, that relationship had been determined previously not by the exercise of free consent between partners, but rather by exterior considerations such as the acquired privilege of a man to possess a woman, or else by such factors as cohabitation or consummation.[11] During the

8. The pioneering study of the fairs is by Félix Bourquelot, *Etudes sur les foires de Champagne*, 2 vols. (Brionne: Le Porgulan, 1865). For a more recent bibliography, see R. Bautier, "Les foires de Champagne, recherches sur une évolution historique," in *Recueils de la Société Jean Bodin* 5 (1953). *La Foire*, 97–147.

9. On the justice of the fairs, which was administered jointly by Henri and by the monks of Saint-Ayoul, see Bourquelot, 2, 257–59.

10. Raymond de Roover, *La pensée économique des scolastiques: Doctrines et méthodes* (Montréal: Institut d'études médiévales; Paris: Vrin, 1981), 58–59; see also *The Cambridge Economic History of Europe*, ed. M. M. Postan, E. E. Rich, and Edward Miller (Cambridge: Cambridge Univ. Press, 1971), vol. 3, 15–18.

11. The best account of shifts in the conception of marriage that occurred in the twelfth century remains, I believe, that of G. Le Bras, "Mariage," in *Dictionnaire de théologie catholique*. See also John T. Noonan, Jr., "The Power to Choose," *Viator* 4 (1973), 419–34; Marie-Odile Métral, *Le mariage: les hésitations de l'occident* (Paris: Aubier, 1977); Georges Duby, *Le chevalier, la femme et le prêtre* (Paris: Hachette, 1981); Jean Leclercq, *Le Mariage vu par les moines au 12e siècle* (Paris: Le Cerf, 1982).

twelfth century (when marriage also became a sacrament) free consent between legitimate partners became the sole basis of the marriage relationship. It would seem, once again, that mutations in the theology of marriage closely attended social progress occurring in the economic sphere, even though this economic substratum is not, itself, directly expressed in discussions of marriage.

What I am suggesting is simple: the multiple discourses that constitute any given speech community not only develop together, they also act upon and interfere with each other, even though we cannot always be sure in which discourse new concepts first arise, and even though certain innovating discourses of the past are not audible to us now. There obviously *was* a specifically mercantile discourse in the twelfth century, and the *oratores* obviously *heard* it, if from a distance. Hugh of St. Victor describes commerce, which he calls *navigatio*, as a peculiar discourse, and not only as a class of action:

> Commerce contains every sort of dealing in the purchase, sale and exchange of foreign goods. This art is beyond all doubt a peculiar sort of rhetoric—strictly of its own kind—for eloquence is in the highest degree necessary to it. Thus the man who excels others in fluency of speech is called a *Mercurius*, or Mercury, as being a *mercatorum kirrius* (*kyrios*)—a very lord among merchants.[12]

Just as the sociolinguist William Labov gives evidence for the socioeconomic motives underlying linguistic change at the level of *phonetic* patterns,[13] so too, I would argue for the socioeconomic basis for mutations, both syntactic and semantic, occurring at the level of *discourse*. Labov's claim that linguistic change occurs most massively in the middle classes, where social mobility is most pronounced, is pertinent to twelfth-century Champagne, where a powerful bourgeois class was beginning to emerge from the lower ranks, and where the lesser nobles, on their side, were beginning to lose or forsake their inherited martial privileges. It was within the cultural turmoil surrounding the emergence of new economic priorities, I would propose, that a new chivalric discourse constituted itself, entailing a whole new ethics, and a new poetics as well: we call this discourse "romance," signalling, thereby, a new alliance between a vernacular language and writing, *grammatica*.[14] It is with this new discourse that I shall henceforth deal, taking Chrétien's *Yvain* as my example.

12. Hugh of St. Victor, *Didascalicon: De studio legendi*, ed. Charles Henry Buttimer (Washington: Catholic Univ. Press, 1939), vol. 2, viii; trans. Jerome Taylor, *The Didascalicon of Hugh of St. Victor* (New York: Columbia Univ. Press, 1961), 91–92.

13. William Labov, *Sociolinguistic Patterns* (Philadelphia: Univ. of Pennsylvania Press, 1972), ch. 1.

14. For a recent study of Chrétien's "textual" poetics, see my forthcoming study, *From Topos to Tale: Logic and Narrative in the Middle Ages* (Minneapolis: University of Minnesota Press, 1986).

By its very name, "romance" may be understood to exist more as a language (*lingua*) and a discourse (*sermo*) than as a form, and in the prescriptive terms of twelfth- and thirteenth-century rhetorical theory, this discourse was to conform to what was called the *stylus nobilis* or *gravis*. Medieval rhetoricians defined the *stylus nobilis* according to two main criteria: first, it follows rules of decorum proper to the sphere of the *miles*, or the chivalric nobleman; second, it is marked by an abundance of tropes or "figures of thought." The term used by rhetoricians to designate this resource of the high style is *ornatus difficilis*.[15] Surely one of the purposes of romance as "troped" narrative was to give to chivalric combat a new *telos*, in other words, to accelerate the transformation of twelfth-century chivalric conduct into a class emblem entitling its bearer to become a lover of noble women. In short, the semantic function of metaphor, or *translatio* (understood as the generic term including all figures of thought) in the narrative discourse of chivalric romance is to "translate" warlike impulses into the impulse to love, that is, to subvert the *proprietas* of chivalric war by making it "figurative." The *semiotization* of chivalry—that is, the tendency for courtly art to make the gestures of the knight into signs of something *else*—is a type of subversion closely linked to the monetarization of twelfth-century economy: money too summons forth and expresses the significations of valor as *value* precisely so that it can be exchanged.

In the prologue of *Yvain*, Arthur's court is portrayed as a place of readily expended (as opposed to hoarded) wealth, and such abundance is the just reward of adventuring knights who circulate through the world and gather together at Pentecost to exchange not exotic commodities, but marvelous tales:

> Artus, li buens rois de Bretaigne,
> La cui proesce nos ansaingne,
> Que nos soiiens preu et cortois,
> Tint cort si riche come rois
> A cele feste, qui tant coste,
> Qu'an doit clamer la pantecoste.[16] [Vv. 1–6]

Arthur, the good king of Brittany, whose prowess teaches us to be bold and courteous, held a very rich, royal court, which *cost* very much, that we call Pente*cost*. [Italics mine]

The idea that verbal art might constitute a kind of wealth is not at all farfetched, at least in medieval terms. If discourse in the high style may be

15. Edmond Faral, *Les arts poétiques du XIIe et du XIIIe siècles: recherches et documents sur la technique littéraire du moyen-âge* (Paris: Champion, 1924), 86–87, 90.

16. Chrétien de Troyes, *Yvain, ou le chevalier au lion*, ed. W. Foerster (Halle: Niemeyer, 1906), vv. 1363–68. Further references to this edition are included in my text. Translations are my own.

considered as "aureate," words themselves, in Boethius's mind, could be considered as a kind of coin.[17] Arthur's fictional court reflects a utopian ideal of prosperity and abundance characteristic of Henri le Libéral's own court in Champagne,[18] but the real character of the noble, chivalric *bellator* in that same historical world was far different from that of his fictional counterpart. In general, the second half of the twelfth century was a time of radical change in the technology of arms (for instance, the deadly crossbow, wielded by non-nobles and bourgeois, became important in France after 1185)[19] in both the technology of assault and defense (now centered upon the stone fortifications built by towns)[20] and, just as importantly, in the *sociology* of *combat personnel:* by now, non-noble armed horsemen were both far more numerous than the noble *milites*,[21] and, especially in Champagne, were in administrative positions of great political prestige,[22] which is to say that, in Champagne, functionally speaking, *bellator* was now in the service of *mercator* and his interests.

The solitary, errant knight of romance who wanders in a marvelous forest in quest of personal honor, fame and love may be a pure fiction, at least with regard to the *miles* as a social creature in the late twelfth century. However, the *fictive* errant knight of romance is strikingly similar to the *real* travelling merchant as a new and important person in the social horizon of Champagne. If the heroic story of the fictive knight contains disguised applause for the new heroism of the real merchant, an *orator* such as Hugh of St. Victor could be more forthright in his admiration of the merchant as a hero who moves in a world of marvels, and the spirit of Hugh's description (2, viii) of the merchant is strangely consonant with that of chivalric romance:

> Commerce penetrates the secret places of the world, approaches shores unseen, explores fearful wildernesses, and in tongues unknown and with barbaric peoples carries on the trade of mankind. The pursuit of commerce reconciles nations, calms wars, strengthens peace, and commutes the private good of individuals into common benefit of all.

17. Brian Stock, "Medieval Literacy, Linguistic Theory, and Social Organization," *New Literary History* 16 (1984–85), 13.

18. John F. Benton, "The Court of Champagne as a Literary Center," *Speculum* 36 (1961), 551–92.

19. Philippe Contamine, *La Guerre au moyen-âge* (Paris: Presses Universitaires de France, 1980), 165.

20. J. F. Finò, *Forteresses de la France médiévale. Construction-attaque-défense* (Paris: Editions A. et J. Picard, 1977) 3rd ed. rev.; Contamine, 207–23.

21. Contamine, 159–63; 192–93. Not only were non-nobles gaining access to the ranks of mounted combatants, but nobles themselves were declining to be dubbed and to fight. Military service by knights was being transformed into financial obligations.

22. The guardians of the fairs were both noble and non-noble, and the mounted sergeants were non-noble. Bourquelot, vol. 1, 94; see also Elizabeth Chapin, *Les Villes de foires de Champagne* (Paris: Champion, 1937).

However, knights gather in Arthur's court at Pentecost to exchange not marvelous commodities from Italy and the Mid-East for English wool and Flemish textiles, but marvelous stories of war and love. It is not the just monetary price or wage of an *aventure* that is the major concern in Arthur's court, but its truth value; and "aureate" language, not gold, is its medium. When, in fiction, *bellator* becomes *miles amans*, he abandons a whole ethics of coercive exchange based upon pillage, ransom, and revenge in favor of another more profitable ethics of exchange founded upon freedom of consent, measure, service, and just prices and wages—and above all on the eternally negated (and therefore eternally renewable) hope of *joie*. Chrétien underscores the similarity—and above all, the difference—between the two systems of love and war when Yvain falls in love with the widow of the knight he has just slain:

> Bien a vangiee, et si nel set,
> La dame la mort son seignor.
> Vanjance an a prise greignor,
> Qu'ele prandre ne l'an seüst,
> S'Amors vangiee ne l'eüst,
> Qui doucemant le requiert,
> Que par les iauz el cuer le fiert.
> [Vv. 1363–68]

The lady surely has revenged the death of her lord. She has taken greater vengeance than she would have been able otherwise if Amor had not avenged her, who sweetly exacts it when he strikes the heart through the eyes.

The villain in such a courtly economy is not a cheater or counterfeiter, but a liar and a *médisant* who tampers with and diminishes conventional courtly language as a medium of exchange.[23] In *Yvain*, the *médisant* Keu not only violates courteous language, but obstructs the commerce of good stories.

Chrétien's concerns with the *justesse* of language—with the accountability of his vernacular *romans* was certainly shared by his patrons, for whom a policy of language was now a properly economic policy as well. Just as there was competition between political leaders in the twelfth century to promulgate this or that coinage as the dominant currency of commerce (Provins, in Henri's Champagne, was the seat of an important money aggressively promoted by the counts of Champagne in Chrétien's time)[24] there must also have been (as there is nowadays) competition to

23. On the dramatic function of the *médisant* in the courtly system, see Eugene Vance, "Freud, Greimas and the Story of Trouvère Lyric," in *Lyric Poetry: Beyond the New Criticism*, ed. Patricia Parker and Chaviva Hosek (Ithaca: Cornell Univ. Press, 1985, forthcoming).

24. Bourquelot, vol. 2, 38–64. The Champenois currency was so influential that the

make this or that language (or dialect) the dominant language of commerce.[25] Wasn't one of the motives for which Henri and his wife Marie so eagerly promoted high quality poetry along with the minting of good money that of enhancing the value of their language?

WOMEN, RINGS, AND THINGS

If it is accurate to claim that woman in Western society (as elsewhere) is central to any system of exchange, whether as an object of exchange or as a medium of exchange (or both), the women of Chrétien's romance are no exception. Indeed, the principal heroines of *Yvain* (Laudine, who becomes Yvain's wife, and her servant Lunette) express, by their actions in the romance, contrasting modalities of exchange in twelfth-century culture as Chrétien seems to have understood them.

Yvain's relationship to Laudine begins on something of an archaic note when he conquers her husband Esclados in combat, thereby depriving the lady and her magic fountain of a defender and also making her more than simply lawfully eligible to marry another good knight—for instance, Yvain himself. In *Erec et Enide* (vv. 4770–4852), when the Count of Oringle, believing that Erec was dead, had scandalously tried to compel Enide to marry him by force, Chrétien had already tested and rejected an older concept of marriage based upon coercion or upon external rights of a man to claim a woman, and was championing consent as the only valid criterion of marriage. In *Yvain*, a marriage will indeed occur between a widow and her husband's slayer, and the acquisition of property will indeed accompany his right to possess the woman's body; however, in this romance, such transactions are made conspicuously subject to the free consent of the woman as marital partner, and, even *after* their marriage, their relationship will continue to be mediated by an elaborate economy of measured values of time and services. Paradoxically, with this new role of woman in marriage came a new ideal of woman as a creature of constancy, and not of change. To be sure, Chrétien puts in Yvain's own mouth the old Ovidian doctrine of female changeability (vv. 1437–39); however, it will be Yvain himself who undergoes shameful change with regard to his constant wife Laudine.

If Chrétien exalts a new relationship of marriage based on the equality

---

Italians not only used it upon their return from the fairs of Champagne, but they imitated it in Rome with a coin called the *provinois du sénat*. This in turn became the official money of the Vatican in 1188, that is, during the height of the Champenois poetic movement.

25. Ian Parker, of the University of Toronto, has kindly passed on to me an unpublished essay entitled "The Rise of the Vernaculars in Early Modern Europe: An Essay on the Political Economy of Language." Parker probes the "economics" of the emerging vernaculars in the late Middle Ages, and I have gained much from discussing these points with him.

and constancy of partners, and if the negotiation of that relationship trans-
pires without any consideration of money, a medium of exchange is hardly
lacking. To the contrary, the role of another *un*married, subordinate woman, Lunette, is prominent throughout the romance, both as middleperson
and as designator of *valor* as exchangeable *value.*

Let us consider more closely Lunette's role as a mediatrix of change
and exchange. One will recall that, after Yvain defeats Esclados by the
marvelous fountain in the forest of Brocéliande, Esclados flees mortally
wounded to his castle. Having followed Esclados into his castle, where he
is now trapped, Yvain finds himself in a room sumptuously decorated with
gold and with finely wrought, brightly colored murals. This eminently
artistic spot is already a sign of Chrétien's partisanship of the economy of
love. Yvain has scarcely begun to apprehend his predicament when, quite
suddenly, Lunette appears through a narrow door (v. 971) to apprise him of
his situation and to bestow upon him a magic ring.

Let us examine the situation in more detail. Although she is the
intimate attendant and *confidante* of Laudine, who is the widow of the
man whom Yvain has just slain, Lunette is also openly indifferent to the
grief of Laudine, who is now burying her husband. Indeed, although Yvain
is now Laudine's worst enemy, Lunette has a long-standing obligation to
him. She now intends to repay in *servise et enor* [service and honor, v.
1002] the service and honor (v. 1013) that Yvain had previously rendered
her when he alone, of all the knights of the court, had deigned to speak to
her, she being at the time only a novice in the art of *cortoisie.* Lunette, who
has now "arrived," declares that she is returning his *guerredon* (v. 1015).

Lunette is equally devoted, in other words, to two potential partners
who have something of *value* to offer each other, yet who are bitterly
opposed, and in the story that follows, Lunette will repeatedly function as
a middleperson and even as a kind of human currency whose service to
truth includes the art of lying.

Lunette's *guerredon* to Yvain is a magic ring that makes its bearer
invisible to others at will. Lunette's ring, which symbolizes a miraculous
power of change and exchange, had many possible sources and analogues
in a more immediate context of Celtic legend and folklore. However,
Chrétien's classicizing propensity may also have made him the heir, even
if indirectly, of another tradition of thoughts about magic rings stretching
back through the Elder Pliny to Herodotus and Plato. The insoluble question of "influences" aside, certain aspects of that tradition are instructive
in their own right. Lunette's ring has striking resemblances, functionally
speaking, with the ring of the tyrant Gyges as evoked by Herodotus and
Plato. As Marc Shell has shown in his book, *The Economy of Literature,*
the fable of the talismanic ring of Gyges, which transforms invisibles into
visibles, and visibles into invisibles, was instrumental as an early (meta-

phorical) understanding of the power of money at a time when Greek culture was undergoing economic transitions similar to those of mid-twelfth-century French culture. Shell writes:

> The ring of Gyges controls the opposition of visibility to invisibility, which concerns the definitions of tyranny and economic exchange, especially during the transition from barter to money. Why did Plato choose a ring as the talisman of the person whose way of life he tries in the Republic? If Plato did adopt the ring from previous accounts of the reign of Gyges, he did so with reason. Rings played several roles in the economic development of money and in the opposition of *ousia phanera* to *ousia aphanes*. First, rings were among the most common symbols before the introduction of coinage. Second, some of the first coins were ring-coins. Third, the die by which coins were minted was originally the seal of the ring of the king (or *symbolon*, as Pliny calls the royal seal). To some Greeks, a coin (as money) may have appeared to play the same role as a *symbolon*.[26]

Lunette and her golden ring express a similarly terrifying, yet marvelous, power of change and exchange. They not only transform the earlier "service" of Yvain into a spontaneous abundance of new commodities, but they disguise and conceal repugnant actions (Yvain's slaying of Esclados) so that their perpetrator may reappear in a new social context, clean, beautiful and useful as potential spouse and protector of Esclados's widow. This new power, which is the secret power of capital, defies earlier customs and norms of justice, yet it also inaugurates a new casuistry based upon the rigorous perception of equivalences of value among people, services or objects to be metamorphosed or exchanged in an economy of love. I am suggesting that the marvels of capital money and commerce are at the very the heart of Chrétien's romanesque *merveilleux* in Yvain.

Since Esclados's corpse begins to bleed in the presence of its slayer, the power of Lunette's ring to make Yvain invisible is timely, to say the least, and Laudine's servants, who are trying to capture the killer, correctly conclude that the power he possesses is both "marvelous and diabolic" (*Ce est mervoille et deablie*, v. 1202). The ring conceals its bearer, we are further told, exactly as bark conceals the pith of a branch (vv. 1028–29). That this metaphor of inner/outer is also a commonplace in medieval thoughts about the relationship between rhetoric and truth is worth emphasizing here, since, as Marc Shell shows, early thoughts about rings or money as a social force were likewise inseparable from "the study of other media of symbolization and transfer, such as verbal metaphor. *Symbolon*, in fact, meant not only pactual token but also word; and, as Plato knew, the development of money corresponds to the development of a new way

26. Marc Shell, *The Economy of Literature* (Baltimore: The Johns Hopkins Univ. Press, 1978), 41.

of speaking."[27] Bearing in mind that the *stylus gravis* was defined by twelfth-century rhetoricians as an "ornate" discourse where *translatio* is prominent, there is pertinence in Marc Shell's suggestion that "There is a ring of Gyges secretly at work within the minds of men: it is the money of the mind" (36).

Lunette, Chrétien tells us, "speaks with covered words" (*parole par couverture*, v. 1938). If one will grant that not only Lunette's ring, but also her rhetoric, her timely appearances and vanishings, and her powers to conceal and reveal, have meaning within a fictive economy of love principles that really do (or should) prevail in an emerging international mercantile economy based on money and middlemen and motivated by profit and capital gain, how far, one may ask, does this system go in *Yvain?*

From her first appearance in the poem, Lunette is associated with marvels whose economic significance is readily perceptible. For instance, after Yvain receives Lunette's magic ring, he reclines on a couch that is covered with a quilt so lavish (*riche*, v. 1041), we are told, that not even the Duke of Austria could afford one like it. Since we may properly assume that the good Duke would indeed want such a quilt, even if he did not need it, we may see that mediated consumer desire is now at the heart of a new heroic ethics. Indeed, textiles were also at the heart of the rising mercantile economy of Champagne.

The main points here are, first, that consumer desire is now a properly heroic sentiment, and second, that like the international trade that excites it, such desire knows no national boundary.

Lunette now asks Yvain if he would not like to dine, and suddenly Yvain is hungry! Just as suddenly, Lunette vanishes and reappears with a sumptuous meal of capon, cakes and good wine (*de buene grape*, v. 1050), the latter already being a status symbol in feudal France. The accessories include a white goblet and even a tablecloth. The emphasis in this scene is on abundance, decorum and spontaneity, and Chrétien refuses (here, at least) to take into consideration any questions about who raised the capon, who made the wine, who wove the tablecloth, or who prepared the dinner—in short, questions as to how all of these fine commodities found their way into the little room at exactly the right time. The secret of such magic is not hard to guess: isn't money marvelous?

Purveying men to women, however, calls for subtler mediations, all the more because in this case the beautiful woman whom Yvain is about to love (and finally wed) is the widow of the knight he has just slain. Fortunately, Lunette is entirely competent to perpetrate this improbable transaction between mortal enemies. Not only does her ring absolve Yvain

27. Shell, 36. On the relationship between money and language as modes of communication, see Genevieve Vaughan, "Communication and Exchange," *Semiotica* 29 (1980), 113–43.

from the brutal justice of revenge that the widow and her club-wielding retenue would customarily exact from him, but Lunette herself will conceal Yvain in a "little room" (*chanbrete* v. 1579) in which she provides everything he needs, no matter how much it costs, on credit (*créance*, vv. 1578–83). Thanks to her slyness, Lunette will spare Yvain the humiliation of sneaking away from the castle at night (*nuitantre*, v. 1577), and she will orchestrate, instead, a spectacular daylight epiphany of his person before Laudine—*precisely at the right time and place*. If ever a man's past were laundered of its harmful deeds it is Yvain's, and his appearance, after three days of invisibility in Lunette's *chanbrete*, is a miracle of social and economic spendor that falls just short of the miracle of Christ's resurrection:

> Si le fet chascun jor beignier
> Et bien laver et apleignier.
> Et avuec ce li aparoille
> Robe d'escarlate vermoille
> De ver foree a tot la croie.
> N'est riens, qu'ele ne li acroie,
> Qui covaingne a lui acesmer:
> Fermail d'or a son col fermer,
> Ovré a pierres precïeuses,
> Qui fot les janz mout gracïeuses
> Et ceinture et aumosniere,
> Qui fu d'une riche seigniere.
> Bien l'a del tot apareillé . . .
> [vv. 1881–93]

Thus she has him bathed each day and washed well and groomed. And she provides him a robe of crimson lined with powdered fur. There is nothing that she does not lend him in order to decorate him: a golden collarpin studded with precious stones, which makes people appear very gracious, a girdle and a purse made of a rich brocade. She equips him well with everything.

Yvain's heroism is above all the heroism of a young and hardy economy, and we may be sure that any of the fineries that Lunette provides Yvain could now have been purchased right in the fairs of Troyes or Provins.

In Chrétien's fiction Lunette, and not money, is the mediator of marvels. The *chanbrete* in which Yvain is so abundantly fed, clothed and bejewelled is a kind of womb, not unlike that of Nature in Alain's *De planctu naturae*, or perhaps even a kind of purse, through whose coinage beings pass in order to be transmuted and reborn. By her very name, Lunette is associated with the moon, that is, with a principle of ordered, cosmic, monthly and menstrual change. As a moon figure, Lunette's light or *san* is reflected light, and her main function in *Yvain* is to reflect or engender fantasms in the desiring minds of those whom she serves. For

example, Lunette's repayment for Yvain's earlier courtly "service" includes placing him by the little window through which he first glimpses
and desires the grieving Laudine: this is a properly courtly payment that
brings not *joie,* but rather more desire. Not only does Lunette reflect
images of lovers back and forth between each other, but when she herself
becomes an object of love for Gauvin, who is Yvain's closest friend, we are
told that Gauvin's glory is like that of the sun itself, and that Lunette is the
"moon" of this cosmic couple—hence, Gauvin's mirror, both because of
her *san* and *cortesie,* and because her name is "Lunette" (*por ce que
Lunette a non,* v. 2414). In my eyes, Lunette looks and acts very much like
a coin.

If Lunette is a mediatrix of exchange, she becomes, herself, unjustly
devalued by Yvain's breach of credit and is condemned by Laudine to be
burned as a traitor. (Bad coins always go back to the refining fires of the
mint.) Lunette's impending death threatens not only her new role in the
more secret economy of love between a knight and a lady, but a more
traditional economy of patronage and gift-giving within the court as a
social group. Lunette's fellow attendants in Laudine's court lament their
mistress's tyranny as follows:

> "Ha! Deus, con nos as obliëes!
> Con remandrons or esgarees,
> Qui perdomes si buene amie,
> Et tel consoil et tel aïe
> Qui a la cort por nos estoit!
> Par son consoil nos revestoit
> Ma dame de ses robes veires.
> Mout changera or li afeires;
> Qu'il n'iert mes, qui por nos parot . . .
> N'iert mes, qui die ne qui lot:
> C'est mantel ver et cest sorcot
> Et ceste cote, chiere dame,
> Donez a cele franche fame!
> Que voir, se vos li anvoiiez,
> Mout i sera bien anploiiez;
> Que ele an a mout grant sofreite".
> Ja de ce n'iert parole treite;
> Car nus n'est mes frans ne cortois . . .
> [Vv. 4361–81]

"Ah, God! How you have forsaken us! How desolate we are, now that we
are losing such a good friend, who gave counsel and aid on our behalf in
the court. By her counsel our lady clothed us with her grey and white
dresses. Now things will change, since there will no longer be anyone to
speak for us. . . . There will no longer be anyone to plead, 'This grey and
white, mantle, this cloak, and this coat, dear lady, give it to this honest

woman. For surely, if you send it to her, it will be well used, for she needs
it dearly.' Surely no longer will such words be spoken, for there is no
longer anyone left who is frank and courteous."

Yvain, for his part, responds to his discredit more in tune with the
times, more as a debt to be liquidated than as the failure of a feudal patronage system. Indeed, one may consider the anonymous fame that Yvain
earns as a kind of *solvency* that he accrues by his services until such time
as he may rightly be *absolved* of his disservice to Laudine. After the
chevalier au lion rescues Lunette from the stake and encounters Laudine,
Laudine asks the nameless lion-knight to tarry longer by her side, but he
declines. Laudine pleads that he at least reveal to her his name, and then he
will be "free" (*quites*, v. 4608) to depart. Yvain quickly overdetermines her
notion of "freedom" by bewailing his pending debt to his lady: "Fully paid,
lady? I shall not do it: I owe more than I can ever pay." (*"Toz quites, dame?
Non feroie. / Plus doi, que randre ne porroie"* vv. 4609–70). Yvain's services as the *chevalier au lion* give rise to a new and abstract solvency that
will make him once again worthy of Laudine's love when the time is right.
Yvain performs no less than six honorable services to different causes
(including that of his lion) in payment for his breach of contract with
Laudine, and Chrétien clearly enjoys putting such an exhorbitant price on
aristocratic *joie d'amour* precisely to distance his art from the baser casuistry of just prices that preoccupied less courtly souls pondering the ethics of
real commerce in Chrétien's milieu. Finally, at the very end of the story,
Yvain's penitence as a sinner against love is deemed complete: he has had
to pay, he says, and to pay dearly, for his folly (vv. 6780–83). We are not far,
in this romance, from the new Cisctercian Purgatory.

LOVE, CREDIT, AND TIME

The economy of desire that Lunette and her fellow women serve is one
where not only the exchange value of people, objects and services is quantified, but so too is time. The notation of precise temporal perspectives
originates in the very tense structure of Chrétien's narrative discourse and
extends to the surface of narrative events and of heroic motivations as
well. Laudine, desiring to meet the knight she loves (but has not yet seen)
insists that she cannot *possibly* wait five days for Lunette to convey Yvain
to her domain (we, of course know that he is already there, hidden by
Lunette). However, Laudine settles for three. In another episode, when the
daughters of Noire Espine quarrel over their heritage, one demands that
the other defend herself with a champion *right away;* the king grants her
forty days to find her champion. Or again, after he has begun his series of
good works to redeem himself from his breach of contract with Laudine,
Yvain discovers that he has exactly one day to finish his exploit against

Harpin de la Montagne if he is to rescue Lunette from being burned at the stake. How different from the world of the *Roland*, where oaths and promises engage a hero's honor in commitments that are as timeless as the God by which they are sworn. If time in *Yvain* has precise value, timeliness is a great virtue. Missed deadlines can kill. Laudine is meticulous in measuring the duration of Yvain's absence from her, and when he runs over his limit, he is exiled. As Lunette explains to Yvain when she reminds him of his truancy:

> "Jusqu'a la feste saint Jehan
> Te dona ele de respit,
> Et tu l'eüs an tel despit,
> Qu'onques puis ne t'an remanbra.
> Ma dame paint an sa chanbre a
> Trestoz les jorz et toz les tans;
> Car qui aimme, est an grand porpans,
> N'onques ne puet prandre buen some,
> Mes tote nuit conte et assome
> Les jorz, qui vientent et qui vont.
> Sez tu, come li amant font?
> Content le tans et la seison."
> [Vv. 2750–61]

"She gave you your freedom until the feast of Saint John, and you held her in such contempt that you never remembered her. My lady marked in her chamber every one of the days and the whole time; for he who loves is very thoughtful, and cannot rest, but during each night counts and adds up the days that come and go. Do you know how lovers do? They count the days and seasons."

In contrast with the world of epic, time is now *interest*ing, and good heroes should never be early or late, but punctual. The implantation of this temporal dimension in the mentality of the aristocratic *bellator* of romance reflects the implantation, in twelfth-century culture, of what Jacques Le Goff calls the "merchant's time."[28]

In the *Roland*, the verb *creire*, "to believe," tends to express above all a hero's engagements, which are imposed and not chosen, in a vertical hierarchy of being. In *Yvain*, by contrast, *créance* implies an act of choice on the part of individuals within a horizontal framework of specific dimensions determined by arbitrary but fixed bonds of time, space and human disposition. That is to say, *créance* inclines toward a more modern notion of *credit*. Credit depends, to be sure, on the constancy of partners, and the ring that Laudine gives to Yvain as he sets out on his *aventure* is a symbol of that constancy; however, credit also implies futurity, growth, and

28. Jacques Le Goff, *Time, Work and Culture in the Middle Ages*, trans. Arthur Goldhammer (Chicago: Univ. of Chicago Press, 1980), 35.

change (though within limits), and the ring that Lunette gives to Yvain in the *chanbrete* is a symbol of that potential. Yvain's transgression of his agreement with Laudine is a breech of *créance* which puts him in her "debt," but we find an even clearer expression of *créance* as credit in lending when Yvain, as he awakens from his folly in the forest, asks that a horse be "lent" on credit (*créance*), and Yvain makes a clear distinction between such credit and an outright gift (*dons*, vv. 3070–73).

That the once delinquent Yvain deserves such credit is quickly borne out when he finds himself protecting the castle of the palfrey's donor, the Dame de Noroison, for he fights, we are told, with an energy surpassing even that of Roland at Ronceval (v. 3235). As Robert Lopez writes, "Unstinting credit was the great lubricant of the Commercial Revolution. It was altogether a novel phenomenon."[29]

DEPRESSIONS

If the pursuit of *joie* in love brings abundance in the economy, what happens to the economy when a knight falls out of love's good graces? Right after Yvain breaks his contract with Laudine agreeing to his absence for one year's time, Lunette characteristically appears out of nowhere to denounce Yvain. Yvain promptly goes mad, and drops out of circulation— both that of love and of commodities. First, he loses his speech; next, he forsakes his chivalric arms for a mere peasant's bow; finally, he leaves the company of his fellow men (and women) in order to forage naked and alone in the forest, where he eats his game raw. At this degree zero of love and of material well-being, Yvain chances upon a hermit dwelling in the forest, and from this moment forward an interesting twofold process of recovery begins. The first step occurs when the hermit, in a gesture of charity, gives mouldy bread and cold water to the wild man; the wild man in turn brings the hermit wild game from the forest. Primitive as it is, this exchange marks a threshold between bestial foraging and primitive barter as a minimal social activity. Now the hermit cooks the game that Yvain had previously eaten raw, and the passage from raw to cooked marks another threshold of human culture one signalling the mastery of fire as a basis of technology (and, metaphorically, of love). The next step is, for us, truly surprising: the hermit goes to town to sell the skins from Yvains's game in order to buy better wheat and to bake better bread. Suddenly, emblems of a divided labor force, money, middlemen and of an economy of surpluses (but not of profit) have emerged before our very eyes.[30] If knights can act like merchants, the clergy can too.

29. Robert S. Lopez, *The Commercial Revolution of the Middle Ages* (Englewood Cliffs: Prentice-Hall, 1971), 72.
30. See Peter Haidu, "The Hermit's Pottage: Deconstruction and History in *Yvain*," in

However, Chrétien's endorsement, within the codes of courtly aristo-cratic discourse, of the new mercantilism of his age is not unqualified. It does not take a Marxist eye to discern that the economic message of the Château de Pesme Aventure is a thinly veiled criticism of the exploitation of labor in a nascent textile industry lying just to the west of Champagne in Flanders. In this episode, Yvain and his lion deliver three hundred damsels held captive by two sons born of the devil and a woman (v. 5271), and their triumphant release may have called to mind equally triumphant scenes of the resurrection of the dead in Romanesque tympani. Chrétien and his powerful patron were quite capable, it seems, not only of revindicating certain commercial values in the dominant discourses of their time (those of the clergy and the knights) but, just as importantly, of calling for limits in the exploitation of the *laboratores* by a rapacious new middle class.

Though earlier in *Yvain* Chrétien seemed to applaud the marvels of a monetarized world, in the Pesme Aventure, Chrétien depicts the poet himself as another potential victim of exploitation as a new kind cultural *laborator*, perhaps in Court Henri's and Marie's own chancery or some *scriptorium* where beautiful texts, not textiles, were woven. The linking of weaving and writing, of textile and text, is hardly a modern critical trick. Brian Stock, who has studied the association, writes: "The idea of a text as a material replica of a woven literary composition, whether originating in words or in writing, made perfect sense to a society in which orality still played a large role in cultural communication."[31] Here in the same Château de Pesme Aventure where three hundred starving, poorly clad damsels weave beautiful silk cloth, an extremely refined and courteous lord and lady recline (on covers of silk!) in a peaceful garden while their ravishing daughter of sixteen reads aloud an anonymous romance (*ne sai de cui*, v. 5366). Refracted through Yvain's eyes, we are encountering in this romance what is in reality a second fictional reader (hence, a fiction of ourselves) capable of stirring—rather, of troubling—a heroic soul. One will recall that, earlier in the romance, Yvain had fallen in love with Laudine precisely when he glimpsed her reading a golden Psalter while she grieved for Esclados. Now, however, this adorable implicit reader is a consumer of vernacular romance, and is presumably closer to Chrétien's own authorial fantasies—or phobias—than was the reader of Scripture. This first insight of a European vernacular writer of fiction into authorial fantasies about his readers is worth exploring:

> Et s'estoit si bele et si jante,
> Qu'an li servir meïst s'antante

The Sower and the Seed. Essays on Chrétien de Troyes, ed. Rupert T. Pickens (Lexington: French Forum, 1983), 127–45.
    31. Stock, "Medieval Literacy," op. cit., 21.

> Li Deus d'Amors, s'il la veïst,
> Ne ja amer ne la feïst
> Autrui se lui meïsme non.
> Por li servir devenist hon,
> S'issist de sa deité fors
> Et ferist lui meïsme el cors
> Del dart, don la plaie ne sainne,
> Se desleaus mires n'i painne.
> [Vv. 5375–84]

And she was so beautiful and noble that the God of Love, if he saw her, would devote himself wholly to her service, nor would he make her fall in love with anyone but himself. He would become a man to serve her, and would abandon his godhead and strike his own body with that dart whose wounds may never be cured, unless by some disloyal physician.

This virginal reader of romance is a source of profound ambivalence, both in Yvain's eyes and in the author's own. She is at once perfectly innocent and perfectly threatening: innocent because she rightly loves and consumes a well-wrought courtly fiction about desire that is beautiful and seductive in its own right; threatening because she and her audience can remain so wholly unconcerned with the marvels of romance (just as they are with the silken rug) as a product woven by a real but nameless human being with compelling desires of his own. The textile of romance competes with its own weaver when it begins to circulate as an autonomous, voiceless stimulus of readerly desire.

Chrétien's sublimely beautiful reader of romance is of course part of Chrétien's fictive universe, and is therefore a figuration of his own desire as a writer of stories about desire. The author of such fiction is analogous to *li Deus d'Amors* that Chrétien mentions as another willing victim of the erotic process that the god himself provokes: for the god of love to become a man (rather, the *fiction* of a man) in order to experience his own darts of desire for a (fictive) woman is very much the same gesture as that of the author who stages in his characters his own desires for an equally seductive reader. I would propose that the underlying terms of reference of Amor's passion (which is now mere "myth") are nothing less than the God of Christianity who created the world, allowed sin into that creation, and who then, for love of sinners, translated himself into the supreme fiction of a man in order that he could die for sinners and redeem them with his own passion.

If it is true that Western literature "in general" (if such a thing may be said to exist) is a discourse whose presuppositions about artistic "creation" entail the occultation of a metaphysical creation, Chrétien's "trivialization" of metaphysics is an important inaugural, downward movement from the true God to mythical Cupid and finally to the poet as "maker" of a fictive world by which he mediates to himself his own autoerotic desire.

Yvain, it would seem, is more intelligent than both Chrétien and Amor, since he spurns adultery with the lord's reading daughter in order to pursue his quest for reunion with his true wife Laudine. One last ordeal, however, separates Yvain from Laudine, and this is a combat with an anonymous knight who happens to be his best friend, Gauvin. Each knight defends a woman who is litigating with her sister over an inheritance. Since Gauvin seems to function in this romance as a kind of chivalric norm, the stalemate that results from their duel confirms Yvain's worthiness both to be reintegrated into the aristocratic world of the court and to be rehabilitated as Laudine's spouse. The laws of love's economy may be invisible and mysterious, but they do adequately account for good deeds and services rendered. It is fitting to the milieu of Champagne that a fictive chivalric quest should end with a combat that justly mediates between a man and a woman, and that the combat should involve neither fatalities nor even the making of enemies. Indeed, the combat transforms itself into a duel of courtesy where each warrior tries to outdo the other in proclaiming his adversary the true victor. In contrast with the earlier combat between Yvain and Esclados, which was fatal, and which involved a process of exchange based on real violence, this combat is more of a class activity or ritual which determines which warriors are worthy of becoming breeders. Chrétien is carefully undermining an obsolete ethics of a de facto warrior class in order to promulgate a new ethics based upon the peaceful transfer of wealth through judicial process and through legitimate inheritance and succession. Chrétien's story brackets the chivalric ideal in a principle of higher justice without destroying, however, those traditional values of courage, generosity and honor which are still commensurate with the new social order, and Chrétien's tact as a partisan of new social values is remarkable. Yvain's marriage with Laudine is ultimately restored, not as it was first instigated, by raw victory at arms, but by the gentler ruse of Lunette, who now tricks her mistress into pledging that she will do everything she can to help the anonymous (but totally creditable) *chevalier au lion* to regain his lady's love which is of course Laudine's very own. True to her character as a mediator without desires of her own (except for the vicarious pleasure of seeing love's accounts settled so that others can be united), Lunette is duly fulfilled by her final "exploit": *Or a bien Lunette esploitié; / De rien n'avoit tel coveité, / Con de ce que ele voit fet* (vv. 6659–61). [Now Lunette has performed well; she had never coveted anything so much as what she has just accomplished.]

If there is any warrant for my claim that the poetics of desire in *Yvain* is distilled from the values of a nascent mercantile economy in Chrétien's Champagne, then the happy narrative closure of that text is an ideological gesture confirming both the possibility and the means of overcoming depression, whether psychic or economic. This recovery depends upon respect for contracts, and such respect was high among the new ethical priorities of Henri's domain. Chrétien's narrative closure is a fulfillment of his own private contract with his reader as well, to the extent that narrative, as a system, involves transformations or exchanges of terms within a determined structure. On that narratological score, Chrétien's credit is high. His closure reinforcess an ideology of *success.*

We may assume that like most patrons of art, whether ancient or modern, Henri le Libéral and his wife Marie knew very well where their interests as patrons of a great literary court lay. Even if it is true that Yvain and Laudine are only a knight and a lady of Chrétien's story, and not merchants, and if it is true that Lunette is only a female servant, and not a piece of money, it is just as true that none of these characters acts as husbands, wives and servants, noble or otherwise, act in the ordinary world. It is precisely their *un*reality that compels us to seek elsewhere than in ordinary affairs of the human heart for the informing paradigms; and if these are still enjoyed by us today, it is no doubt in part because they convey a system of human values that our world still shares with those which motivated Chrétien to become the first great master of romance vernacular fiction.

NANCY FREEMAN REGALADO

Effet de réel, Effet du réel: Representation and Reference in Villon's Testament*

Henri d'Andeli, in his thirteenth-century *Bataille des sept arts*, called upon Grammar, *Madame la haute science,* to lead out the troups of the humanities against the onslaughts of Parisian logic. The anonymous muse of Grammar is invoked as well in the title above, which records a grammatical slip found in some recent critical works in English, in which citations of the well-known article by Roland Barthes on "Effet de réel,"[1] the expression "effet *de* réel" has, at times, been transcribed as "effet *du* réel." This fortuitous error, which transforms the "reality effect" into the "impact of the real," offers a set of opposing terms which may serve to define crucial problems of representation and reference in Villon's *Testament.*

These problems are raised by the numerous historical names and dates within the *Testament* that have led many readers to declare that they could not read Villon without knowledge of the historical context of his works, as did Clément Marot, in the prologue to his 1533 edition of Villon: "As for the matters in the legacy stanzas of his 'Testaments,' to truly understand it one would have to have lived in Villon's time in Paris, and have known the places, things, and men of whom he speaks."[2] It is in the very article where Paul Valéry declared, "Que me font les amours de Racine! C'est Phèdre qui m'importe!" [What importance can Racine's love-life have for me; it's Phèdre I care about!] that he said of Villon: "In this case the biographical question is inescapable. . . . It is essential to inquire into the life and adventures of François Villon and to reconstruct

*I am grateful to the National Endowment for the Humanities for a summer stipend grant supporting preparation of this essay for publication.
    1. Roland Barthes, "Effet de réel," *Communications* 11 (1968).
    2. In *Oeuvres complètes de François Villon,* ed. Pierre Jannet (Paris: Librairie Marpon and Flammarion, 1881), 3.

them. . . . All that is inextricably incorporated into his poetry, inseparable from it, and makes it often virtually unintelligible to anyone who does not represent in his mind the picturesque, sinister aspects of Paris at that period."[3]

Valéry's word *représente* recalls now familiar models describing a text's relation to its reader and the reader's reading to the historical world. Words in texts have been seen as having the power to move our minds to *represent,* that is, to construct scenes, to imagine feelings, characters, ideas, worlds. What we represent while reading may well be quite unrelated to historical circumstances: we may represent impossible events, unknown worlds and characters. On the other hand, our representation may seem to have or may in fact have reference, that is, explicit, purposeful, and verifiable connections with historical circumstances. Representation is thus taken here as our imaginative construction, to be distinguished from reference, which describes the relation between representation and what exists in the historical world.

The term *effet de réel* or reality effect serves to draw our attention as critics to the processes of representation within texts, to the lifelike, convincing, plausible representation of objects, characters, actions, and emotions. Yet the *effet de réel* speaks not only of a text's power to represent what could well be; for Barthes, it leads the reader to experience parts of the text as directly designating "the real." The *effet de réel* thus creates within our representation an impression of reference, which Barthes calls "l'illusion référentielle." The *effet de réel* facilitates the reader's representation by drawing its elements from the familiar, easily imagined everyday world, but it also shortcircuits the reader's awareness of the artful processes of representation by leading the reader to believe the text is referring directly to what *is.*

The new term, *effet du réel,* on the other hand, brings into focus entirely different questions concerning the relevant connections between the historical world and literary texts: the effect of historical events upon a text; the polemical intent of the author; the political impact of a work. The *effet du réel* assumes reference and therefore seeks to verify historical facts and experience apart from the text and to analyze their expression in the text.

Villon's *Testament* contains many elements common to historical documents; real proper names, places, and dates invade the poem and overwhelm the reader. It has seemed natural, therefore, that the *Testament* be consistently read in terms of *effet du réel,* that is by verification of its references to a historical context. Critics, novelists, and readers con-

3. Paul Valéry, *Oeuvres,* "Villon et Verlaine" (Paris: Gallimard, 1957 [1937]), 427–43. Translation mine.

sistently try to reconstruct the historical context around the poem; in turn, the *Testament* has often been used as a springboard for surveys of fifteenth-century history, like the one Jean Favier published in 1982.[4] The *Testament* is often read as if it were a document, that is, as if it offered evidence equivalent to police or church records, which enable us to fix historical facts and circumstances with some degree of certainty. Moreover, there are undeniable coincidences between recorded historical facts and seemingly referential elements in the *Testament* to be accounted for.

Efforts at historical reconstruction, however, have invariably resulted in fragmented readings of the *Testament*. As its verses have been traced piecemeal into archives, the complete poem of the *Testament* has been left pecked apart like the faces of the hanged men in Villon's *ballade*. Few studies indeed have attempted to account for the *Testament* as a poetic whole; fewer still have attempted to understand the poetic function of the elements of historical reference within the *Testament*.

Although it is currently fashionable to think of reading as a construction of a text, it may be seen that works like the *Testament* also construct and determine our reading. Even if the historical documents which have filled out the biographical and historical accounts of Villon had not been recovered in the nineteenth century, comparison to a contemporary poem shows how the *Testament* in and of itself thrusts every reader towards a referential reading.

The initial verses of Charles d'Orléans's *ballade* 98 could be read in terms of reference[5]:

> En tirant d'Orléans a Blois,
> L'autre jour par eaue venoye
> Si rencontré, par plusieurs foiz,
> Vaisseaux, ainsi que je passoye,
> Qui singloient leur droicte voye
> Et aloient legierement,
> Pour ce qu'eurent, comme veoye,
> A plaisir et a gré le vent.
>
> Mon cueur, Penser et moy, nous troys,
> Les regardasmes a grant joye,
> Et dit mon cueur a basse vois:
> "Voulentiers en ce point feroye,
> De Confort la voille tendroye,
> Se je cuidoye seurement
> Avoir, ainsi que je vouldroye,
> A plaisir et a gré le vent." [Vv. 1–16]

4. Jean Favier, *François Villon* (Paris: Fayard, 1982).
5. Charles d'Orléans, *Poésies*, CFMA, ed. P. Champion (Paris: Champion, 1923–27).

> Going by water the other day from Orleans to Blois, several times I met boats as I passed, which sailed straight along and made their way easily because they had, as I saw, the wind in their favor.
>
> The three of us, my heart, Thought, and I, contemplated them with great joy, and my heart said in a low voice: "I would willingly do likewise, I would spread the sail of Consolation, if I could be sure of having, as I would wish, the wind in my favor."

The elements here strongly marked by geographic referentiality are set into the text in ways that complement the reader's imaginative representation of boats carried along a river by wind, oars, and currents. Blois and Orleans are commonly recognized as referring to river towns or, alternatively, to princely residences. Any inclination to verify historical reference, however, is effectively damped by the identity of the three in the boat ("My heart, Thought, and I, we three") that shifts the reader's representation, his imaginative construction, away from referentiality towards introspective moral reflection. This movement is repeatedly confirmed by the abstract nouns that modify every concrete image in the poem except those of *bateaux, nefs,* and *vent* [boats, wind]: "la voille de Confort; l'eaue de Fortune, le bateau du Monde, les avirons d'Espoir, les vagues de Tourment." [The sail of Consolation, the water of Fortune, the boat of the World, the oars of Hope, the waves of Suffering.] These abstractions do not weaken the reader's mental representation of the river scene, but they do hold in check his urge to seek reference. It would be difficult to speak of Charles d'Orléans's poem in terms of *effet du réel,* of referentiality. But the text leads us gently and easily to enjoy the *effet de réel,* the veil of familiar scenes and images which both clothes and represents the inner meditation.

The *Testament's* opening *huitain,* in contrast, leads the reader to a very different process of imaginative construction.

> En l'an de mon trentiesme aage,
> Que toutes mes hontes j'euz beues,
> Ne du tout fol ne du tout saige
> Non obstant maintes peines eues,
> Lesquelles j'ay toutes receues
> Soubz la main Thibault d'Aucigny . . .
> S'esvesque il est, signant les rues,
> Qu'il soit le mien, je le regny. [Vv. 1–8]

> In my thirtieth year of life
> When I had drunk down all my disgrace
> Neither altogether a fool nor altogether wise
> Despite the many blows I had
> Every one of which I took
> At Thibault d'Aussigny's hand

Bishop he may be as he signs the cross
Through the streets, but I deny he is mine.[6]

The first movement of this huitain does incline us towards moral reflection relatively unmarked by reference to history. A voice speaks of his age and moral condition and our imaginative representation requires only the most general human understanding of disgrace, folly, wisdom, and what it's like to be over thirty.

The words *Thibault d'Aucigny* in the sixth line, which the reader identifies as a "real" proper name, open up the possibility of reference to a historical context. With the words *Thibault d'Aucigny* Villon could intend either to represent a fictional character with a realistic name, an *effet de réel*, or to refer to a real person, an *effet du réel*. Two additional elements in the *Testament* push towards an *effet du réel* and a reading in referential terms.

First, textual cues like past tenses stir up the reader's propensity for stories, incite him to undertake a narrative representation. The opening stanzas of the *Testament* link *Thibault d'Aucigny* to the poetic I in a burst of feelings and events; blows are taken, authority is denied. Something terrible happened to Villon, we think; *Thibault d'Aucigny* did it. Moreover because such a narrative representation has a strong, agglomerative pull, subsequent passages in the *Testament* that seem to fit the "story" will be readily added to it: the bread and water diet of the second huitain (vv. 13–14) is Thibaut's doing as is the stay in the Meung prison (v. 83); the "story" explains the vindictive last stanzas of *Testament*'s penultimate *ballade* addressed to the "traitres chiens matins / Qui m'ont fait ronger dures crostes, / Mascher mains soirs et mains matins, / Que ores je ne crains troys crottes" [the sons-of-bitches / Who made me shit small and gnaw / Crusts many a dusk and dawn / Who don't scare me now three turds (Vv. 1984–87)]. Readers of Villon do not usually read the *Testament* itself as a narrative; but they typically dip into narrative representations made up from elements of the poem to understand its apparently disjointed content.

A second factor thrusts a reader's "story" towards history: the verses and stanzas about *Thibault d'Aucigny* in the *Testament* seem quite incomplete. The sentence which forms the initial stanza, "En l'an de mon trentiesme aage," never ends; no main clause ever comes, only digressive subordinates which trail out over some seven stanzas. We get crumbs of events, dates, places: "Tel luy soit Dieu qu'il m'a esté!" [God be to him as he's been to me (v. 16)]; "Escript l'ay l'an soixante et ung, / Lors que le roy

6. François Villon, *Le Testament Villon*, vol. 1, *Texte*, TLF, ed. J. Rychner and A. Henry (Geneva: Droz, 1974). All English citations of Villon are taken from the translation by Galway Kinnell, *The Poems of François Villon* (Boston: Houghton Mifflin, 1977).

me delivra / De la dure prison de Mehun." [Written in the year sixty-one / When the good king set me free / From the hard prison at Meung (vv. 81–83)]. The seventy-third *huitain* reads like a series of muttered fragments, emphasized by the modern editors' punctuation:

> Dieu mercy . . . et Tacque Thibault,
> Qui tant d'eau froide m'a fait boire,
> En ung bas, non pas en ung hault,
> Menger d'angoisse mainte poire,
> Enferré . . . Quant j'en ay memoire,
> Je prie pour luy, *et relicqua*,
> Que Dieu luy doint, et voire, voire,
> Ce que je pense, *et cetera*.
> [*Testament*, vv. 737–44]

> Thanks to God and Tacque Thibault
> Who made me drink all that cold water
> Locked in a dungeon, no upper room
> And eat all those anguish-pears
> In irons . . . Whenever it comes back to me
> I pray for him *et reliqua*
> That God may give him oh yes, oh yes
> What I'm thinking of *et cetera*.

These verses reiterate suggestive allusions, seem to recall a past history ("quant j'en ay memoire") which is then broken off or smudged out with ellipses. Apparent incompleteness frustrates the reader's impulse to find coherence: terms like *et cetera* imply that there is more to be said; yet words like "voire voire" give little nourishment to imaginative representation. A reader who feels he has not learned enough from the poem's own content to understand it, that is, to make a satisfactory mental representation, may well seize upon proper names of a historical type such as *Thibault d'Aucigny*, thinking that understanding must depend on knowledge of the historical context, where the allusions to events may be explained, the persons found who bore the names incorporated in the *Testament*. Moreover, the familiar Romantic myth of poetry fed by the poet's lived pain enhances the reader's readiness to use history to account for a poem whose themes are precisely the pain of living and experience. Thus through the combination of apparent referential allusion and of apparent incompleteness, the language of the *Testament* orients readers strongly towards the pursuit of historical reference.

In their effort to make sense of every line of the *Testament*, scholars have indeed often had recourse to narrative constructions based first and foremost on the elements in the poem that could have reference to historical people, places, events. A Thibaut d'Aussigny did exist; the real prison at Meung was actually under his legal jurisdiction as bishop of Orleans from 1452–1473. Narrative conjectures have served to fill in the gaps between historical information and the *Testament*. To account for the tone and content of Villon's verses on *Thibault d'Aucigny*, André Burger suggests that Villon must have been defrocked and imprisoned by Bishop Thibaut d'Aussigny, although not legally under his jurisdiction, and that Villon might have been driven by poverty to joining up with the *Coquillards*, a notorious band of thieves.[7] Jean Dufournet elaborates a different hypothetical story: Villon might have been deeply disappointed in Thibaut's refusal to be his spiritual father and resented Thibaut's refusal to recognize him as a *clerc* and as a poet.[8]

It is possible that discrepancies between such conjectural stories might be resolved by new historical evidence. Why should history not be accepted, the *effet du réel* acknowledged, these stanzas of the *Testament* read as referring to facts, what David Kuhn has called "les faits de Mehun," represented in a problematically obscure language?[9] Do not overwhelming chains of coincidence keep the *Testament* irrevocably bound to historical reference to explain the presence in both the *Testament* and police archives of names like Guy Tabarie, Jean Mautaint, Colin des Cayeux, and the identity of age, condition, criminal past of the François de Montcorbier of record and of the "je, François Villon, escollier" of the poetry?

First, the historical facts known do not fit with elements of the text. Although many proper names appear in both the *Testament* and in documents of historical record, Pierre Demarolle has demonstrated that there is no overlap between events recorded in the archives and those suggested in the *Testament*.[10] Although archives verify the criminal record of Maître François, no word outside the *Testament* confirms that Villon was imprisoned in Meung or connects him in any way with Bishop Thibaut.

Second, the verified facts of historical reference marshalled in massive array behind the *Testament* have been of surprisingly little use in helping readers make better sense of this difficult text. There remains a striking disparity between the characteristically coherent smoothness of hypothetical narratives written about Villon from a historical perspective and the broken, discontinuous surface of the *Testament* itself. Paradoxically it is the very lines that seem to fairly bristle with referentiality that are the hardest to read in historical terms. The factual background for many apparent references seems quite complete, as for those in the legacy stanza to Maistre Guillaume de Villon.

7. André Burger, *Studi . . . Siciliano* (Florence, 1966).

8. Jean Dufournet, *Recherches sur le "Testament"* (Paris: SEDES, 2nd edition, 1971), vol. 1, 162–63.

9. David Kuhn, *Poétique de François Villon* (Paris: Colin, 1967), 229.

10. Pierre Demarolle, *Villon: un testament ambigu* (Paris: Larousse, 1973), 61–64.

Je lui donne ma librarye
Et le roumant du Pet au Deable
Lequel maistre Guy Tabarye
Grossa, qui est homs veritable.
Par cayeulx est soubz une table;
Combien qu'il soit rudement fait
La matiere est si tres notable
Qu'elle admende tout le mesfait. [Vv. 857–64]

I give him my library
Including "The Tale of the Devil's Fart"
Which that truthful fellow
Master Guy Tabarie clear-copied
It's in notebooks under a table
Although the style may be crude
The matter itself is so potent
It makes up for the defects.

The *Pet au Deable* was a boundary stone recorded in police reports on students who in rioting bands carried it to the Mont Sainte Geneviève from the dwelling of Mademoiselle de Bruyère, who owned the stone and who is herself another legatee within the *Testament* (v. 1508). Historians have essentially recovered all that can reasonably be known now about Guy Tabarie; every twist of the rack produced more facts in his confession to the Collège of Navarre theft and about his acquaintance with "maistre François Villon," who participated in the crime. But all the laboriously reconstructed information does not seem pertinent to the *Testament*, does not match this *huitain* in a way that clarifies its meaning. Why is the "Roumant" left to Guillaume de Villon? What does it mean to say Guy Tabarie made a fair copy of it? and that he is an "hom veritable"? Why is it under the table? Such problems of sense reinforce the persistent belief that there is some yet uncovered referent that will enable these lines to be better understood, perhaps some clue to a joke understood by the poet's acquaintances. Some have thought that the stanza secretly refers to the Collège de Navarre theft. Dufournet and Villon's most recent editors propose to read "cayeulx" (v. 861) as an allusion to Colin de Cayeulx, implicated in the Collège de Navarre theft and "skinned" (i.e., hanged) in v. 1675 of the *Testament*.[11] Such connections, however, lead again to conjectural reconstruction within history, and not to either an accounting for the inner structure of the *Testament* nor even for the sense of this stanza. For what would it mean to say: "By Colin de Cayeux it is under a table?"

It may be seen, too, that verification of reference does not, in fact,

11. Dufournet, *Recherches*, vol. 1, 251–57; Rychner and Henry, *Testament*. Vol. 2, *Commentaire*, 128–29.

bring the reader to an essentially different reading of a typical legacy stanza than that he might make without any footnotes from history.

> *Item*, a maistre Jacques James,
> Qui se tue d'amasser biens,
> Donne fiancer tant de femmes
> Qu'il voudra, mais d'espouser, riens!
> Pour quy amasse il? Pour les sciens?
> Il ne plaint fors que ses morceaux;
> Ce qui fut aux truyes, je tiens
> Qu'il doit de droit estre aux pourceaulx. [Vv. 1812–19]

> *Item* to master Jacques James
> Who kills himself acquiring wealth
> I give all the women he wants
> As fiancées but not one as wife
> For whom is it all for, his family?
> He whines for nothing but his junk[12]
> What was for the sows I reckon
> Belongs by rights to the pigs.

The stanza names a gentleman, maistre Jacques James (called "homme de bien" in v. 1944 of the *Testament*), gives him "nothing" (*riens*), and associates him with pigs to boot. What can be learned of Maistre Jacques from the archives, that he was a man of property and a bureaucrat in the Buildings Department of Paris, adds an additional fillip of specificity, but does not change the essential shape of the stanza which is identical to that of the legacy to Guillaume de Villon and many other legacy stanzas as well: a proper name, that of a historical contemporary (usually a man of substance), is associated with grotesque, even obscene motifs and derisive first-person commentary. The legacy stanzas thus follow a poetic pattern whose spaces can be filled with real proper names, incongruous legacies, and wry, jeering asides.

Confirmation that the choice of elements having potential reference is determined by poetic design within the poem comes with recognition of other combinations of literary patterns and elements of historical reference inserted into the mock legacies. For example, Villon sets a proverb into the stanza to Jacques James, punning on a place name associated with Maistre Jacques, who owned a house in la rue aux Truyes (Sow Street): "Ce

---

12. Dufournet notes an early nineteenth-century explanation of this expression: "Plaindre les morceaux: N'estre pas content qu'un autre mange." ["To resent what others eat."] *Recherches*, vol. 2, 510. Rychner and Henry gloss differently: "il ne lésine, il ne mesure avec économie que ce qu'il mange lui, et nourrit largement les siens." ["He's only stingy with his own food and feeds his family well."] *Commentaire*, 253.

forfait la truye, que les pourceaux le compeiront." [The piglets pay for the sow's misdeeds.][13] Other texts confirm the fifteenth-century taste for fictional fantasies made up from street names, tavern signs and the like, as in *The Marriage of the Parisian Street Signs,* celebrating the wedding of tavern signs like *The Four Sons of Aymon* to *The Three Daughters of Dan Symon* and *Saint George's Maiden.*[14] Such texts provided a model for this stanza as they did for the *Pet au deable* (also a street sign of sorts) in the legacy to Guillaume de Villon. Between the *Testament* and history, then, must be discerned layers of literary patterns that admit yet also deform reference to history.

The fifteenth-century texts that are really determined by an *effet du réel,* that do depict specific historical events and persons or that are intended to actively, polemically affect historical events, are utterly unlike the *Testament.* Within the contemporary Burgundian court, for example, political events and intentions provide a constant grain for the mills of Rhetoriqueur poets to grind out in glittering verse. Description of insignia of the Order of the Golden Fleece, wórn by thirteen notables who visited the Flanders border on behalf of Charles le Téméraire, is straightforward in the chronicle of Olivier de la Marche: "Et furent les officiers habillez et vestuz de robes longues d'escarlate. . . . Tous avoient le collier d'or faict de fusilz et garniz de leurs flames au col, auquel pendoit la noble thoison d'or." [The officers were garbed and dressed in long scarlet robes. . . . All had the gold collar made of steels and adorned with their flames at the neck, from which hung the noble Golden Fleece.][15] Molinet's poem of occasional verse, "Le Bergier sans solas," transforms the ambassadors' garb into a glorious mythological riddle: "Treize bergiers portans zone aureÿne, / A leur poitrine ung mouton de Colcos," [Thirteen shepherds, girt with an aureate zone, / upon their breast a sheep of Colchis (vv. 235–36)]. Reading such works one may successfully seek information about the referent as well as study the representation of history within the text; factional or polemical aims can be identified which attach the work to a group, an interest, or to political events and questions of patronage and diffusion must be discussed.[16] The panygerics celebrating the victories of the *lion rampant* of Burgundy, the polemical machines like Molinet's *Naufrage de la pucelle,* are texts sweltering in what Zumthor has called *le*

13. *Proverbes français antérieurs au XVe siècle,* ed. J. Morawski (Paris: Champion, 1925), no. 320.

14. Cited by P. Champion, *François Villon* (Paris: Champion, 1913), vol. 1, 61.

15. Cited by Noël Dupire, ed., *Les Faictz et dictz de Jean Molinet* (Paris: SATF, 1936–39), vol. 3, 969–70.

16. Jane Tompkins's fine essay "The Reader in History" defines such matters of *effet du réel* from a solidly historical perspective. *Reader-Oriented Criticism* (Baltimore: The Johns Hopkins Univ. Press, 1980), 201–32.

discours de la gloire [the discourse of glory].[17] They typically costume historical events and political ambitions in a heavy cloth of fifteenth-century rhetorical *poeterie*, a gloss of fiction, myth, and allegory utterly unlike the poetic manner of the *Testament*. These factional pieces are the poetic complement to the Burgundian chronicles, parallel modes of discourse for representing, recording, and glorifying historical events: the chronicles overcoat the confusion and contradictions of events with what Auerbach called "the smoothness of legend"; the verses disguise and transform referentiality in order to engender poetic effects of admiration appropriate to the celebration of princely power.

Given the ease with which the referential framework of such occasional verse can be established, it is all the more striking that studies of the *Testament* have failed to identify conclusively any political, polemical, factional, or satirical interests consistently served by the *Testament*'s mode of ironic *vituperatio*. It is difficult to stabilize the tone of the *Testament* within any of the rhetorically determined schemes of praise or blame typical of fifteenth-century political eloquence. Within the *Testament*, moreover, we cannot grasp the sense of the allusions to historical circumstances around the poetic I that might correspond to an *effet du réel*. Its intense emotions—humor, disgust, resentment, vengeance, warning, regret—are puzzling; they seem purposeful, but cannot be coherently linked to historical events or partisan purpose nor even to the self-advocacy evident in Villon's occasional verse: his praise of Louis XI (*Test.*, vv. 55–72), the *Louange à Marie d'Orléans, Requête à monseigneur de Bourbon, Louange et requête à la Cour.*

In marked contrast to the Rhétoriqueurs, however, stand those fifteenth-century works and genres that commonly represent their themes in terms of highly mimetic creatural realism, as distinct from those that refer specifically to History. This kind of vivid, convincing representation, this taste for *effet de réel*, is characteristic of almost every literary genre in the fifteenth century but lyric love poetry. From farce to mystery, from the *Cent Nouvelles Nouvelles* to chivalric biographies, from the familiar metaphors of Charles d'Orléans and the lugubrious *Danse macabré* to Coquillart's dramatic monologues, all are strongly marked by what C. S. Lewis calls "presentational realism."[18] In such works, elements of historical reference are an integral element in their *effet de réel*, as in the dramatic monologues of the braggart soldier where allusions to famous real officers and battles provides an element of convincing characterization. "I campaigned with Captain La Hire at the siege of Orleans," says the Franc

17. P. Zumthor, *Le Masque et la lumière* (Paris: Seuil, 1978).
18. C. S. Lewis, "On Realisms," *An Experiment in Criticism* (London: Cambridge Univ. Press, 1961), 57–73.

Archer de Baignollet, "I was at Ancenis with La Rochefoucault and the bastard of Bourbon." "You don't believe me?" asks the Franc Archer de Cherré, "Cela est aussi vray que histoire" [It's as true as history.][19]

Only those texts most closely bound to historical circumstances, the Burgundian *poèmes de circonstance* and the political *sotties*, paradoxically escape the pervasive fashion for detailed representation of every literary theme in plausible, recognizable, everyday garb of character, setting, and event. The *effet de réel* or representational realism is, therefore, weakest in those fifteenth-century works most strongly tied to history, strongest in works whose themes are literary commonplaces of love, death, and trickery.

Villon's poetry intensifies and particularizes to an extraordinary extent certain aspects of presentational realism typical of this period, not by multiplying the clutter of everyday objects as does Guillaume Coquillart in his dramatic monologues, but by multiplying the instances of reference to historical persons and places. Such references added an extra *effet de réel* to works like *Petit Jehan de Saintré*, where several characters including the hero bear historical names or like the *Cent Nouvelles Nouvelles*, represented as tales told by real members of the Burgundian court.

Contemporary imitations of the *Testament* confirm that it was indeed viewed as a playful juggling of referential elements within the fixed literary patterns of the mock will: the legacy of a trivial or impossible item to real people. Contemporary works that explicitly reuse the *Testament*'s "formula" all play with mentions of historical referents. The compelling force of referentiality is diminished in these, however, because the authors reduce the number of proper names and specific allusions. The "Testament Ragot," that declares, "J'ay excedé maistre François Villon," addresses "ces procureurs et jeunes avocats," not, as does Villon, "mon procureur Fournier" (*Testament*, v. 1030). In the *Testament Levrault* "taverniers" get a legacy not "Robin Turgis" (tavernkeeper of "le trou de la Pomme de Pin," the Pine Cone Hole Tavern, *Testament*, v. 1045).[20] In the *Testament*, on the other hand, elements of reference cannot be confined to a few categories of literary themes and structures. They are not there reduced to setting, as in the *Cent Nouvelles Nouvelles*, to characterization as in the *Franc Archer*, to exemplary tale as in *Saintré*, nor to motif as in the *Testament Ragot* but invade every domain of form and subject.

The distinction between representation and reference thus demarcates two groups of fifteenth-century texts that have very different rela-

19. L. Polak, ed., *Le Franc Archier de Baignollet*, TLF (Geneva: Droz, 1966), 67, v. 548.
20. "Le Testament du hault et notable homme nommé Ragot " (St. 6) and "Le Testament et Epitaphe de Maistre Françoys Levrault, Sergent-Royal en la Sénéchaussée de Guyenne," (St. 33), ed. A. de Montaiglon, *Anciennes poésies françoises*, vol. 5, 151 and vol. 10, 137–38.

tions to the historical world and entirely dissimilar modes of representation. Moreover, the *Testament* seen as a member of the group ruled by *effet de réel* opens it up to a study not of referents but of the effect of referentiality created by the power of the poet's language.

Freed of the need to verify reference in history, critics can at last undertake evaluation of the essential poetic function served by all the elements of *effet de réel* in the *Testament:* the characterization of the poetic I that constitutes from first to last its true center and real subject. It is this poetic I, the voice that speaks in the poem, that gives it the coherence which is not to be found in historical reference.

There is much yet to be said about this voice, the key starting point for new readings of Villon. One could speak of the biographical mode of the *Testament* that continues the genre of the *vida* and *razo*, which created a biographical or narrative setting for lyric texts, a tradition developed in works like Machaut's *Voir dit* and Christine de Pisan's *Livre du Duc des vrais amants.* The *Testament*'s greatly expanded representation of such a biographical frame is cast in realistic terms unknown to the courtly tradition, but familiar enough within the fifteenth-century dramatic monologues to which the *Testament* has not yet been fully compared. Lawyers, policemen, whores and thieves swirl around the poetic I; the spaces evoked to surround the voice that speaks are not *La Forest de Longue Attente* but the Innocents Cemetery, the Threadmarket of Paris. This voice acts as a vehicle for an anthology of poetic modes from the lyric stanzas of plaintive regret to the obscene *sotte chanson* of la Grosse Margot, to the *Lais* of Villon himself, cited and rewritten in the *Testament.* The voice in the *Testament* speaks a richly varied poetic language, can, indeed, speak of anything, for "Qui meurt a ses loix de tout dire " [A dying man should have his say (v. 728)].

The insistent first-person singular marks every line, intrudes into every poetic register, subordinates to itself every lyric piece. The three *ballades* of yesteryear are grasped by the poetic I: "Puis que pappes, roys, filz de roys / . . . . / Moy, povre marcerot de regnes, / Morrai ge pas?" [Since popes, kings, and kings' sons / . . . / I a poor packman out of Rennes / Won't I also die? (vv. 413, 417–18)]; the I adds himself to the enumeration of celebrated lovers in the *Double Ballade:* "De moy, povre, je vueil parler" [Of my poor self let me say (v. 657)].

The initial *Thibault d'Aucigny* matter serves to immediately characterize the poetic I in social and affective terms as a clerical voice, subordinate to and defiant of ecclesiastical authority, knowledgeable in literary matters. It establishes an initial tone of injury and outrage that is recalled and sustained throughout the *Testament* and that serves both to characterize the speaker and to carry all the themes of the poem. To this single voice are attributed the regrets for a wasted youth, the sardonic legacies, the vile disgust of the *Ballade des langues envieuses*, the gaudy defiance of the *Ballade de la Grosse Margot:* "Ordure amons, ordure nous assuit" [On filth we dote, filth is our lot (v. 1625)].

Syntactic patterns representing familiar speech both characterize this voice and create a sense of immediacy and presence; effects of spoken language like ellipsis, digression, and cursing frequently intrude into poetic diction within the *Testament.* The even tone and language, the smooth matching of clauses, phrases, and verse length in Charles d'Orléans's *ballade* contrast with the characteristic jolting rhythm and low talk of Villon's huitains, as in the conclusion to the final verses to *Thibault d'Aucigny* and his "chiens":

> Je feisse pour eulx pez et roctes,
> Je ne puis, car je suis assiz.
> Auffort, pour esviter rïoctes,
> Je crye a toutes gens mercys. [Vv. 1988–91]

> I'd raise for them farts and belches
> But as I'm sitting down I can't manage
> Anyway to avoid starting a riot
> I cry everyone's pardon.

Such language and such prosody is part and parcel of the poetic intention of the *Testament*, that seeks to characterize and immortalize a voice, to fix it into memory: "Au moins sera de moi memoire / Telle qu'elle est d'un bon follastre" [So that at least there'll be some memory left / Such as may be of a wayward one, (v. 1883).] Villon's typical colloquial language is a further element of characterization, consistent with the classical conception that equated low style with humble subject; the *Testament*'s rasping, vulgar talk suits its representation of a *bon follastre*'s voice: "Je suis paillart, la paillarde me suyt. / . . . / c'est a mau rat mau chat" [I'm a lecher, she's a lecher to match / . . . / like unto like, bad rat bad cat (vv. 1622, 1624)].

The apparently referential content of many verses, which leads readers to locate the voice within historical circumstance, is, therefore, a complementary means of representing lived experience, which the poem attributes to the poetic I. In the *Thibault d'Aucigny* stanzas as throughout the *Testament*, the abundant display of historical terms are not a tangle of references to unknot, but a poetic element characterizing the memorable voice that fills the *Testament*.

The extraordinary success of the dense poetic characterization of voice in the *Testament* can be measured by its transformation from voice to character. "Villon" is first the trickster hero of the *Repues franches* who reappears in Rabelais's *Quart Livre*, then the somber rogue poet, *poète maudit*, in both scholarly books of historical reconstruction and in dozens of nineteenth- and twentieth-century sketches, novels, plays and films about "François Villon" by poets, novelists and biographers like Rimbaud, Théophile Gautier, Robert Lewis Stevenson, D. B. Wyndham Lewis, Babette Deustch. The *Testament*'s powerful characterization of voice persuaded Ezra Pound that Villon "lilted his heart out" without mask, achieving sincere self-expression unmediated by thought, art, imagination, or literary self-consciousness.[21]

The *Testament* is not, however, a work determined by sincerity and *effet du réel* and written to recount historical experience but a poem that represents a voice speaking of experience in such convincing terms, with such *effet de réel*, that we attribute to it historical existence. The poem forces us into a referential reading, into the *effet du réel*, as the best possible *effet de réel*, that which makes us believe that a text is not only true to life but also true to fact. The slant towards referential reading in Villon criticism that intrudes at every point upon our perception of poetic structures is a construction imposed on our reading by the *Testament* itself. The short circuiting, the conjuring away of our awareness of the poetic process of representation that hides its *effet de réel* under a cover of *effet du réel*, is indeed the key to the poem. For the *Testament* contains and displays lyric poems, but, unlike Villon's *Lais* it conceals its own poetic structure and substitutes a documentary for a literary shape. But reference serves representation, not history in the *Testament*. In order to read the *Testament* to its fullest as a poem, we must see it as well as believe it.

The slip from *effet de réel* to *effet du réel* recalls Pliny's famous story of the contest between the rival Greek painters of antiquity, Zeuxis and Parrhasius. The grapes painted by Zeuxis were so realistically represented that birds flew to peck at them. But then Zeuxis turned condescendingly to Parrhasius and asked him to draw aside the curtain covering his painting. "Ah," responded Parrhasius, "the curtain is the painting!" Have we long been trying to draw aside the curtain of Villon's poetry instead of seeing it?

---

21. *A Lume Spento* (New York: New Directions, 1965), 120; see George J. Bornstein and Hugh H. Witemeyer, "From *Villain* to Visionary: Pound and Yeats on Villon," *Comparative Literature* 19 (1967), 308–20.

II. Imaging the Text

R. HOWARD BLOCH

Silence and Holes: The *Roman de Silence* and the Art of the Trouvère

Among the little-known works of the Middle Ages none has been the object of greater neglect than the *Roman de Silence*. So complete, in fact, has been the silence surrounding this thirteenth-century verse romance that it was not edited in toto until 1972, has occasioned no major critical effort (article or book), and—*mirabile visu*—is not even mentioned in Volker Roloff's thematic study of speech and silence in Old French.[1] That *Silence* has elicited so little attention is all the more startling given the eloquence with which it speaks to issues crucial not only to a hypothetical medieval audience, but to the present day. The explicitness with which *Silence* probes the relation between nature and culture, the precision of its reflection of social context—in short, its historical mimetism—make it a keystone in the anthropology of the High Middle Ages.[2] More important, the complex series of articulations which the text establishes between language and desire, between writing and sexual difference, between poetry and power (economic, military, political) pressures a reading of the *Roman de Silence* toward the modes of textual production inherent to every age. And if *Silence* constitutes a guide to the understanding of medieval culture and poetics, it also reads uncannily like a programme for the

---

1. *Reden und Schweigen. Zur Tradition und Gestaltung eines mittelalterlichen Themas in der französischen Literatur* (Munich: Fink, 1973). Those interested generally in silence should see B. P. Dauenhauer, *Silence: The Phenomenon and its Ontological Significance* (Bloomington: Univ. of Indiana Press, 1980); A. B. Greene, *The Philosophy of Silence* (New York: Richard Smith, 1940); M. Picard, *The World of Silence* (Chicago: H. Regnery, 1952).

2. This is the subject of a book I recently published and which forms the background of this essay: *Etymologies and Genealogies: A Literary Anthropology of the French Middle Ages* (Chicago: Univ. of Chicago Press, 1983). For a discussion of the *Roman de Silence*, see 195–97.

interpretation of modernism. Silence is golden—a gold mine of insight into medieval and modern discursive theory as well as practice.

Superficially, the central focus of *Silence* is prepared by an almost incidental subplot in which the quarrel between two counts over which will marry the eldest of two sisters and thus inherit the larger of two holdings (*la maisnee*), results in the death of both and a royal prohibition of cognatic succession. "Never again," proclaims King Ebain, "will a woman inherit in the realm of England as long as I hold land."[3] The exclusion of females, which angers those anxious to endow younger sons through affiliation, thus lays the groundwork for an elaborate biopolitical drama whose resolution occupies the rest of the romance. For when King Ebain then seeks to marry off the only daughter of the Duke of Cornwall and to invest the dead duke's son-in-law with the paternal duchy, that investiture, by Ebain's own decree, depends upon the production of a male heir (vv. 1295, 1455, 1588, 1684). The subsequent birth of a daughter to Eufemie and Cador (Ebain's nephew) poses the dilemma of lineal interruption which the author, who twice identifies himself as the otherwise unknown Heldris de Cornuälle (vv. 1, 6682), conceives simultaneously in genealogical and linguistic terms. That is, the parents decide to name their daughter Silentius, to hide her sexual identity, and, if the deception is ever discovered, simply to change her name to Silentia (see below p. 86).

Silence, raised in isolation (a medieval Wild Child), becomes aware, around the time of puberty, not only that she is a female "trapped in a male body," but that she is inexplicably attracted to poetry, more specifically, to a troupe of itinerant jongleurs with whom she escapes. So skilled in fact does she then become at the art of singing that she outperforms and out-earns the jealous poets who plot to kill her. Meanwhile, Ebain's wife Eufeme has fallen in love with Silence and, failing twice to seduce her, succeeds in having her exiled to France armed with forged letters requesting her execution. The King of France, suspicious of Ebain's intention, learns the truth and houses Silence at his own court until Ebain recalls her to fight in the wars against rebellious barons. Peace restored, Eufeme again tries to seduce Silence and, again rebuffed, denounces her to Ebain. The King this time substitutes for exile an expiatory ordeal—to capture Merlin who, according to legend, will only be taken by a woman, as Silence, who succeeds in bringing the magician under her spell, is entrapped by the revelation of her true gender. Ebain is furious at his wife's perfidy, executes her, and marries Silence, daughter of his own nephew and the woman whose name—Eufemie—differs but by one letter from that of his former wife.

3. *Le Roman de Silence*, ed. L. Thorpe (Cambridge: Heffer and Sons, 1972), v. 314. All references are to this edition.

This summary (reminiscent of the old SATF introductions?) behind us, we can begin to read the *Roman de Silence* which in fact begins to read itself, for the medieval text prescribes the parameters of its own interpretation; and the theory and praxis of such a reading are intertwined. We begin, then, by noting that *Silence* participates in a long and respected Latin and vernacular tradition according to which nature, writing, and sexual difference are allied. Alain de Lille, for example, associates the "lawful path of sure descent" with Nature, who, in order to insure genealogical succession, endowed her handmaiden Venus with two instruments of rectitude—*ortho*graphy, or straight writing, and *ortho*dox coition, or straight sexuality:

> Also, I appointed for her work anvils, noble instruments, with a command that she would apply these same hammers to them, and faithfully give herself up to the forming of things, not permitting the hammers to become strangers to the anvils. For the office of writing I provided her with an especially potent reed-pen, in order that, on suitable leaves that desire the writing of the pen . . . she might, according to the rules of my orthography, trace the nature of things, and might not suffer the pen to stray at all in the trackless diversion of false style away from the path of proper description. But since for the production of progeny the rule of marital coition, with its lawful embraces, was to connect things unlike in their opposition of sexes. . . .[4]

Licit intercourse thus preserves the continuity of lineage and is indissociable from correct writing, or grammar, which excludes diversion from the "path of proper description," that is to say, linguistic property. Nouns and adjectives copulate according to the rules of heterosexual combination,[5] and people conjugate according to the precepts of regular construction.[6]

For Jean de Meun (inspired by Alain), Nature is the earthly agent of generational continuity, the guarantor of the species despite the death of individuals. Nature's confessor, Genius, is the "god and master of places and of property."[7] If Nature assures the survival of human lineage, her

4. Alain de Lille, *De Planctu Naturae,* in *Satirical Poets of the Twelfth Century,* ed. T. Wright (London: Longman, 1872), 475.

5. "Furthermore, my command enjoined Cypris that, in her constructions, she have regard to the ordinary rules for nouns and adjectives, and that she appoint that organ which is especially marked with the peculiarity of the feminine sex to the office of noun, and that she should put that organ characterized by the signs of the masculine sex in the seat of the adjective" (*De Planctu,* 476).

6. "Besides this, I added that the Dionean conjugation should not admit into its uniform use of transitive construction either a defective use, or the circuity of reflexiveness, or the crookedness of double conjugation since it is content with the direct course of single conjugation" (Ibid., 477).

7. "Genius, dist elle, biau prestres, / Qui des leus estes diex et mestres, / Et selonc lor propriétés / Toutes en ovre les metés, / Et bien achevés le besoingne / Si cum a chascun le besoingne. . . ." (*Le Roman de la rose,* ed. D. Poirion [Paris: Flammarion, 1974], v. 16285).

vicar preserves the proper places (*leus*) of speech or the order of representation itself ("les figures representables"). Genius embodies the figure of the writer, the scribe of that arch-text of the Middle Ages—the Book of Nature:

> Devant Nature la deesse,
> Li prestres, qui bien s'acordoit,
> En audience recordoit
> Les figures representables,
> De toutes choses corrumpables,
> Qu'il ot escrites en son livre,
> Si cum Nature les li livre.[8]

Before the Goddess Nature the priest, who was very accomodating, recorded in audience the representable figures of all corruptible things, which he wrote in his book as Nature gave them to him.

Proper writing (the discreteness of place) and proper generation (the uninterrupted devolution of things according to their nature or property) are, through Nature and Genius, combined.

The *Roman de Silence* reads in many places like a vernacular version of Alain's *De Planctus Naturae* which its author most certainly knew; Heldris's relation to Jean is, because of the uncertainty of the date of the manuscript, much less certain. Nonetheless, here too Nature embodies the principle of difference, the "mould" of many things from unformed matter synonomous with the discreteness of names:

> Molles i a bien .m. milliers,
> Que cho li est moult grans mestiers,
> Car s'ele n'eüst formé c'une
> Sa samblance estroit si commune
> De tolte gent, c'on ne savroit
> Quoi, ne quel non, chascuns avroit.
> Mais Nature garda si bien
> En s'uevre n'a a blasmer rien. [V. 1887]

There are a thousand thousand moulds of which she has great need, since, if she had only formed one, her image of all men would be so common that one would not know what nor what name each had. But Nature took care that there should be nothing to blame in her work.

The above portrayal of *Natura formatrix* is similar to descriptions found in numerous contemporaneous literary and philosophical texts, descriptions in which the nature or property of an individual thing—the unique nonessential quality distinguishing it from all others in its class—is linked explicitly to writing:

8. Ibid., v. 16278.

> Les orelles li fait petites
> Nature, ki les a escrites,
> Les sorcils brun et bien seöir,
> Nul hom ne puet si bials veöir. [V. 1917]

Nature made her small ears, Nature who wrote upon them such dark and well situated eyebrows that no one could see more beautiful ones.

Nature has literally inscribed Silence's features upon her face and in so doing reproduces the movement of the author whose own corpus of inscription is coterminous with the feminine body of romance.

Such an attempt to "close" the text upon itself is not to deny that the difference or property assured by Nature's names was, for the aristocracy of the thirteenth century, manifestly linked to the real differences of property attached to the patronym. The name of the family holding—its land and castle—was identical to that of the holder of title and of a title which assured the proper (primogenital) transmission of all three. What I am suggesting is that the propriety of names, thus posited at the level of nature, served to guarantee—through writing—what was perceived as a natural social order. This is why, despite the complaint of Nature (vv. 5997 ff.) and despite the elaborate debate between Nature and Nurture (Noreture) that runs throughout the Roman de Silence (vv. 2292, 2423, 2653, 5987) and is even expressed as an opposition between the raw and the cooked (vv. 5997–6114), there is no essential contradiction between heredity and environment. This is also why grammatical irregularity, language which differs, is conceived in terms of an act against nature. For Alain, once again, all rhetoric is the equivalent of social deviance:

> Furthermore, just as it has been my purpose to attack with bitter hostility certain practices of grammar and logic, and exclude them from the schools of Venus, so I have forbidden to the arts of Cypris those metonymic postures of rhetoricians which Mother Rhetoric embraces in her wide bosom, thereby gracing her speeches with many fine touches; for I feared lest if, in the pursuit of too strained a metaphor, she should change the predicate from its protesting subject into something wholly foreign, cleverness would be too far converted into a blemish, refinement into grossness, a trope into a fault, ornament into a show. [De Planctu, 478]

Grammatical and sexual prohibitions work hand in hand to prevent the use of "too strained a metaphor," which amounts to verbal and moral vice. Viciousness, in the tradition passed to the Middle Ages from Latin grammarians, is a rhetorical concept designating incorrect usage (barbarism and solecism) and carrying the bivalent resonance of a confusion of active and passive functions—a "retaining under the letters of the passive the nature of the active," that is, "an assumption of the law of the deponent"—and a confusion of genders. The homosexual, for example, is thus "both predicate and subject, he becomes likewise of two declensions, he pushes the laws of grammar too far. He barbarously denies that he is a man. Art does not please him, but rather artifice; even that artificiality cannot be called metaphor; rather it sinks into vice" (*De Planctu*, 429).

The association of sophistry and sodomy which lies at the core of Alain's thought is evident in a broad range of both courtly and noncourtly vernacular forms. The rivalry of poets in the fabliau known as "La Contregengle," for instance, produces the charge of faulty logic ("Tu paroles moult folement. / Si me fez .I. argument / Et .I. sofisme tout boçu") alongside that of perversion ("Lez moi que j'avoie à voisins / .II. maus larrons de tes cousins; / Andui furent par bougresie / Ars en milieu de Normendie"); both being assimilable to verbal bestiality: "Tu n'as pas ta borde vendue, / Qui ainsi bestornes les nons."[9]

Nature in the *Roman de Silence* considers her work to have been linguistically perverted ("Que s'uevre li ont bestornee," [v. 2259]) by an act of false naming. As Cador confesses to Eufemie, whose own name suggests euphemistic inflation, the suffix of their daughter's name is against both nature and natural usage:

> Il iert només Silenscius;
> Et s'il avient par aventure
> Al descovrir de sa nature
> Nos muerons cest -us en -a,
> S'avra a non Scilencia.
> Se nos li tolons dont cest -us
> Nos li donrons natural us,
> Car cis -us est contre nature,
> Mais l'altres seroit par nature. [V. 2074]

He will be named Silencius; and if it happens by chance that his nature is discovered, we will change this -*us* into -*a*, and she will be named Scilentia. If we withdraw then this -*us* we will restore natural law (us), because this -*us* is against nature and the other is according to nature.

Silence considers herself the "sophism of Nature" ("Dont se porpense en lui meïsme / Que Nature li fait sofime," [v. 2539]), as the -*us* that is against both custom ("Por che que l'-us est encontre us" [v. 2541]) and nature ("Car cis us n'est pas natureus" [v. 2554]) comes to constitute the gap—or specific minimal difference—within which this drama of language and lineage is played out.

This may seem like an excessive claim. Yet the *Roman de Silence*

9. *Recueil général des fabliaux*, ed. A. de Montaiglon and G. Raynaud (Paris: Librairie des bibliophiles, 1872–90), vol. 2, 257–60. "You speak very foolishly and construct for me an argument and a hunchbacked sophism." "Beside me I had for neighbors those two thieving cousins of yours; both were burned for buggery in the middle of Normandy." "You have not sold your tricks, you who bestialize (pervert) names."

focuses precisely upon the attempt to bring the suffix -a into consonance with the sexual identity of its bearer: "Silence atornent come feme" (v. 6664). No less than Chrétien's *Conte du Graal* (or, it might be argued, any courtly romance) Heldris's text is about the search for ancestral property and a proper name:[10]

> Segnor, que vos diroie plus?
> Ains ot non Scilensiüs:
> Ostés est -us, mis i est -a,
> Si est només Scilentia. [V. 6665]

Lords, what more can I say? Before she was named Scilensius. The -*us* was removed; the -*a* put in its place. And she was named Scilentia.

Once discovered, the proper name, according to the fictional possibility of verbal straightness or rectitude ("droiture"), restores the rule of nature, or sexual difference:

> D'illuec al tierc jor que Nature
> Ot recovree sa droiture
> Si prist Nature a repolir
> Par tolt le cors et a tolir
> Tolt quanque ot sor le cors de malle. [V. 6669]

On the third day after Nature had recovered its straightness Nature began to retool her body and to remove all traces of masculinity.

With Silence's assumption of her name the text also assumes its name, and the author is reduced literally to silence. "Segnor, que vos diroie plus?," Heldris asks, aware of the impossibility of further narrative progression.

To the extent to which the *Roman de Silence* maintains a false appellation and a nominal sexual difference ("Il a us d'ome tant usé / Et cel de feme refusé / Que poi en falt que il n'est males " [He has followed the custom of man for so long, and refused that of woman, that but for a little he is a man v. 2476]), in the interest of a true and real inheritance it symptomizes that which constitutes the proper of romance. That is, romance is written in the interstices between nature, an assumed propriety of names, sexual difference, and the rule of primogenital inheritance, on the one hand, and, on the other, the ruses of language expressed as artifice or hiding (and including silence), transgression of grammatical property, sexual inversion, and the deflection of a proper succession.

The impossibility of distinguishing the denotative impropriety of the heroine's name from its connotative propriety points, moreover, in the

---

10. See R. Dragonetti, *La Vie de la lettre au moyen âge* (Paris: Seuil, 1980); A. Leupin, *Le Graal et la littérature* (Lausanne: L'Age d'Homme, 1982); Ch. Méla, *Blanchefleur et le saint homme ou la semblance des reliques* (Paris: Seuil, 1979), 13–46; *Etymologies and Genealogies*, 203–12.

direction of a fundamental indeterminacy, the kind of indeterminacy which Alain identifies with the heteroclitic (and essentially dangerous) nature of poetry:

> Of such of these men as profess the grammar of love, some embrace only the masculine gender, some the feminine, others the common or indiscriminate. Indeed, some, as if of heteroclite gender, are declined irregularly, through the winter in the feminine, through the summer in the masculine. Some, in the pursuit of the logic of love, establish in their conclusions the law of the subject and the predicate in proper relation. Some who have the place of the subject have not learned how to form a predicate. Some only predicate and do not await the proper addition of the subject's end. Others, scorning to enter into the court of Dione, devise a miserable sport below its vestibule. [*De Planctu*, 463]

It is, ultimately, the mobility of poetic language and of sexual identity that represents for Nature the most potent threat to the *straight*ness—*correct*ness, *regular*ity, *ortho*doxy—of grammar and to the continuity of lineage. A lack of definition—and it should be remembered that the grammar of this early period was based upon the *recti*tude of definition—is tantamount to the dissolution of paternal relations and the transgression of Nature's and society's most sacred taboo. What this means is that the *Roman de Silence* represents an occulted attempt to transform poetry into grammar, or, put another way, to recuperate the oxymoronic impossibility of the hermaphrodite—the "malle de femiele," the "vallés meschine" (vv. 2041, 3763)—by the straightness of proper imposition: " . . . Nature/Ot recovree sa droiture." To the modern dictum "Nature abhors a vacuum" Alain and Heldris might have preferred "Natura abhoret hermaphroditos," with the understanding that the poet is himself the polyvalent figure who, in the words of the troubadour Bernart Marti, "will transform a bitch into a sire and raise today until tomorrow."[11]

Silence represents the systematic refusal of univocal meaning. A multiform figure like Merlin whom she captures, she is the liar, the deceiver and trickster—a "bel semblant" (v. 5001) who wears other clothes and takes other names in defiance of Nature's rule of difference: "Car cil a fait de son non cange, / Si l'a mué por plus estrange" (v. 3175). [For this one has changed his name and has thus made it stranger.] Silence embodies the pluralistic possibilities of fiction whose multiple functions she assumes. She both listens ("Silence entent et escolte," [v. 3403]) and is deaf ("Silence lor fait sord orelle," [v. 3533]). Silence silences ("Et c'on nos fait por lui taizir" [v. 3312]) and is silent. She speaks ("C'onques ne fu tels abstinence / Com poés oïr de Silence" [v. 2659]) and is even garrulous ("Dont respondi la dame fole: / Silence, trop avés parole!" [v. 6273]).

---

11. "Far vos a de gossa can / Et d'eyssa guiza levar / Lo dia tro l'endeman. . . ." (*Les Poésies de Bernart Marti*, ed. E. Hoepffner [Paris: Champion, 1929], 5).

The very undetermined nature of Silence, and in particular her un-
defined sexuality, transforms "li vallés qui est mescine" (v. 3785) into the
object of universal desire. Queen Eufeme tries three times to seduce her,
the King of France is enthralled, King Ebain eventually marries her. Such
generalized desire for Silence again thematizes the writer's desire for the
proper name enabling closure; it makes the possibility of an "outside" or a
"beyond" language both the object of and the catalyst to eroticism. And
while, for example, Euphemie may enjoy speaking to Cador ("Tant croist
l'Amor plus a plenté / Car puis qu'en parler ont delit" [v. 752]), it is silence
or that which is not said that nourishes passion:

> Car cho fait Eufemie irer,
> Que cascun jor voit que desire
> Et de son desir se consire.
> Ele desire qu'il seüst
> Qu'ele altre ami que lui n'eüst:
> Mais qu'en li tant de cuer n'a mie
> Que die a lui qu'est s'amie.
> Dirai jo dont qu'ele ait delit
> Quant el ne fait, grant ne petit,
> De quanque li siens cuers desire,
> Fors lui amer sans ozer dire? [V. 760]

This upset Eufemie, since each day she sees that which she desires; and
she is confused by her desire. She desires that he know that she would
have no other friend but him. But she lacks the courage to tell him.
Should I say that she is happy when she doesn't do in any way what her
heart desires, but instead loves him without daring to speak?

What is remarkable here is neither that the nature of Silence's mother
causes her to remain silent ("Cil l'aime et dire ne li oze" [v. 405]), nor that
silence increases desire, but that the drama of speech withheld by the lover
is set against—indeed is virtually indistinguishable from—the poet's hesitation before his own language: "Dirai jo dont qu'ele ait delit . . . ?"

The chiasmatically impossible effects of speech withheld make the
lover analogous to the poet. For if Eufemie's desire is fed by the gaps or
"trous" of that which remains unsaid, Cador recognizes the difficulty of
silence, which makes of him a trouvère: "Ne li os, las! amor rover; / Nel
taisir ne puis bien trover" (v. 663, see also v. 768). [Alas, I do not dare ask
her for her love, nor can I find any good in silence.] The desire of the lover is
a desire to speak, to avow, just as the desire of the poet is to break silence—

> Maistre Heldris de Cornüälle
> Escrist ces viers trestolt a talle.
> A çals quis unt commande et rueve,
> El conmencier dé suns qu'il trouve . . . [V. 1]

> Master Heldris of Cornwall wrote these verses such as they are. To those
> who have the power and command, in the beginning out of sounds he
> invented. . . .

—and to speak of Silence: "De la meschine vus voel dire . . . " (v. 753). In
short, the erotic struggle to speak, which occupies such a large portion of
the beginning of the romance (vv. 406–1119), encapsulates the arch-strug-
gle of the poet or jongleur to articulate his own desire for silence. The
dictum "Nel taisir ne puis bien trover" applies equally to Heldris and
Cador and can be understood alternately as "there is no profit" and "there
is no poetry" in silence.

The troubadour or trouvère is one who attempts to fill the silences or
"trous" in speech (which he also makes by speaking). Similarly, the lover
is one who desires the other, but only in so far as he or she desires speech.
Sexual desire is ultimately a desire for language, which explains the emphasis throughout the *Roman de Silence* upon the word *golozer* meaning
"to dispute," "to be jealous of," "to desire," and "to gloss." Eufemie is
jealous of an imagined rival ("De l'une est Eufemie gloze" [v. 987]) but does
not dare to break silence ("Qu'en li n'en a pas tant d'ozer / Qu'ele sor li
l'oze glozer" [v. 989]). Both lovers are jealous and desirous of the speech of
the other ("Et l'uns et l'autres le golouse" [v. 1340]), and their desire remains indissociable from that of the poet to speak of Silence ("A parler de
l'enfant goloze" [v. 2345]). This may seem like a minor philological point
hidden in a canonically minor work, but its implications in fact extend to
much of what we understand about poetic elaboration in the High Middle
Ages. It virtually stands on its ear that which positivist scholarship has
from the beginning considered to be the medieval writer's servile glossing
of Classical texts, the *locus classicus* of which is the Prologue to the *Lais* of
Marie de France:

> Custume fu as ancïens,
> Ceo testimoine Precïens,
> Es livres ke jadis feseient,
> Assez oscurement diseient
> Pur ceus ki a venir esteient
> Et ki aprendre les deveient,
> K'i peüssent gloser la lettre
> Et de lur sen le surplus mettre.[12]

> As Priscian bears witness, it was the custom of the Ancients to speak
> obscurely enough in their books so that those who came afterward and
> would be obliged to teach (or learn) them would be able to gloss the letter
> and with their sense fill in the rest.

12. Marie de France, *Lais*, ed. J. Rychner (Paris: Champion, 1981), v. 9.

According to our reading of the couple "gloser/golozer," the poet (like the philologist) actively seeks the text's points of resistance—the holes or silences that have through time become elusive and obscure. The desire "to supplement sense," or to fill in such gaps, is, as R. Dragonetti and others maintain, ultimately a desire for the letter that is inseparable from the desire for poetry itself.[13]

Poetry is in the *Roman de Silence* thematized in terms of seduction. Silence, like Dante's Paolo and Francesca or the heroine of Marie's *Guigemar*, is allured by books. She is naturally attracted to letters ("Li enfes est de tel orine / Que il meïsme se doctrine") [The child's origin is such that he teaches himself (v. 2385)]) and to the trouvères whose skill she quickly surpasses. When, in fact, her talent comes to be recognized as an abundant source of income, it incites the jealousy of her teachers and underscores yet another resonance of the verb "trouver" with which the romance begins:

> Un clers poroit lonc tans aprendre
> Por rime trover et por viers,
> Tant par est cis siecles diviers,
> Qu'ançois poroit rime trover
> Qui peüst en cest mont trover
> Blos solement un sol princhier. . . .
> Volés esprover gent avere?
> Servés lé bien, come vo pere:
> Dont serés vus li bien venus,
> Bons menestreus, bien recheüs.
> Mais, puis qu'il venra al rover,
> Savés que i porés trover?
> Bien laide chiere et une enfrume,
> Car cend est tols jors la costume. [Vv. 14ff.]

A Cleric might learn for a long time in order to compose rhyme and verse; yet this world is so debased that even if he composes rhyme he might stumble upon a stingy prince. . . . Do you want to test stingy people? Serve them well, like your father; for you will be a good and well received performer. But when it comes to asking for a reward, do you know what you might find? Hard times and miserliness, for this is always the custom.

If the trouvère is the one whose invention fills holes, it is the holes in his own pocket that he would like to fill. "Trouver"—"to find," "to invent"—also means "to earn." There is literally no profit in silence (see above p.

---

13. See Dragonetti, *Le Gai savoir dans la rhétorique courtoise* (Paris: Seuil, 1982), 111–30.

90), as linguistic and economic value are assimilated to each other. Silence, the inscription of the poet within the text, is, like Balzac's Sarazine (see Barthes's *S/Z*), a virtuoso who, as the object of universal desire, also becomes the source of seemingly limitless wealth. Silence is golden.[14]

Poetry, like money, represents the possibility of self-creating, purely specular and speculative value whose very lack of origin signals the impossibility of reproduction or genealogical succession:

> Car qui violt avoir amasser,
> Quant il n'en ist honors ne biens?
> Assés valt certes mains que fiens.
> Li fiens encrassce vials la terre,
> Mais li avoirs c'on entreserre
> Honist celui ki l'i entasse. [V. 46]

For who wants to amass wealth when neither good nor honor can come from it? It is certainly worth less than manure. Manure at least enriches the earth. But the money one buries shames the one who hoards it.

The "honors" or "biens" mentioned above are the equivalent of a fief or of what in legal terms was known as a "propre"—immovable property, real estate, tangible wealth attached to a name quite literally rooted in the soil that also bears it. Money, on the other hand, represents a mobile personal good—that which potentially renders a propre saleable, nominalizes title. Because it is unattached, without origin, it is also considered sterile. "Pecunia quantum est de se per seipsam non fructificat," claims St. Bonaventure, echoing the dictum that can be traced all the way back to Aristotle and according to which "nummus non parit nummos."[15]

To cause money to parturate constituted an act against nature analogous to poetic invention. This is why, as A. Pézard and E. Vance have shown, Dante associates blasphemy, sodomy and usury, and why, as Nicholas Oresme—the most important medieval authority on minting—claims, currency manipulation is essentially the incorrect imposition of a name: "And besides, in these changes by which profit accrues, it is necessary to call something which is not a penny, a penny, and which is not a pound, a pound."[16] The usurer and the poet are colleagues—fellow disruptors of genealogy through monetary and verbal impropriety, interest (liter-

14. "Et se l'estorie ne me ment, / Il a des estrumens apris / Car moult grant traval i a mis, / Qu'ains que li tiers ans fust passés / A il ses maistres tols passés, / Et moult grant avoir lor gaägne" (v. 3138). [And if the story does not lie, he learned to play instruments. Because he worked hard at it, before three years had passed he had surpassed all his teachers and earned them great wealth.]

15. See *Etymologies and Genealogies*, 164–74.

16. Nicholas Oresme, *De Moneta*, ed. C. Johnson (London: Thomas Nelson, 1956), 26. See also A. Pézard, *Dante sous la pluie de feu* (Paris: J. Vrin, 1950); E. Vance, "Désir, rhétorique et texte," *Poétique* 42 (1980), 137–55.

ally the production of difference) and metaphor. Both meet, moreover, in the figure of Silence who produces song from the soundlessness of her name and money from song. Like the counterfeiter, she engenders herself, becomes, in the final account of her adventures, the author of her own tale.[17]

Silence's autochthonous invention of herself makes her the object of universal desire and incurs the enmity of her fellow poets who can only conceive of her unnatural musical skill in terms of plagiarism or theft: "Cis a emblé nostre savoir. . . . / Nostre damages doblera, / Car nostre avoir enportera" (vv. 3268, 3277) [This one has stolen our knowledge. . . . He will double our loss, for he will take away our wealth.] The *Roman de Silence* thus inscribes its own origin from which we can deduce an important element of external literary history in the rivalry of jongleurs whose competing accounts—like the rival counts with which the tale begins— make them sufficiently jealous of Silence to attempt to silence her: "Pur quoi iriens nos en Espagne, / Compaig, por golozer gaägne? / Nostre espoir gist en lui ocire" (v. 3329). [Why should we go to Spain, friends, to earn wages? Our hope is in killing him.] Here we glimpse the hidden agenda of such an inscription—the author's own relation to the text; for what is rhetoricized as the poet's desire for gain ("golozer gaägne") reflects ultimately what we have identified as Heldris's own desire to speak of Silence ("A parler de l'enfant goloze" [v. 2345]) and his jealousy of her.

This suggests that the *Roman de Silence* is essentially about the writer's relation to writing. And if the process of poetic production is mediated through a variety of metaphors of impropriety (perversion, sophistry, excrement ["li fiens," cf. above p. 92], money, and theft), the impropriety of metaphor traces a closed circuit of specific textual effects. The transgression of verbal, economic, and sexual property provokes an indeterminacy that within the world of romance occasions desire, which in turn produces the unnatural and heteroclitic language of poetry. As Cador confesses, desire denatures: "Mais jo sui tols desnaturés / Et si cuic estre enfaiturés"

17. Silence to Ebain: "Sire, se Dex bien me consente / Il n'est pas drois que je vos mente. / Mes pere fist de moi son buen. . . . [in text] / Et quant jo ving a tel aäge / Que gent comencent estre sage / Mes pere me fist asavoir / Que jo ja ne poroie avoir, / Sire, ireté en vostre tierre. / Et por mon iretage quierre / Me rova vivre al fuer de malle, . . . / A. XV. ans vig a cort, bials sire. . . . / Vos m'envoiastes dela mer. . . . / Puis reving jo en vostre tierre, / S'aidai a finer vostre guierre. . . . / La vertés nel puet consentir / Que jo vos puisse rien mentir, / Ne jo n'ai soig mais de taisir" (v. 6590). [Sire, as God well desires, it is not right that I lie to you. My father made me his heir. . . . And when I reached the age at which people begin to be wise, my father explained to me that I could never have an inheritance in your country, Sire. And in order to seek my inheritance, he commanded me to live in the guise of a male. . . . At the age of fifteen, I came to court, beautiful sire. . . . You sent me across the sea. . . . Then I returned to your land and helped to end your war. . . . The truth cannot permit that I lie to you about anything. Nor have I cared ever to remain silent.]

(v. 1031). And, as Eufemie discovers, what it denatures is language itself:

> Li jors apert et Eufemie
> Saut sus que ne s'atarja mie.
> Vient en la cambre a son ami.
> Dist li: "Amis, parlés, haymmi!"
> Dire li dut: "Parlés a moi,"
> Mais l'Amors li fist tel anoi
> Que dire dut: "Parlés a mi,"
> Se li a dit: "Parlés, haymmi!"
> "Parlés a mi" dire li dut,
> Mais, "haymmi!" sor le cuer li jut.
> Si tost com ele ot dit "amis,"
> En la clauze "haymmi!" a mis.
> "Ami" dut dire, et "haymmi!" dist,
> Por la dolor qui en li gist. [V. 889]

The day broke and Eufemie who did not delay jumped up. She came to her beloved's room and said to him: "Friend, speak, hate me." She meant to say, "Speak to me," but Love pulled such a trick as to make her say "Speak, hate me" instead of "Speak to me." But "hate me" remained on her heart. As soon as she said "amis" she said "hate me!" She should have said "Ami," and she said "hate me!" because of the pain that is in her.

It is hard to imagine a more eloquent expression of desire and the desire for speech ("Amis, parlés. . . . Parlés a moi") as catalysts to linguistic distortion ("Si tost com ele ot dit 'amis,' / En la clauze 'haymmi!' a mis"). Desire alienates language which, alienated, becomes an even greater source of desire and the desire for language: "Cis mos 'amis' fait esperer / Cador qu'or pora averer" (v. 903).

Two metaphors of dislocation and distance dominate the *Roman de Silence* above and beyond the ways in which the process of poetry is thematized. The first has to do with clothing and has a long history in the Middle Ages, one evident in both popular and learned traditions. The author of "La Vieille Truande," for example, assimilates fables and fabliaux to "cloth, shoes, and songs":

> Des fables fet on les fabliaus,
> Et des notes les sons noviaus,
> Et des materes les canchons,
> Et des dras, cauces et cauchons. [Montaiglon and Raynaud, vol. 5, 171]

Out of fables one makes fabliaux; out of notes, new sounds; out of material, songs; and out of cloth, socks and shoes.

Within the realm of high culture Macrobius (fifth century) claims that "a frank and open exposition of herself is distasteful to Nature, who, just as she has withheld an understanding of herself from the uncouth senses of man by enveloping herself in variegated garments, has also desired to have her secrets handled by more prudent individuals through fabulous narratives. . . . In truth, divinities always have preferred to be known in the fashion assigned to them by ancient popular tradition, which made images of beings that had no physical form, represented them as of different ages though they were subject neither to growth nor decay, and gave them clothes and ornaments though they had no bodies."[18]

The relation of truth, Nature, to its representation or image is thus that of the body to the clothes which are a potent paradigm of representation in Macrobius's terms—bodiless, empty, less capable of expressing a reality exterior to it than of covering up an absence that is also, finally, scandalous, Macrobius continues: "Numenius, a philosopher with a curiosity for occult things, had revealed to him in a dream the outrage he had committed against the gods by proclaiming his interpretation of the Eleusinian mysteries. The Eleusinian goddesses themselves, dressed in the garments of courtesans, appeared to him standing before an open brothel, and when in his astonishment he asked for the reason for this shocking conduct, they replied that he had driven them from their sanctuary of modesty and prostituted them to every passer-by." Beneath the garment of representation lies the scandal of courtesans, just as beneath the ill-fitting masculine clothing of Silence lies a female anatomy: "Il est desos les dras mescine" (v. 2480).

It may be argued that what we find beneath the robe of Silence is not an absence but the presence of the body, which, Heldris maintains, is merely another layer of clothing: "Li cors n'est mais fors sarpelliere" (v. 1845). What remains essential, however, is not whether or not Nature lurks beneath the veil of representation, but the incongruity of the rapport between the body and that which covers it. Clothes are for Heldris the equivalent of a refusal of nature: "Quant li enfes pot dras user, / Por se nature refuser / L'ont tres bien vestu a fuer d'ome" (v. 2359, see also v. 2826). [When the child could use clothes to refuse her nature, they dressed her well in the guise of a man.] Clothes, like the letter that masks sense, serve more to obscure than to make plain. As Silence admits, they merely patch that which they cannot contain: "Vos savés bien de ma nature: / Jo sui, fait il, nel mescrées, / Com li malvais dras encrées" (v. 3640). [You know well my nature: do not be deceived, I am like bad cloth which is patched.]

The second major articulation of the effects of desire upon language has to do with wax, letters, and heat:

18. Ambrosii Theodosii Macrobii, *Commentarii in Somnium Scipionis,* ed. J. Willis (Leipzig: Teubner, 1970), 7–8. See also the representation of Nature's garment in Alain de Lille's *De Planctu.*

> Escriziés moi ens en le cire
> Letres que om bien puisse lire.
> Faites le cire dont remetre.
> Enne perist donques la lettre?
> Oïl, par Deu! par le calor.
> Nient plus n'a cuers d'amant valor
> De bien retenir s[a] mimorie,
> Que cire encontre fu victorie
> De retenir la lettre escrite.
> Qu'angoisse d'amor n'est petite
> Car cho qu'est voirs cho fait mescroire,
> Et tenir fause coze a voire; . . . .
> Si en sunt mult en grant batalle
> Que al sorplus ne facent falle [Vv. 1169, 1187]

Write for me thus in wax letters that we can read. Remelt the wax. Does the letter perish? Yes, by God, because of the heat. No more does the heart of a lover have the power to retain its impression (memory) than the wax the written letter. For the pain of love is not small and makes one mistake the truth and hold false things for true. . . . They are so troubled that they almost missed love-making (surplus).

Just as heat melts the inscription upon wax, desire erases memory, which produces the effect of paranoia. Not only is cognition troubled ("Car ki bien aime n'est sans dote, / Ne ne puet tenir droit rote, / Ne cho qu'il set ne puet savoir" [For whoever loves well is not without doubt, nor can he hold a straight path, nor can he know that which he knows] (v. 1165), but all interpretation, because of the multiplicity of its possibilities, becomes impossible ("Car cho qu'est voirs fait mescroire, / Et tenir fause coze a voire" [For it makes one disbelieve that which is true, and hold a false thing as true]). It is, finally, the inaccessibility of univocal and stable knowledge that renders meaning, identified above with Marie de France's "surplus sense of the letter," fallacious: "Si en sunt mult en grant batalle / Que al sorplus ne face falle." [They are so troubled that they might miss the surplus.]

The wax, letters, and heat paradigm points in the direction of a literal dislocation: "Li frois ne puet avoir valor / Ki puisse vaintre my calor" (v. 1019), complains Cador, playing upon the difference of only one letter between his own name and his desire for Eufemie and drawing our attention to the omnipresence of such wordplays. Read at the level of the letter, the *Roman de Silence* can be said to be based upon a series of graphemic displacements—of prefixes (Nature/Noreture, ozer/glozer, medecine/mescine); of suffixes (Eufeme/Eufemie, Silentius/Silentia); of accents (conte/conté); of accents and letters (oire/oirre/oir/oïr), etc. And it can be said to be about a series of stolen letters.

The central section of the romance turns around an exchange of forged, misplaced, and misinterpreted letters between Ebain, his wife, and the King of France.[19] Here historical mimetism joins the problematics of displacement outlined above, for rarely do we catch such a profound look at the workings of the medieval chancellery. Yet rarely do we find a more conscious rendering of the deliberate and unwitting errors of sense produced by the office responsible for the composition, transcription, transmission, and interpretation of letters. Thus Eufeme's desire for Silence leads her to intercept and alter the letter of safe conduct Silence carries into exile:

> Pense que se li briés esploite
> Que li rois violt en cire metre
> Qu'ele mesme fera tel letre
> Dont cil avra grant dostorbance,
> Sel puet quil portera en France. [V. 4276]

She thinks that she will distort the letter that the king wants to put into wax and that she will make a letter that will cause great harm to the one who carries it to France.

As in the Pauline dictum, the letter kills: "Car sa mort porte escrite en cire." (V. 4374). [For he carries his death written in wax.] It literally prescribes dismemberment—

> De par roi Ebayn, son segnor,
> Escrist al roi de France un brief
> Qu'il tolle al message le cief
> Qui les lettres a lui enporte. [V. 4320]

From King Ebain, her lord, she wrote a letter to the King of France that he should cut off the head of the messenger who brings the letter to him.

—and is itself dismembered:

> Que il por rien ne l'en deporte,
> Car il a fait al roi tel honte
> Qu'il ne le violt metre en conte. . . .
> Cest brief a la roïne escrit. [Vv. 4324, 4331]

For he (the King of France) should not fail in this for any reason for he (the messenger) has done to the King (of England) such shame that it cannot be put into writing. . . . Such is the letter the queen wrote.

The "shame of Silence" ("Car il a fait al roi tel honte") cannot be detached from a certain textual fissure—the scandal of that which cannot be said

---

19. For a contemporary discussion of the problematics of letters, see J. Lacan, "Le Séminaire sur 'La Lettre volée'" in Ecrits 1 (Paris: Seuil, 1970), 19–78; J. Derrida, "Le Facteur de la vérité," Poétique 21 (1975), 96–147; B. Johnson, "The Frame of Reference: Poe, Lacan, Derrida," Yale French Studies 55/56 (1977), 457–505.

("Qu'il ne le violt metre en conte"), which is that the letter is always already dislocated and that silence, spoken, always distorts. This is the secret contained in the letter's fold and why the folding and sealing of letters comes, in the exposure by Ebain's priest of Eufeme's forgery, to occupy such a large place:

> Quant ele clost et mist en ploi
> Tolt alsi qu'ele n'eüst cure
> Que jo veïssce l'escriture! . . . .
> Et quant ele ot mon brief ploié
> Sil me rendi bien ferm loié
> Et je l'enseëlai en oire. [Vv. 4990, 5073]

When she closed (the letter) and folded it she made sure I did not see the writing! . . . And when she had folded my letter she returned it to me well closed, and I sealed it in haste.

Folded and sealed, the letter signals a specular reversal of the historically mimetic conditions of its production. Put in other terms, the tale does not simply reflect the distortions of human intention it supposedly portrays but actually produces them, as the Queen's defense makes clear: "Dist que li brief vint par un conte. . . . Et c'un cuens paltoniers fallis / Canja les letres par envie / Por tolir a l'enfant la vie" (vv. 5100, 5112). [She says the letter came from a count (tale). . . . And that the felonious count (account) changed the letters out of jealousy in order to have the child killed.] Taken literally, the felonious tale ("cuens paltoniers") perverts the letter because of jealousy or desire ("Canja les letres par envie"), which, because it is also the sign of desire for the letter, transforms the romance into a map of its own misreadings.

The *Roman de Silence* is in fact all about misreading. Silence is a female version of Alexis with whom she shares a common parental name, Eufemie, Eufemiien (Alexis's father). Both refuse the law of the father, depart and return to the paternal roof where they encounter the problem of recognition. Together they summon the spectre of troubled reading. Cador, informed of his daughter's return in the guise of one of the jongleurs he has banished ("Veés la vostre fil Silence, / Si a apris des estrumens" [Here is your son Silence; he has learned to play instruments (V. 3539)], fails to see: "Son fil demande et il le tient: / Il le convoite et nel voit nient" (v. 3619). [He asks for his son and he is holding him: he desires him and does not see him at all.] This failure of vision is at bottom a matter of reading in which the count (as well as the tale) is blind to his (its) own progeny (or meaning) and in which Silence becomes the very figure of Alexia. All of which transforms the problem of indeterminacy with which we began into the perceptual and cognitive impossibility of seeing, reading, hearing, or speaking the silence whose transgression is the premise of fiction.

In conclusion, the *Roman de Silence* symptomizes the paradox of the poet who speaks the impossibility both of silence and of an always already dislocated speech. Its heroine, by her own account, represents the specular image of that which poetry cannot say, which is that to speak the truth is to be disinherited:

> Ne li vallés ki est mescine
> Ne violt pas dire son covine,
> De sa nature verité,
> Qu'il perdroit donques s'ireté. [V. 3871, see also v. 4169]

The squire who was a girl did not want to tell the secret of her true nature, for she would lose her inheritance.

To name oneself—"Silence ai non . . ." (v. 6140)—is to contradict oneself, as the myriad of contradictions attached to the name joins what we might think of as the fiction of fiction or the poet's desire "to begin without making a sound" ("Car moult grans volentés me point / De muevre rime et conmencier, / Sans noise faire, et sans tenchier" [v. 104]) to the critic's desire to have the last word by making Silence speak and, finally, to silence her.

MICHEL ZINK

The Allegorical Poem as Interior Memoir

The allegorical poem deals by definition with the present of subjectivity from the moment that it assumes the form of a psychomachia. That is to say, psychomachia understood in the broadest sense as a description of the movements and the conflicts within psychological as well as moral consciousness. It is worth reflecting, in this context, on the complex relations between the subject and time, the time of dream, of reality, of literary expression, at the beginning of the *Roman de la Rose*. In the first fifty lines of Guillaume de Lorris's poem, the reader is ushered from dream to reality, from present to past, in a back and forth motion so rapid and so deft that he is disoriented without noticing it: the text appears to be transparent, even though it is extremely dense. The poet begins by evoking the dream that he had at the age of twenty and its circumstances. He then shifts to a presentation of the poem that he is undertaking in the present, five years later, giving its title, addressing its public, mentioning for whom it is intended. Finally, he comes back to his dream, to the period when he had it, to the season of the year and the hour of the day when he fell under its spell.

The poem's insistence on temporality and on dates is an insistence on the suspense of love. In the present when the poet undertakes to compose the narrative of this dream from the past, he is compelled to write by a new fact, namely the actualization of the dream and of love. He must recall it to memory, this dream from his twentieth year, this tribute paid to Love in his youth, he must subject it to literary elaboration in the light of the new reality of love, in order that the dream may flow into this reality and allow it to pursue its course beyond the dream's limits. Everything is a question of time: the affective and poetic personality designated by the *je* in the poem is fashioned by the clash and the blend, reproduced in the text itself, of recollection and the present, of memories resuscitated by writing and the incomplete reality in whose development they are meant to assist, of the dreamer in love and the poet in love, who are the same "person," but separated by five years.

It is not sufficient, however, to say that the poem plays on the expression of time in order to create the image of a subjectivity. Not everything, in fact, is confined to happening in between the past dream, actualized by writing, and present reality, of which one knows only that it corresponds in every detail to what the dream had shown. For what it shows is not simply an anticipation of reality. The dream in the *Roman de la Rose*, as everyone knows, is an allegorical dream which requires an interpretation. This interpretation, as the author announces in a sort of parenthesis at the opening of Love's discourse, is to be given at the end of the poem. The reader must wait until then for an explanation of the meaning of the dream (*dou songe la senefïance*, v. 2070):

> La verités, qui est coverte,
> vos sera lores toute overte
> quant espondre m'oroiz le songe [Vv. 2071–73]

> The truth, which is hidden, will be quite open to you
> when you hear me explain the dream. . . .[1]

This promise, unfortunately, is not kept, since Guillaume de Lorris's poem is unfinished. But it is clear that the dream is not a first, illusory version of the real events that occurred five years later. It renders in advance the meaning of these events. In this way, the back and forth motion between present and past, already evident in the prologue, is completed. Present reality gives to past dream the weight of truth. But it receives its own meaning from this dream. The truth and the pertinence of the allegory, that is, its aptitude for giving an account of experience, for formalizing it, for making its meaning apparent, are confirmed by the actualization of the dream. Conversely, only the interpretation of the dream and the establishment of its *senefïance* make it possible to recognize the dream's actualization in the experience of love. This exchange is accomplished, of course, through the writing of the dream, writing which is, in all senses of the term, a reflection on the dream; in other words, the exchange is accomplished through the poem. The literary undertaking, therefore, makes the allegorical universe into a subjective experience of the poet and sets it beside his equally subjective experience of reality. And this undertaking uses the expression of time as a means of revealing not only subjectivity, but also the link between allegory and subjectivity. Now, this link is not self-evident, for it does not coincide in any way with the venerable association between allegory and the expression of psychological realities.

1. Guillaume de Lorris and Jean de Meun, *Roman de la Rose*, ed. Felix Lecoy, (Paris: Champion, 1966–70), 3 vols.; Guillaume de Lorris and Jean de Meun, *The Romance of the Rose*, trans. Charles Dahlberg (Hanover and London: Univ. Press of New England, 1983), 59.

Taken by itself, this last statement is of course too brief. Allegory is not limited to the field of psychology. The personifications which, in classical literature, we view as allegory, are not at all restricted to the field of sentiments, passions and thought. Furthermore, they are generally the object of religious beliefs and are for this reason objectified. From still another perspective, allegory undergoes a sort of inverse reduction the moment that it is viewed as a literary technique: Quintilian and his successors consider it only as a rhetorical ornament.[2] It is certainly true, however, that allegory has always been a privileged means for describing and even for investigating the movements of the soul and of the inner life. This truth asserts itself regardless of the angle from which one tackles the question. From a point of view that is both general and fundamental, it has been known since the classic work of Dodds[3] that, already in Homeric literature, the representation of gods is a means of accounting for the obscure forces and passions that dominate the human soul; it is a means of making comprehensible, while avoiding ineffectual rational analysis, the notions covered by words such as *atè* or *thumos*. To be more precise, it is not simply that the myths used by Plato to reveal, for example, the nature of love or of the soul are dependent upon allegory, since they give a concrete image to abstract realities. In addition, Plato's representations of the conflict between the soul and the bodily passions or between the two parts of the soul, the one a prey to obscure and irrational passions and the other determined to dominate them, are the point of departure for all subsequent psychomachia. He illustrates them twice, moreover, in the *Phaedo* and in the *Republic*,[4] by the same quotation from Homer, which is in this regard significant: "Smiting his breast, he reproached his heart with word . . ." (*Odyssey*, 20, 17).[5] Through Neo-Platonism and through Saint Augustine, this form of thinking spread to Christian literature, which provided a very favorable environment for its subsequent development. The Christian reader was, indeed, accustomed by the New Testament to decipher parables and generally to search for truth behind appearance; or, to employ the Pauline language which having first been used to assimilate the Law was then made applicable to all reading, the Christian reader was accustomed to go beyond the letter in order to discover the spirit. He was equally

2. Quintilian, *Instit. orat.* 9, 2, 46, where, in a famous formula, allegory is defined as an extended metaphor. Cf. Augustine, *De Trin.* 15, 9, 15: "What therefore is allegory, if not a trope in which one thing is understood from something different?" There are analogous formulations by Isidore of Seville (*Etym.* 1, 37, 22) and by the Venerable Bede (*De schem. et tropis sacrae script.* 2, 12), whose definition ("a trope by which something other is signified than what is said") is, moreover, taken word for word from Donatus.

3. E.-R. Dodds, *The Greeks and the Irrational* (Berkeley: Univ. of California Press, 1951).

4. Plato, *Phaedo* 94, c, d; *Republic* 4, 441, b, c. Cf. Dodds, 213.

5. Plato, *Republic*, trans. Allan Bloom (New York: Basic Books, Inc., 1968), 68.

accustomed to a representation of the world in which the forces of good confronted those of evil and, once again through Saint Paul, then through the interpretation of the historical books of the Old Testament and of the Psalms, he was used to the figurative description of this confrontation in the form of a battle.

It should be observed that in the Platonic perspective evoked above, then in the Augustinian conception of the battle against demoniacal forces, then in the description of the *bellum intestinum* by the pseudo-John Scottus Eriugena, the first Neo-Platonic theologian of the Middle Ages, it is not merely the individual soul which is at stake. Just as the *Timaeus* proceeds from the world soul to the human soul and body, in the same way the Christian battle for salvation is acted out in world history and in each individual human destiny. The parallel is not in any way gratuitous. Just as medieval historians made an effort to reconcile the chronology of pagan antiquity with that of the Bible, in the same way the theologian-poets of the twelfth century tried to unite the Platonic vision of the universe with the one proposed by the Bible in their allegorical works, the *De mundi universitate* and the commentary on the *Aeneid* by Bernard Silvester, the *De planctu Naturae* and the *Anticlaudianus* by Alan of Lille. When Bernard sees in the city that Aeneas wants to establish an image of the human body, with each category of inhabitants corresponding to an organ whose place it occupies and whose function it fills, it is difficult not to think of the *Republic* as well as of the *Timaeus*. When, according to both Bernard and Alan, Nature needs help in order to create mankind and to breathe life into him, help obtained (after a voyage among the celestial spheres) either from the intellectual faculties (in Bernard) or from Faith which obtains from God the gift of a soul able to animate an inert body, it is at once Plato's demiurge and the Christian God that one sees at work. Genius, who appears at the very end of the *De planctu Naturae* before his well-known appearance in Jean de Meun's *Roman de la Rose*, is

> The spirit of God, conceived as a demiurgic power, which imposes on matter the *figura*, the types, the seals of forms. . . . We recognize here a coherent doctrine, anchored both in antiquity and in Alan of Lille's contemporaries. It comes, of course, from the *Timaeus*, passed along by Seneca's *Letter* 65 and by Boethius. It is continued in Neo-Platonism and notably, as M. T. d'Alverny has shown, in the *Theophania* of the pseudo-John Scottus, where the term "genius" appears. It blossoms finally in the School of Chartres. Let us add, to return to antiquity, that the same philosophy, extending from Plato to Seneca, is found at the source of Ciceronian rhetoric and esthetics. Alan was undoubtedly aware of this. He certainly knew of it through the Augustinian tradition, which was joined to the same current, thanks to Varro. The profound unity of the Occidental poetic tradition here makes itself manifest in a striking fashion. The ugliness and the beauty of the images, of the allegories and of the

figures constitute a divine language. This is accomplished in theophany, a direct and intuitive form of knowledge, which serves to complete theology.[6]

Thus, the reflection of the macrocosm in the microcosm, of the destiny and functioning of the universe in the destiny and functioning of the individual, invites us to see in each a meaning transposed from the other. In addition, poetic language, by rendering this transposed, universal meaning perceptible, reveals the presence of the divine. Allegory is the privileged mode of expression for the relations of the individual soul with the principle of the universe and with God.

It is clear, therefore, that medieval allegory cannot be reduced to personifications, but that on the contrary these are only its ultimate manifestations. Personifications are of course quite striking in Prudentius's *Psychomachia* and in Martianus Capella's *De Nuptiis Philologiae et Mercurii*, two works essential, as one knows, to the development of the medieval allegorical world. But Prudentius seems to see in the struggle of the virtues against the vices both the struggle of the soul and that of the Church throughout its history. And the work of Martianus Capella, which the manuscripts often group with Macrobius's commentary on Scipio's dream and with the *Timaeus*, was glossed in the Middle Ages by numerous commentators, including John Scottus Eriugena. In his interpretation of the celestial voyage undertaken by Apollo and Mercury to obtain Philology from Jupiter as Mercury's bride, John Scottus Eriugena speaks at length of the double voyage of the soul through the celestial spheres, first to be incarnated in the human body, then to reach the heavens once again after death.[7] This confers on Martianus Capella an importance different from that given him within the restricted domain of literary history, for having mingled the gods of antiquity with personifications of abstract notions, as was later done so often in the Middle Ages, or for having been the first to devote seven books of his work to the seven Liberal Arts, which established him as a kind of patron of the medieval *cursus studiorum*.

It is also clear why medieval literary allegory is so deeply rooted in religious thought. This is not at all because secular literature transposed or adapted for its own purposes the methods of Biblical exegesis, based on the elucidation of the three (or the four) meanings of Scripture, and based in a more essential way on the idea that since divine revelation is able to occur, on account of mankind's imperfection, only by the indirect means of human language or human history, there is nothing in Scriptural sym-

6. Alain Michel, "Rhétorique, poétique et nature chez Alain de Lille," in *Alain de Lille, Gautier de Châtillon, Jakemart Giélée et leur temps,* comp. H. Roussel et F. Suard (Lille, 1980), 117–18.

7. See Marc-René Jung, *Etudes sur le poème allégorique en France au Moyen Age* (Berne: Francke, 1971), 43–44.

bolism which is not at once *res et signum,* to use Saint Augustine's vocabulary. All of this has in itself nothing to do with the personifications or the extended metaphors which establish allegory as a literary technique.[8] Moreover, one finds in the Middle Ages a very careful distinction between the composition of a work of fiction which conveys allegorical meaning, the allegorical commentary on a text whose literal level is true, such as the Bible, and the allegorical commentary on a text whose literal level is fictitious, for example that of Bernard Sylvester on the *Aeneid* and those of Remigius of Auxerre or John Scottus Eriugena on the *De Nuptiis Philologiae et Mercurii.* Meanwhile, one has only to compare the *Roman de la Rose* with any Scriptural gloss in order to ascertain that there is no relation between them, aside from the fact that both presuppose the existence of a transposed meaning in addition to the literal one. The deep roots of allegory within the religious sphere probably have a much more general explanation. It lies in the fact that the concrete representation of abstract realities, by means of personifications or by any other means, has enjoyed a special connection since the beginning, one might say since Homer, with the most abstract and elusive domain of them all and the one which for that very reason most needs such a link: the domain of the soul, with its obscure movements, its nature, its ties to the universe and to the sacred. If allegorical literature, at least until the *Roman de la Rose,* shows a predilection for religious subjects, this is therefore not because it is inspired by Scriptural exegesis. It is rather because, by adhering to the psychological domain as firmly as it has always done, even while using its own techniques drawn from linguistics, rhetoric and poetics, allegorical literature easily returns in this oblique manner to its religious preoccupations, since in the Christian world the psychological cannot be separated from the moral nor from the eschatological.

That allegory depicts the amorous soul, and no longer the religious soul, does not therefore constitute, from the viewpoint of its literary implementation, a genuine rupture. However, as was emphasized above, the depiction of the psychological sphere does not in itself imply a subjective viewpoint. On the contrary, allegory appears to be in itself a generalizing exploration and description of consciousness. In personifying, for example, the forces which confront each other within consciousness, allegory renders them independent of the subject who is the theater for their struggle, and it perceives in this struggle the application of permanent and nontemporal laws much more than it sets forth the particular accidents, the circumstances, the immersion in the present of a subjectivity, which experiences this struggle each time as if it were unique. It is therefore not

---

8. See Armand Strubel, "'Allegoria in factis' et 'allegoria in verbis,'" in *Poétique* 23 (1975), 343.

surprising to find in early medieval French literature, not allegory's grasp of the present state of a subjectivity, but the confrontation of a subjectivity with allegory.

From the beginning of the thirteenth century on, the means that is nearly always used to place the subject into the allegorical world is the dream. For the dream allows one to confirm subjective experience, or the reality of what has been lived, without insisting on the reality of its content. At the same time, the dream is by nature the purveyor of a truth which is its meaning and which is therefore in itself analogous to the truth of allegory.

Macrobius, whom Guillaume de Lorris does not invoke by chance at the beginning of the *Roman de la Rose*, defines the nature of this truth and the conditions of its unveiling in terms which make understandable the association of allegory, not only with the dream, but also with the subjectivity of the dreamer. It is well known that he distinguishes, at the beginning of his commentary on Scipio's dream, among five kinds of dreams. He immediately brushes two of them aside: *insomnium* (Greek *enupnion*), which designates agitated dreams, either nightmares or erotic dreams, produced by worries of the mind or disorders of the body; and *visum* (Greek *phantasma*), which designates the disjointed or indistinct images that present themselves in the intermediate state between waking and slumber, at the moment of falling asleep. These two categories of dreams allow no interpretation and conceal no truth. At the other extreme are two further categories which are characterized by the limpidness of their relation to reality. The *oraculum* (Greek *chrematismos*) is a direct prediction or warning given to the sleeper by one of his relatives, by a venerable and important person, by a priest, or by God Himself. The *visio* (Greek *horama*) is a dream which is realized exactly as it has been dreamed. But the fifth category, that of the *somnium* (Greek *oneir*), in which Macrobius places Scipio's dream, is the most interesting:

> Somnium proprie vocatur, quod tegit figuris et velat ambagibus non nisi interpretatione intelligendam significationem rei quae demonstratur.

> By an enigmatic dream we mean one that conceals with strange shapes and veils with ambiguity the true meaning of the information being offered, and requires an interpretation for its understanding.[9]

Thus, the *somnium* is in itself the figurative or indirect representation of a meaning which only the decipherment resulting from interpretation is able to make apparent. It is by nature the framework for allegory. But at the

9. The edition that has been used is the one printed by Sébastien Gryphius (Lyon, 1550), where the passages in question are found on 19–21. Macrobius, *Commentary on the Dream of Scipio*, trans. William Harris Stahl (New York: Columbia Univ. Press, 1952), 90.

same time, Macrobius distinguishes several subcategories of the *somnium*, each defined by the degree of the dreamer's participation in the action of his dream:

> Huius (*i.e. somnii*) quinque sunt species: aut enim proprium, aut alienum, aut commune, aut publicum, aut generale. Proprium est, cum se quis facientem patientemve aliquid somniat. Alienum, cum alium. Commune, cum se una cum alio.

> There are five varieties of it (*i.e. somnium*): personal, alien, social, public, and universal. It is called personal when one dreams that he himself is doing or experiencing something; alien, when he dreams this about someone else; social, when his dream involves others and himself. . . .

The *somnium publicum* is a dream which has a public place for its setting, the *somnium generale,* a dream characterized by the intervention of parts of the universe, such as the sun, the moon, the stars, etc. Thus, the criterion for classifying the different kinds of *somnium* is the dreamer's presence or absence as an actor in his own dream, from the most intimate kind, which he fills entirely, to the most general kind, offering a panorama of the universe from which he is totally absent. Macrobius therefore includes within his definitions of the dream both allegory and the staging (*la mise en scène*) of the subject. The literature of the Middle Ages, one perceives, remains faithful to him when it sees in the first of these terms an instrument specially designed for arranging the encounter of the two others.

This encounter takes at first the form of contemplation by the subject, that is, by the dreamer, of an allegorical world which presents itself for his interpretation. This is the situation which was described above by saying that the theater of allegory is outside the subject or, similarly, that instead of representing the subject, allegory is confronted by the subject, which keeps itself set apart. This is the case in the poems or in the Latin prosimetra referred to earlier. The very title of the *Consolatio Philosophiae* of Boethius is in this regard exemplary: Philosophy, personified, is the subject's interlocutor and consoles him. However, when this situation appears in French poetry, the impersonal and nontemporal character of the allegory is counterbalanced not only by the fact that it is the subject's dream, but also by the presence in this dream, intermingled with the allegorical world, of references to the real and contemporary world, in conformity with the new poetics of the thirteenth century. Thus, in the *Songe d'Enfer*, Raoul de Houdenc places personifications beside real characters. A little later, Huon de Méry uses the same procedure in the *Tournoiement Antechrist,* which does not claim, admittedly, to be the narrative of a dream, but rather that of events actually experienced by the poet. But the fountain of Baranton, near which Huon encounters the chamberlain of the Antichrist, is a place as propitious for meaningful (*signi-*

fiante) adventure as is the time of dream. We will return to this point. In itself, certainly, the intermingling of personifications with characters entirely outside the allegory is nothing new. Thus, at the time of his descent into Hades, Aeneas, in the *Aeneid* (6, 273–81) just as in the French romance of *Eneas* (vv. 2401–12), encounters Old Age, Fear, Hunger, Poverty and Suffering, his companions, his enemies, his lover and, finally, his father. But these personifications are nothing other than images which present themselves to the hero's view at the threshold of his expedition, and they have nothing in common with the characters who concern him later, in the dwelling place of the dead. Raoul de Houdenc and especially Huon de Méry, on the contrary, deal on the same footing with all their characters, allegorical, Biblical, mythological, literary—i.e., borrowed from the contemporary French literature in which Huon was steeped— and they assign to all these characters the same status within the allegorical narrative. In addition, however, Raoul de Houdenc mixes real, contemporary figures into this motley crowd, while Huon de Méry makes multiple allusions to contemporary events or to ethnic stereotypes, satirizing for instance the Poitevins, the Normans, the English. These two poets therefore do not place allegorical narrative farther from reality than fictional mimetic narrative, but on the contrary closer to it. Closer to it not only because the allegory renders the meaning of reality, but also because reality is present in the allegory. Its presence is that of the author, who is the spectator of the allegory, and that of the real characters, with whom he is acquainted and who are included within it. Huon de Méry even plays the two roles at once, since he intervenes episodically in the allegorical combat and there receives a wound. On this subject, it has been observed that in the *Tournoiement Antechrist* "pour la première fois, le poète choisit le cadre du poème allégorique pour raconter une aventure personnelle"[10] [for the first time, the poet chooses the framework of the allegorical poem in order to recount a personal adventure]. This is true, but one must remember that Huon de Méry's "personal adventure" lies in having witnessed the confrontation between the legions of the Antichrist and the sacred hosts, and in having even played a small part in it. This is certainly not insignificant, and it is not granted to everyone. But there is a considerable difference between this and the position of the narrator of the *Roman de la Rose*, who is both the center (with regard to the signifier), and the stage (with regard to the signified) of the allegorical theater. The combat of the forces of Evil against those of Good would take place in any case, whether the poet, who found himself there by chance, participated in it or not. By contrast, in the *Roman de la Rose*, it is the poet's love which sets in motion the forces that confront each other around him. The wound re-

10. M.-R. Jung, op. cit., 290.

ceived by Huon in the course of the combat does not suffice to make the *Tournoiement Antechrist* anything other than a particular case of the type of poem in which the narrator is the spectator of the allegorical representation. But Raoul de Houdenc and Huon de Méry, in mingling the allegorical world with the contemporary world, with their world and their contemporaries, both show that allegory touches reality and touches it through their own mediation.

Since a dream is involved, this mediation is by definition essential, because the whole allegorical representation comes into play in the consciousness of the dreamer. Further, the reader must take care not to forget this; that is, he must keep his attention directed toward the relation between the dreaming self and the waking self who is supposed to be the narrator of the dream. His attention is, in fact, so directed when the poem describes the process of falling asleep and the birth of the dream or raises questions concerning the nature of the dream. This description and this questioning, moreover, are closely associated. For on the one hand, medieval commentators engaged in profound reflections on the definition of visions and of dreams, on their differences, on their connections, on the nature of their truth; numerous episodes from the Bible, from saints' lives and from classical literature invited them to do so. On the other hand, poets transformed into a literary motif, developed in an increasingly explicit way, the description of a state which originally resulted from a technique used by horsemen, both in the West and in many other places (e.g., among the Mongols), a technique designed to permit the rider, as Corneille later wrote, to "Passer des jours entiers et des nuits à cheval." [Pass entire days and nights on horseback.] This state, sometimes called *dorveille,* is a sort of drowsiness in which the mind maintains only a distant relationship with reality or even loses contact with it, but without actually giving way to sleep.[11] It is probably this state that Guillaume IX, the first troubadour, refers to when he claims to have composed a poem *en durmen / Sobre chevau* [while sleeping on horseback.] It is this state that fosters those amorous ecstasies in the course of which the heroes of romances, Lancelot, Perceval, Durmart le Gallois, lose all contact with outside reality. It is this state, finally, that allows passage into another world, the frontier of which is crossed by means of the half-sleep of the horseback ride. It is thus used at the same time as a motive for romance narrative, as a means of access to inner adventure, and as a medium of poetic creation, if it is legitimate, as it probably is, to interpret in this way the verses of Guillaume IX. The original meaning of *rêver,* of course, is to wander about,

11. The present discussion on this point is inspired by the analyses of Michel Stanesco in "Aspects ludiques de la fonction guerrière dans la littérature française à la fin du Moyen Age," Diss. Toulouse 1982, 280–314, an excellent work which, it is to be hoped, will soon be published.

to roam the mental and physical countryside:* it is the activity of the horseman and, during the same interval, of his mind. Under these circumstances, the relation between the literal and the figurative sense of *rêver* is a relation both of simultaneity and of causality. As for the result of the daydream,† it may be designated equally well as the conclusion of the horseback ride—the arrival in another world—, as the affective state and the imaginary aspect of the dream—the amorous ecstasy—, as the poem which may involve both the one and the other, and which defines itself literally as the product of the waking dream.

To raise questions about the nature of such a dream, whose incorporation into sleep is denied, placed in doubt or passed over in silence, to speculate about its reality, to describe the conditions of its appearance before recounting it as a personal experience: the vogue of this literary exercise grew continually, even when the initial cause and justification of *dorveille,* travel by horseback, was forgotten. The growth of this vogue took place in conjunction with the development of poetry devoted to personal narration, for the reasons given above. To focus on the vision's mode of appearance means to reveal the relation between its general meaning and the particular conditions of the subjectivity which is at once its source and its beneficiary, and through which it is communicated to the reader of the poem.

One would have to give numerous examples in order to show the extraordinary degree to which this process was used, almost as a rule of the genre, from the second half of the thirteenth century until the end of the Middle Ages. At the beginning of this period, certain poems by Rutebeuf, such as the *Dit d'Hypocrisie* or the *Voie de Paradis,* are particularly well suited to this kind of analysis. For our present purposes, however, a single example will have to suffice: the poet Watriquet de Couvin, who was active in the first third of the fourteenth century. Several of his poems will be cited in order to show both the constants and the variants in the process. In every case, an impression or a preoccupation which haunts the wakeful poet at the poem's beginning, finds it correlative, its prolongation, its fulfilment or its explanation in the vision which comes to him. But the linking of one state to the other is suggested in a variety of ways. Here are three examples, in which the poet emphasizes the continuity between waking and daydreaming or dreaming.

Thus in the *Dit de l'araignée et du crapaud:*

---

* The original text plays here upon the ambiguity of the thirteenth-century verb *rêver* and of the expression *battre la campagne:* taken literally, they mean *to roam, to explore the territory;* understood figuratively, they are *to daydream, to reflect in disordered fashion on a variety of things.*—Translator's note.

† In order to reflect the consistent terminology of the French text, I have always translated *rêverie* as *daydream* and *rêve* as *dream.*—Translator's note.

Par .I. mardi au point du jour,
Me levai sans faire sejour
L'an .XXIX. ou mois de juing,
Si m'en aloie tout enjuing
Parmi .I. vergier vert jouant,
Et le chant d'un oisel sivant,
Qui moult me faisoit esjoïr,
Car gracieus iert a oïr.
De branche en branche voletoit,
Et de chanter s'entremetoit
Si forment qu'a son joli son
M'endormi desouz .I. buisson,
C'onques l'oiselet n'eslongai;
Mais en cest dormant je songai
Que j'estoie a Bec Oisel
Ou Charles et maint damoisel
Iert alez pour esbanoier.
La trouvai desouz .I. noier,
Seant assez pres de la porte,
Raison. . . . [Vv. 1–20][12]

Poem of the Spider and the Frog
On a Tuesday at daybreak, in June of the year 1329, I arose without delay
and, without breakfasting, went on my way; I went gaily through a green
orchard, following the song of a bird, a song which filled me with joy, for
it was charming to hear. The bird fluttered about from branch to branch
and set itself to singing so loudly that at the lovely sound I fell asleep
beneath a bush, from which the little bird never strayed; in this sleep I
dreamed that I was at Bec Oisel, where Charles and many damsels had
gone to amuse themselves. There beneath a walnut tree, sitting rather
close to the gate, I found Reason. . . .

Having followed the singing bird, the poet falls asleep while listening to it,
only to rediscover immediately, transposed into his dream, all that he has
just left behind. The bird itself, of course, is not left behind (v. 13): the
poet's dream, in fact, transports him not only to a castle named Bec
d'Oiseau, but also into the midst of the games of a troop of children, an
image which could have been suggested to him by the bird's carefree
cheerfulness, the whimsical vivacity of its flight, its chirping. Children are
involved, in fact, because the Charles in question, second son of Guy de
Blois and future duke of Brittany, was ten years old in 1329. Similarly, the
trees of the orchard, in whose branches the poet observed the bird, are
represented in his dream by the walnut tree beneath which he finds Reason. The latter, having been driven out of the pontifical court, and having
taken refuge at the court of the Count of Blois, bursts into complaints and

12. Auguste Scheler, *Les Dits de Watriquet de Couvin* (Brussels, 1968), 65.

tears. When she goes away, the poet turns his head, and this movement wakes him:

> A itant de l'aler s'atourne
> Dame Raisons, et je retourne
> Mon chief aussi comme estourdis,
> Si m'esveillai. [Vv. 209–12][13]

> Then Lady Reason turned to go, and I turned my head as if I were dazed; thus I woke up.

The transition from dream to awakening is therefore indicated, as was the falling asleep and the plunge into dream, by a movement that begins in the dream and then interrupts it by waking the dreamer; it is also indicated by the dizziness of the dreamer, who has trouble regaining mental control and whose uncertain consciousness still hovers between the two states. Once again, the poet, in his role as Reason's confidant, confronts entirely from the outside an allegorical world which is not his own. But he compensates for the passivity of his role by emphasizing the contingency of this encounter and the subjectivity of his viewpoint. The precise dating—a Tuesday in June, 1329, at daybreak—, the careful descriptions of falling asleep and of awakening, the projection into the imaginary dream world of the circumstances of waking reality, all aim to produce this effect. In contradistinction to what happened in the preceding poem, these circumstances and these contingencies justify by the "logic" of free association the allegorical argument of the dream, or at least its point of departure. Falling asleep at the song of a bird, the poet dreams of the castle of Bec d'Oiseau [Bird's Beak] and of the young Charles de Blois; from there, his mind passes to the political activity of the Count of Blois, whose court is the refuge of Reason.

The same process is used in a much more detailed and more explicit fashion in the *Tournoi des dames*, whose introduction Scheler summarizes as follows:

> On a winter day, in the pavilion of a tower of the castle of Montferrant, the poet is reflecting on the meaning of a stained glass window which represents the victorious struggle of a group of ladies against their knights, when he falls asleep. In his sleep, Lady Truth, driven out of every other place, comes to him and urges him to follow her. After having helped him to grasp the hidden meaning of the singular tournament depicted on the window (*the struggle of the flesh against the soul*), she proceeds on her way accompanied by the poet. . . . But this introduction is itself preceded by a fairly long description of the place where the author had his vision: it is Montferrant, a castle in the country of Blois, where he was visiting the count, as he says himself, in October of 1327. The charms of the site, the luxuriousness of the château, the surrounding

13. Scheler, 72.

forests filled with game, these form the subject of the first 120 verses, which thus assume the character of a dedication to the castle's lord, in whose service Watriquet was engaged.[14]

This long prologue is not only a dedication: the stained glass window of the tower's pavilion, described after all the marvels of the castle of Montfer-rant, appears unexpectedly and enigmatically as their crowning feature. Its secret is, as it were, the secret of the castle, to which the poet has access only after having been exposed to its other charms. There is continuity leading from the description of the castle to that of the stained glass window and from the latter to the vision which explains its meaning and which results directly from the poet's fascinated contemplation of the strange tournament represented in the glass:

> Ceste oevre moult m'esbahissoit
> Comment ce pooit avenir.
> Tant i pensai que soustenir
> Ne me poi plus, ançois me couche
> Seur mon bras (n'i oi autre couche),
> Si fui si qu'entre dor et voille
> Touz raviz. Or orrés merveille
> Qu'ilec en ce penser m'avint.
> A moi une dame là vint
> Où j'estoie, en celle tornelle. . . . [Vv. 166–75][15]

This work astonished me greatly and made me wonder how it had come about. I meditated upon it so much that I could no longer remain stand-ing, so I laid my head down on my arms (there was nothing else to rest on), and there between sleeping and waking I was completely entranced. Now listen to the marvelous thing that happened to me while I was in this meditation. A lady came to me, to where I was in that little tower. . . .

The state of the poet who is submerged, entranced within his con-templation is explicitly defined as a *dorveille*. Truth, when she appears to him, addresses him moreover in these terms:

> ". . . A quel matere
> Penses tu, compains, biaus amis;
> Di moi qui en ce point t'a mis
> Que tu ne dors ne tu ne veilles." [Vv. 186–89]

"What are you thinking of, my companion, my good friend? Tell me what has put you in this state in which you are neither asleep nor awake."

He is not asleep, he does not rediscover in a dream the distorted echo or the transposed image of impressions from his waking state. He continues to

14. Scheler, 473–74.
15. Scheler, 236–37.

pursue the same thoughts. But his unrelenting concentration and the resultant fatigue cause a slackening of the attention, a relaxation of the body (turned inward upon itself) and of the mind (no longer conscious of exterior reality) which gives rise to the eagerly desired elucidation in the form of the allegorical vision. The scene continues in the same setting, in the same little tower, before the same window, and yet it is in another world. By definition, the lessons that Truth teaches to the poet by means of five parables are of a general nature, just as truth is general. But the long description of the activities and preoccupations of the poet at the castle of Montferrant, in this month of October, 1327, the care with which he presents the vision as their consequence and their prolongation, the attention given to his state of consciousness at the instant when the vision appears, all function to present the universal teaching of the allegory as the result of chance circumstances and subjective impressions.

Finally, in the *Miroir des Dames*, Watriquet rediscovers the original association of *dorveille* with horseback riding. But he inverts the effects and the causes:

> De maintes biautez me souvint,
> De dames et de damoiseles,
> Gracieuses, plaisans et beles,
> De gens cors, de douces veües,
> Et des biens que j'en ai eüs,
> Et fui si de joie esmeüs
> C'onques si liez n'avoie esté.
> Ce fu le premier jour d'esté
> Que cis pensers me vint devant,
> Aussi qu'entour soleil levant,
> Qu'iere levez au point du jour;
> Si pensai tant et sans sejour
> Qu'en cest penser fui si pensis,
> Que mors sembloie estre ou transis
> Et ensement que touz muïz.
> Et ou penser me fu avis
> Que fusse en une grant forest,
> Si chevauchoie sanz arrest
> Parmi les bois moi deduisant.
> Li rai du cler soleil luisant
> S'espandoient parmi les buissons,
> Et cil oiselet a douz sons
> S'esforçoient de haut chanter:
> C'iert melodie a escouter. [Vv. 24–48][16]

I remembered many beauties, ladies and damsels who were gracious, pleasing and beautiful, with lovely bodies and sweet glances; and I re-

16. Scheler, 2.

membered the favors I had had from them; and at this I was so moved by joy that I felt happier than I had ever been before. It was on the first day of summer that this thought came to me, around the time when the sun was rising, for I had risen at daybreak; I reflected so much and so steadily and was so absorbed that I appeared to be either dead or transfixed, and as if completely transformed. And in my thoughts it seemed to me that I was in a great forest, riding continuously on horseback, passing gaily among the trees. The rays of the clear, bright sun fell among the bushes, and little birds sang sweetly with all their heart; it was a beautiful melody to hear.

According to the literary conventions of the period, the poet ought to ride through the forest, where the sun on the leaves and the singing of birds would plunge him into an amorous daydream. Here, the opposite occurs: the thought of feminine beauty produces an ecstatic state in which, although he is completely cut off from reality, it seems to him that he is riding in a forest brightened by rays of sunshine and songs of birds. In actual fact, it often happens that in a dream, the narrator finds himself deep within a forest, usually lost there. This is the case, for example, in Froissart's *Temple d'Honneur* and in the *Amant rendu cordelier à l'Observance d'Amour*.[17] This is also the case, in effect, in the *Divine Comedy*, even though its setting is not literally that of the allegorical dream. In Watriquet's *Miroir*, the forest possesses the characteristics of a *locus amoenus*, which is supposed to inspire daydreaming about feminine beauty and not to be its result. But at the same time, the forest is certainly—but within the daydream—the place of beauty's unveiling. Indeed, in this forest, where the singing nightingale does not flee at his approach, the poet encounters Adventure, who proposes to initiate him, to guide him to where he can contemplate feminine perfection:

> "Je vous menrai o moi veoir
> De biauté le vrai mireoir,
> Le droit compas, le parfait monstre;
> Se je fais tant con le vous monstre,
> Faire en devriez aucun biau dit." [Vv. 117–21]

> "I will take you with me to see the true mirror of beauty, its just measure, its perfect appearance; if I do show it to you, you ought to make a beautiful poem about it."

The poet is in fact led to the castle where this marvel is revealed to him, through the efforts of Courtliness, Largesse, Loyalty, Nature, who created it, and Science, who *"en savait la glose"* (v. 1164) [knew its explanation]. Each of them exhorts him, as Adventure had done, to fashion a poem from the revelation of which they have judged him to be worthy:

17. See Michel Zink, "Séduire, endormir: Notes sur les premiers vers d'un poème du XVe siècle," in *Littérature* 23 (Oct. 1976), 117–21.

> Mais au partir moult me pria [Loyauté]
> Qu'aus dames savoir le feïsse
> Et .I. dit en rime meïsse . . .
> Chascune le me semonnoit. [Vv. 1158–66]

But at our parting [Loyalty] begged me earnestly to reveal it to the ladies,
to make a rhymed poem about it. . . . Each of them pressed me to do this.

Meanwhile, all these ladies call him by name and seem to be well acquainted with him—like Courtliness, who welcomes him in these terms:

> ". . . Qui t'envoia ça,
> Watriquet? Je te cognois bien." [Vv. 402–03]

"Who sent you here, Watriquet? I know you well."

One sees that the relation between the subjectivity of the poetic *moi* and
the allegory is based on a sort of continual reversal (*chassé-croisé*) and,
even more, a sort of interweaving, of interiority and exteriority. Instead of
real, exterior adventure—that is, presumed real by literary convention—
leading to meditation or to ecstasy, as in the case of Lancelot or of Perceval,
it is here meditation which leads to ecstacy, the setting for interior adventure. But this latter is personified, which is to say that if it is not exteriorized, it is at least objectified even within interiority. This play of interiority and exteriority corresponds by its effects to the hesitation that has
been noted in the *Dit des quatre sièges* between that which stems from the
vision and that which stems from the waking state; in both cases, reality,
elusive or indifferent, is as if devalued as a reference point or as a touch-
stone of truth, in favor of the narrator's perceptions and states of consciousness. Similarly, the literary project is revealed at two different points
in the poem. First at the beginning:

> Por ce est mes cuers assentiz
> A ce c'un dit vous conte et die,
> A oïr plaisant melodie,
> De la plus tres bele aventure
> C'onques meïsse en escripture. [Vv. 10–14]

Thus my heart has consented that I should recite you a poem, a melody
pleasant to hear, about the most wonderful adventure that I have ever put
into writing.

Second, it reveals itself within the very framework of the vision, as was
seen above. More importantly, it is at the very interior of the vision that
the text begins to be written. The poet, in fact, immediately acts upon the
advice he has received in the verses already quoted:

> Chascune le me semonnoit,
> Et je du rimer m'entremis,
> Que terme ne respit n'i mis. [Vv. 1166–68]

Each of them pressed me to do it, and I set myself to making rhymes, neither stopping nor resting.

His awakening is described in a manner analogous to the one already found in the *Dit de l'araignée et du crapaud:* awake, he continues what he had begun in his dream and feels as a result a sort of dizziness (*étourdissement*). This time, however, it is not only a question of a movement, but of the effort of literary creation, rendered perceptible in its very expression by the play of *annominatio:*

> Et je en l'ombre d'une tour
> Me tournai ainssi atourné
> S'ai tant tourné et retourné,
> Comme un hons qui est endormis,
> Qu'a moi reving touz estourdis
> En l'estudie et ou penser,
> Si ne voil tant ne quant cesser
> Que celle belle avision,
> Dont dite ai la division,
> En rime n'aie devisee. [Vv. 1274–83]

And, thus equipped, I returned to the shadow of a tower; and there, like a man who is asleep, I tossed and turned about so much that I came to myself feeling completely dazed, deep in study and in thought; and so I have no wish to stop before having cast into rhyme this beautiful vision, which I have described.

He turns over in his sleep: this movement, which in the setting of the vision signals his departure, just after the departure of Nature, wakes him up, and the movement is then interpreted altogether differently, as the agitation of a preoccupied man, a man whose preoccupation is writing. This intimate preoccupation, which has been born of his dream and which has awakened him, is not with writing poetic confidences. Its aim is general and, in its own way, edifying: to make known the canons of feminine beauty and perfection. Further, the source of the vision lies not in amorous sentiment, nor even in admiration for a particular woman, but in the memory of all the beauties that the poet has known. And the revelation that he receives through the vision concerns the nature and the laws of beauty (see above, vv. 118–20), in short, the idea of beauty reflected in each woman. The poem does not progress from the particular to the general, but from a multiplicity to the idea which unifies it. A poem of this type, therefore, does not claim to reveal anything of the poet's sentiments, nor of his life. And yet, it focuses very emphatically on the poet's person and on his point of view. Both emblematically, through the allegorical vision, and explicitly, through its treatment of its own composition, the poem defines itself as the product of a perception and of writing. The recourse to vision, to daydream or to dream is a way of drawing attention to the first of these two components.

It is essentially for this reason that poems which narrate an allegorical dream are based entirely on the narrator's subjectivity. The nature of the allegorical argument may attenuate or accentuate this relationship, but the argument is not the key factor. Either the poet is allowed to contemplate an allegorical system referring to an exterior reality whose meaning is revealed to him, or the allegory reflects his own interiority; the difference between the two is certainly important. H. R. Jauss is right to emphasize that the second approach is adopted for the first time by Guillaume de Lorris and that, in his *Roman de la Rose,* allegory for the first time expresses not the movements of the soul in general, but rather the narrator's own subjectivity.[18] The consciousness of the dreamer in that poem is not only the theater of the dream, but also the object described by its action. This is, for the medieval reader of Macrobius, the most extreme form of the *somnium proprium* and at the same time, for the modern reader, the recognition of what all dreams are in reality. The play on time and on subjectivity in the work's prologue makes evident, as we tried to show above, the introversion of the poetic *je* and the self-referential character of the narrative. The *Roman de la Rose* thus clearly marks the end result of the increasingly close relation between allegory and subjectivity. It is a logical and not a chronological end point, however, because the *dits* of Watriquet de Couvin that we have taken as examples, and the many fourteenth- and fifteenth-century poems that resemble them are from this point of view somewhat retrograde in comparison with the *Rose.*

However, one must not exaggerate the originality of the *Roman de la Rose* on this particular point, for two reasons. The first is that its action is not entirely interiorized, in the sense that, while it is true that the allegory is presented only from the narrator's point of view, this allegory involves some personifications which do not represent elements of his psyche and which are presumed to be exterior to him. In the *Roman de la Rose,* as in all the analogous poems of the time, the allegory deals in the same way with representations of consciousness and with those of the exterior world, both being materialized and objectified in an identical way. The second reason is more important and it leads us back to the preceding analyses. The manifestation of a subjectivity in the poem is less evident in the content of the allegorical narrative than in the expression of the perceptions of the consciousness which introduces it and forms its basis. To describe and define the states of consciousness which lead to daydream or to dream, to investigate the border between these two states, to show that

18. Hans-Robert Jauss, "La Transformation de la forme allégorique entre 1180 et 1240: d'Alain de Lille à Guillaume de Lorris," in *L'Humanisme médiéval dans les littératures romanes du XIIe au XIVe siècle,* ed. Anthime Fourrier (Paris, 1964), 107–44; and "Entstehung und Strukturwandel der allegorischen Dichtung," in *Grundriss der romanischen Literaturen des Mittelalters* VI/1 (Heidelberg: Carl Winter, 1968), 146–244.

their content and their form are neither arbitrary nor foreign to the dreamer, but that on the contrary they are determined by the permanence of waking impressions even when consciousness of the real has been effaced, all this is to show that, whatever constitutes the general truth of allegorical revelation, it exists only through the accidents of a subjectivity and the contingencies of actual experiences. This approach and this concern characterize the whole of allegorical literature from the end of the twelfth to the end of the fifteenth century. The date, the moment, the place, the circumstances, in determining the poet's perception of the world at a given instant, inform the allegorical vision. The prologue of the *Roman de la Rose*, as was suggested at the beginning of this article, applies this principle in a particularly complex and profound manner, by adding to the interplay between reality and dream the interaction of past, memory and present. In this lies the originality of the poem of Guillaume de Lorris, undoubtedly rendered less evident by its incompletion, rather than in the dream's plot itself, whatever may have been its relative novelty in the first third of the thirteenth century.

Thus it is in this way that the relation between allegory and subjectivity is resolved. Allegory, which aspires to convey a general truth, attempts at the same time to be, in its particular expression, the product of the narrator's state of consciousness. The recourse to dream or to waking dream renders this perceptible in the most striking and the most frequent way. But there are other ways, such as that used by Huon de Méry. One may remember that the *Tournoiement Antecrist* does not present itself as the narration of a dream, but as that of a real adventure. Must one regard this difference as a decisive typological criterion? Certainly not. The argument employed by Huon de Méry shows this clearly. In fact, he tells in the prologue that, profiting from his stay in Brittany with the king's army on the occasion of a royal expedition against Pierre Mauclerc, the Count of Brittany, he entered the forest of Broceliande in order to *apprendre la vérité* [learn the truth] concerning the perilous fountain. He finds it after four days, pours water on the *perron* [stone steps], as first Calogrenant and then Yvain had done in the romance of the *Chevalier au Lion* by Chrétien de Troyes, and this action does not fail to unleash a frightful storm. When morning comes and the storm has subsided, there appears a Moor, from Mauritania, who disarms the poet and compels him to proceed to the court of the Antichrist, of whom the Moor is the chamberlain Bras-de-Fer. It is in this fashion that the poet comes to witness the combat between the forces of evil and the holy legions. One should note that Huon several times refers explicitly and admiringly to Chrétien de Troyes, as well as to the *Songe d'Enfer* and to the *Roman des Ailes* of Raoul de Houdenc. He thus aims to be the modest but faithful imitator, both of the romances of Chrétien:

> Pour ce que mors est Crestïens
> De Troies, cil qui tant ot pris
> De trover, ai hardement pris
> De mot a mot meitre en escrit
> Le tournoiement Antecrist. [Vv. 22–26][19]

Because Chrétien de Troyes, who had so often set himself to writing poems, is dead, I have boldly set myself to writing, word for word, the battle of the Antichrist.

and of the allegorical *songe* [dream] of Raoul, who, as Huon continually emphasizes, has already said much better the things that he is merely repeating. However, Huon does not take up the dream setting, and it is an understatement to say that his poem scarcely resembles the romances of Chrétien de Troyes. Why does he feel so strongly his dependence upon his two predecessors? Why does he conclude his own poem with the remark that they have said everything and have left him nothing but some gleanings:

> Molt mis grant peine a eschiver
> Les diz Raol et Crestïen,
> C'onques bouche de crestïen
> Ne dist si bien com il disoient.
> Mes quant qu'il dirent il prenoient
> Le bel françois trestot a plein
> Si com il lor venoit a mein,
> si c'apres eus n'ont rien guerpi.
> Se j'ai trové aucun espi
> Apres la main as mestiviers,
> Je l'ai glané molt volentiers. [Vv. 3534–44][20]

I took great pains to preserve the poems of Raoul and of Chrétien, which no Christian mouth ever told as well as they did. Whatever they said, they took the beautiful French language so well and firmly into their hands, that they let nothing fall behind them. If I have found any grains left by the harvesters' hands, I have been very happy to glean them.

The response to these questions involves two preliminary observations. It is not sufficient, in fact, to say that Huon simply imitates Chrétien and Raoul. It must be added that, on the one hand, he maintains his status as their reader even when writing his own poem, and that, on the other hand, he imitates them conjointly. He maintains his status as their reader, for he quotes them, he explicitly acknowledges borrowing situations from them and, in the case of Chrétien, he substitutes himself for the romance's

19. Georg Wimmer, *Li Tornoiemenz Antecrist von Huon de Mery, nach den Handschriften zu Paris, London und Oxford neu herausgegeben* (Marburg: N. G. Elwert, 1888), 37.
20. Wimmer, 104.

hero and takes his place in these situations: it is Huon himself, and not Calogrenant or Yvain, who unleashes the storm by pouring water on the steps of the fountain. In other words, he is trying less to reproduce his literary model than to prolong by identification the impression that this model produced upon him. His repeated homage to the two poets, his sense of being unable to equal them and of having nothing more to say after them, his difficulty in finding other subjects than those with which they dealt, all of this has the same cause. He is incapable of detaching himself, in order to turn to writing, from the fascination he feels as a reader; for him, to write under the inspiration of Chrétien and of Raoul is to sustain and to express the impressions that he received while reading them. Wace was no better off after his real excursion to the fountain of Barenton. The excursion which Huon imagines while linking it as closely as he can to his real life satisfies him entirely, for it permits him to enter into the world of his favorite authors.

To enter into the world of his favorite authors is a metaphor. One never enters there except by the imagination, which is stimulated by reading. But Huon's reading of Chrétien and of Raoul is prolonged by the writing of a poem, whose argument is precisely that the narrator enters into the world of his two models. His feeling of dependence on them is thus explained, even though his poem bears no resemblance, or no genuine resemblance, to theirs, by the fact that it is the expression of their resonance in his mind. But one can also understand why he experiences this feeling of dependence in regard to the two poets conjointly and without being able to dissociate them. He can enter into the world of Chrétien's romances only by means of the mental leap into the world of allegory, for which Raoul offered him a model. Inversely, he can escape from the admitted unreality of the dream, which is the usual framework for this leap into allegory, only by substituting romance adventure, to which he assigns the same introductory role. On the first point, in fact, whatever may be his desire for identification, the poet cannot claim actually to have experienced an adventure in Brittany: the meaning of the Arthurian world is based on a radical distancing of the past.[21] But he is able, at the very location in Brittany where the Arthurian adventure had taken place, to undergo an adventure that resembles it and that lays claim to truth. This adventure is the subjective experience of allegorical revelation, which invokes as its own truth that which is signified. As for the second point, it illustrates the proposition from which we started, and to which we return

---

21. M.-R. Jung, emphasizing Huon's insistent interest in *ce qui de novel avient* [the new things that happen] (v. 9) and in *une aventure novele* [a new adventure] (v. 11), opposes this attitude to that of Chrétien who, in the prologue to the *Chevalier au lion*, "devant la décadence de son époque préfèrent parler de ceux qui furent" [given the decadence of his era prefers to speak of those which were] op. cit., 288.

after a long detour: the narrator's state of consciousness, which is supposed to call forth the allegorical adventure and revelation, is able to escape from the form of the dream without, however, modifying in any significant way the relation between allegory and subjectivity. The *Tournoiement Antecrist*, in place of the interiorized experience of *dorveille*, of daydream or of dream, substitutes that of the escape resulting from the fascination of literature, which is itself exteriorized and materialized in the form of an unconventional literary pilgrimage. Certainly, in contrast to the poems which depend upon the *mise en scène* of a dream or a vision, nothing in Huon's text itself suggests that the narrative could be literally untrue. Only the chronological references which, so often, as we have already seen, root the allegorical adventure firmly within the lived experience of the poet, pass from simple dating to the symbolic unfolding of liturgical time. The date of the adventure is that of Louis IX's expedition against Pierre Mauclerc. Its time is that of the week before Ascension: the army of the King of the Firmament celebrates its victory and returns to heaven on the seventh day, which is Wednesday, the eve of Ascension, and on Ascension Thursday, Huon enters the convent of Saint-Germain-des-Prés, in a final fusion of the symbolic time of the liturgy and the chronological unfolding of the events of his own life, which he rejoins in extremis. Nothing in the text itself would lead one to doubt the factual reality of the combat between the Antichrist and the King of the Firmament, and nothing would designate it as a vision and as a product of the narrator's mind, if the literary references did not thus define the entire poem: a reader's phantasy, the result of the expansive mimesis of his *moi* which identifies itself simultaneously with the author and with the character. It is in this sense that the initial adventure in Brittany is a substitute for the dream and has, like the dream, the function of subordinating the allegorical narrative to the narrator's psychological state.

This approach is therefore not limited to the cases, although they are very frequent, in which the daydream or the dream serves as *mise en scène* and as framework for the allegory; on the contrary, it is constant and almost obligatory in the allegorical poetry of this period. The allegory is always filtered through a subjective point of view, that of the narrator. It is a perception, that is, a coherent and meaningful organization of the impressions and the sensations experienced by a consciousness that interprets and associates them according to its psychological tendencies, its intellectual patterns, its memories. Therefore, the allegory in no way offers that overly clear simplicity which repels the modern mind, nor does it offer that stable and objective truth which Scriptural exegesis reveals behind the literal meaning. It is the reflection of a truth in a consciousness. A reflection blurred, of course, by the particular conditions of this consciousness. It is this blurring which produces, with the signifier, the allegorical discourse. This discourse therefore reveals just as much about the consciousness that receives and expresses the truth of the signified as about this truth itself. The particular turn which the discourse gives to this truth, its obscurities, its haplologies,[22] its complacencies, each of its choices, make it into a discourse of the self on the self as much as a discourse of a general truth veiled by concrete trappings. This is why allegorical poetry, in relation to the general evolution of poetry from the thirteenth century on, is conceived as personal poetry. This is why it is so careful to show the overlapping and the interaction, within consciousness, of the perception of the exterior world with the perception of meaningful revelation. This is also why it emphasizes the uncertainty of reality through the uncertainty of the boundaries separating perception from revelation. This is why allegorical poetry focuses on describing the fluctuation of states of consciousness and on understanding the present of subjectivity.

In this poetry, however, writing never claims to be simultaneous with the putative experience and state of consciousness that it describes. The poetry preserves their memory. All the cases we have considered above are very explicit on this point. Only the *Miroir des Dames* integrates a preoccupation with writing into the vision itself, and this prior to the awakening, which it causes; but it is not until after this awakening, of course, that the literary project conceived in the dream is put into action. The poem increases in value by implicitly claiming to have been written in the heat of the moment, for example upon the instant of awakening. It is nonetheless a return to a past state of consciousness, barely past, but past all the same. This distance is precisely what supports all the reflective and by the same token retrospective effort of the poem to define the narrator's state of consciousness, daydream or dream, to rediscover the circumstances of falling asleep and of waking up, to understand the relations between the exterior circumstances and the nature of the vision. Once more, the *Roman de la Rose* (characterized, as we have seen, by the prominence it gives to the play of memory), demonstrates its particular insight into this subject, by showing that this relation to the past, a relation that is necessarily operative in all the poems of this type, is not self-evident and by integrating it into the debate on dream and reality, truth and meaning. Thus, this poetry reveals the mediation effected by recollection, even while claiming to follow as closely as possible the flow of consciousness in the perception and in the ordering of the allegorical universe.

22. "Le grammairien Démétrius joint le symbole et l'allégorie pour observer que la force de ces figures, supérieure à celle du langage clair, provient de leur nature brachylogique qui, à partir d'un mot, laisse entendre le reste." [The grammarian Demetrius joins symbol to allegory in order to observe that the force of these figures, superior to that of clear language, comes from their brachylogical nature which, on the basis of a word, allows the rest to be understood.] Jean Pépin, *Dante et la tradition de l'allégorie* (Montréal-Paris, 1970), 16.

This observation calls for two others, one dealing with the link between allegory and the faculty of memory, the other with that between
recollection and self-consciousness.* On the first point, we know that the
method of artificial memory by visualization, set forth in the *Rhetorica ad
Herennium* and later glossed by various medieval thinkers, depends upon
the allegorization of a recollection. The orator, for whom this method is
principally recommended, is asked to imagine, for example, a vast edifice
and to distribute among its different rooms each of the ideas he proposes to
develop, in the form of scenes that are preferably violent or bloody, or of
figures whose beauty or ugliness is extreme, forms that can evoke his ideas
by analogy. Thereafter, it suffices for the orator, while delivering his
speech, to wander by imagination through this edifice in order to rediscover in each room successively the striking scenes representing each of
his ideas. In her masterful essay, the *Art of Memory*, Frances Yates, discussing the medieval avatars of this method and of the theory that it
presupposes in the work of Boncompagno, Albertus Magnus and Thomas
Aquinas, writes:

> The images chosen for their memorable quality in the Roman orator's art
> have been changed by mediaeval piety into 'corporeal similitudes' of
> 'subtle and spiritual intentions'. . . . What becomes of the strikingly
> beautiful and strikingly hideous *imagines agentes* in such a memory?
> The immediately pre-scholastic memory of Bancompagno suggests an
> answer to this question, with its virtues and vices as 'memorial notes
> reminding of the ways to Heaven and to Hell.' The *imagines agentes*
> would have been moralised into beautiful or hideous human figures as
> 'corporeal similitudes' of spiritual intentions of gaining Heaven or avoid-
> ing Hell, and memorised as ranged in order in some 'solemn' building.[23]

This moralization and this Christianization of the art of memory, this
conviction that it consists essentially in the figurative and striking representation of Heaven and Hell, of virtues and vices, in such a way as to keep
constantly in mind that which is to be sought and that which is to be
avoided, lead Frances Yates to suggest that the didactic and edifying literature of the Middle Ages owes perhaps more than one might think to the
Artes memoriae. She also links the striking, hideous or bloody images,
which were favored by those *Artes,* with the predilection of medieval art
for grotesque or terrifying figures. These intuitions are, certainly, au-
dacious; the more so as the author does not develop them. But there is no

*The French text here makes a distinction between *mémoire,* a faculty or capacity of the
human mind, and *souvenir,* the specific, individual product of this faculty. In an effort to
preserve this distinction, I have translated the former term by *memory* and the latter by
recollection.—Translator's note.

23. Frances A. Yates, *The Art of Memory* (Chicago: Univ. of Chicago Press, 1966), 76–77.

doubt that allegory is at once the fundamental process of artificial memory, which replaces ideas with concrete representations that designate them, and the mode of expression most favored by the didactic literature of the Middle Ages. Nor is it excessive to claim that in this last case the function of allegory is to fix more easily in the memory, by stimulating the imagination, the truths that a work aims to inculate. This attribution of a mnemonic function to allegory has as its counterpart the medieval attribution of an edifying function to the art of memory.

These links between allegory and the exercise of memory allow one to elaborate and to complete the analyses proposed above. They suggest, in fact, that the recovery of mental states by means of recollection does not merely make memory the framework of the allegorical poem, but that the allegory itself develops as a function of memory. The allegory is thus bound up with the narrator's consciousness, not only in the cases where the characters constituting this consciousness emanate from it, as in the *Roman de la Rose*, not only, and more generally, because the allegory presents itself as a perception of the consciousness whose conditions and accidents it reflects, but in a still more fundamental way: truth reveals itself to the consciousness in the form of allegory, because it is allegory that fixes truth in the memory. It was the link between allegory and memory which, during the period when prescholasticism and scholasticism revealed or rediscovered it, obliged allegorical poetry, despite its pretensions to generality, to be a poetry of subjectivity.

It is thus that one proceeds necessarily, as outlined above, from the relation between allegory and memory to that between recollection and consciousness. Allegorical poetry assumes that the narrator turns inward upon himself, gives retrospective attention to the circumstances of his life and to their resonance in his consciousness, to the nature and the contingencies of his perception of himself and of the world. It is written as *interior memoirs*. Rooted in the dates and the accidents of life, of which it is the interiorized prolongation, allegorical poetry is the symmetrical counterpart of the personal *dit*, which also dwells upon these dates and these accidents, but in order to define the subject only on the basis of his exteriority. However, having fallen back on the play of consciousness and of recollection, allegorical poetry is paradoxically more sensitive to the function of time in the decipherment of the subject. Claiming to grasp the present of subjectivity through the consciousness of recollection and the recollection of consciousness, it reflects, despite its admittedly fictional component, the most innovative aspect of the interest in autobiography that was emerging in the literature of the period: the attention directed toward the subject in and of himself and not merely as a witness, toward the way that he is marked and molded by events, not only by their succession, but by their meaning—both present and retrospective—with regard to his own life. The narrator of the *Roman de la Rose* proceeds in just this way when he recalls an old dream, because his present life abruptly reveals the dream's meaning and because this present draws its own meaning from the dream.

Translated by Margaret Miner
and Kevin Brownlee

ALEXANDRE LEUPIN

The Powerlessness of Writing: Guillaume de Machaut, the Gorgon, and *Ordenance*

Car il n'est regle qui ne faille[1]

We will here be concerned with measuring the space or the lack of connection between two seemingly incommensurable terms: the essence of power and the essence of poetic language; with tying and untying the knots of their articulations and their disjunctions.

I

Princes proliferate in the corpus of Guillaume de Machaut: friends, silent partners, employers and addressees—that is, characters of written fiction. They seem to exemplify, in the interior of the work, that which would be one or the other of its possible exteriorities: its large, attentive, garrulous and omnipresent public, or, as well, the hierarchial, socialized scene upon which the activity of the medieval poet inscribes itself.

Machaut, faced with this exteriority which is simultaneously power, describes himself as subjected to it as a secretary: he who captures in writing the voice of this power, giving it the form of a decree, a charter, a letter, or a book of records. This function makes him an intimate and servant of the prince, and a confidant to some of his secrets. It gives him the power to reveal them, more clearly than others, within the sin-

---

1. *Remède de Fortune*, v. 2721. Other references will be indicated in the text using the following abbreviations: RF-*Remède de Fortune*, PA-*La Prise d'Alexandrie*, DA-*Dit de l'Alerion*, CA-*Confort d'Ami*, VD-*Voir-Dit*.

The edition of Ernest Hoepffner, *Œuvres de Guillaume de Machaut* (Paris: Didot-Champion, 1908–21), is used for all citations from the following works: *Le Dit dou Vergier*, *Le Jugement dou Roy de Navarre*, *Remède de Fortune*, *Le Dit dou Lyon*, *Le Dit de l'Alerion* and *Le Confort d'Ami*. All citations from the *Voir-Dit* are from Paulin Paris, ed., *Le Livre du Voir-Dit* (Paris: Société des Bibliophiles Français, 1875). All citations from *La Prise d'Alexandrie* are from Louis de Mas Latrie, ed., *La Prise d'Alexandrie ou Chronique du Roi Pierre de Lusignan* (Geneva: Fick, 1877).

uosities of language; as Machaut writes of Jean de Bohème in *La Prise d'Alexandrie:*

> Je fu ses clers, ans plus de XXX.,
> Si congnu ses meurs et s'entente,
> S'onneur, son bien, sa gentillesse,
> Son hardement et sa largesse,
> Car j'estoie ses secretaires
> En trestous ses plus gros affaires.
> S'en puis parler plus clerement
> Que maint autre, et plus proprement. [*PA*, vv. 785–92]

I was his clerk for more than thirty years and thus I knew his habits and his thoughts, his honor, his worth, his kindness, his strength and his generosity, for I was his secretary in all his most important affairs. And so I can speak of them more clearly and more specifically than most others.

In another text, the *Dit de l'Alerion,* the relationship of the prince to his subjects is presented with such clarity that we are almost blind to the wily parabolic character of the *exemplum* used by Guillaume de Machaut.

A bird of prey of an inferior species dares to kill an eagle. The courtiers then praise the bird for attacking such a mighty prey ("Roy des oiseaus, noble et puissant," v. 3044 [King of the birds, noble and powerful]). The "true" king is not taken in and he cuts off the head of the regicide. It could not be more explicit that the fundamental argument which upholds the death sentence is that the bird of prey committed a crime that transgressed the laws of Nature:

> Car li oiseaus se desnature,
> Tant soit grans, ne tant ait de force,
> Qui encontre l'aigle s'efforce. [*DA*, vv. 3390–92]

For a bird acts contrary to nature, no matter how big or how powerful it is, when it attacks an eagle.

At the same stroke (of the sword), the prince symbolically naturalizes power, transforming its arbitrary and artificial character into an eternal and inviolable essence. This violent operation (which in return justifies the mute and gentle obedience to its own betrayal) inscribes itself in a specific space: that of language. The bird's head is, in fact, the emblem of the subversive and destructive word which attacks not the exercise of power, but the tautology which neutralizes it as an essence and as law. The "true" word of power thus comes to detach discourse from subversion and to return it to its frivolous nothingness:

> Sa teste, ce sont ses paroles,
> Nom pas tant seulement frivoles,
> Mais parlers de detraction

> Qui met gens a destruction.
> Celle teste est tost esrachie,
> Par parole bien affichie
> A l'onneur dou seurdit briefment. [*DA*, vv. 3565–71]

(The bird's) head signifies its speech, which is not only frivolous but slanderous, leading people to destruction. This head is quickly severed by the honorable speech briefly mentioned above.

But in the *Dit de l'Alerion*, the bird is also, in a more general sense, a metaphor for every word: not only that of the lie, of the *losangiers* (slanderers) in which case it is an inconstant word (cf. *DA* 824 ff.), but also that of desire. The bird can then symbolize not only power, but the entire space of the poem itself, to the extent that the poem is a vast adventure of desire.

> Volentés qui est par dedens
> Est si a Amour aërdans
> Qu'elle est en un moment volée
> En l'air ou sa dame est montee,
> Non d'estat, mais de melodie.[2] [*DA*, vv. 2599–603]

The (lover's) will is so fired by Love that in an instant it flies up into the air where its Lady has climbed, not in station, but in melody.

(It is interesting to note in this context how Machaut presents a person as equal to something [*à la hauteur*]. It is neither a question of social stature nor of power, but of melody.)

However, this space in Machaut (which he calls *argument* [argument, v. 1635], *comparaison* [comparison, v. 2551], *exemplaire* [example, v. 1639]) is submitted to a systematic covering (*couverture*): that of the *parabole* (parabola or parable). Truth is then curved, and can only be half-said (*DA*, v. 3079: "J'en responderoie briefment / le vray un po couvertement" ["I would answer succinctly and a little covertly with the truth"]). This is the place in the very interior of the word where the supplement of the word's (*de la par/ab/ole*) signifier insinuates itself, this AB(C) where the oblicity and secondary place of every poetic ennunciation is initiated: "La littérature est seconde" ("Literature is second"—M. Blanchot). This obliquity could profoundly affect the word of power (its slicing, cutting power), curving it to another necessity which we will attempt to decipher.

Let us return to the eagle. In the *Dit de l'Alerion* it is also the metaphor for the lady, a comparison facilitated in Old French since the symbol of power was feminine (we will come back to this point):

2. See also vv. 2663–65: Mais loial Volenté d'ami/Et Desirs qui est tout emmy/Le cuer d'ami, volent après./[But the loyal Will of a friend and Desire, who is right in the middle of a friend's heart, fly after.]

> Je di que l'aigle de puissance,
> Que j'ay a dame de vaillance
> Comparé en mainte maniere . . . .[*DA*, vv. 3661–63]

I say that the powerful eagle, which I have in many ways compared to a noble lady . . . .

But it is not only the object of desire which is formulated in the request for love or for power: it refers as well to the subject of this desire—like the other birds of prey—and thus to Guillaume de Machaut, insofar as he is a hunter fascinated by the bait of his prey.[3]

The capture of the first bird of the series is enlightening in this respect: it is thanks to a living bait (another bird) that the narrator captures the sparrow-hawk, which is duly compared to the lady ("a dame comparé," v. 1197). But Machaut does not permit the sparrow-hawk to take hold of the prey—here pointing to the fundamental absence that characterizes the relationship of the bait to desire.

(It should also be noted that the bait, or the prey, is Machaut since he is a hunter who desires: the places whirl around the absent object of desire.)

In this manner, as both object and subject of the request, the birds do nothing more than mark the emptiness that is the distinctive trait of the place of the object (of the phallus: this metaphor is not limited to Boccaccio or Artaud—the *ucello* always takes flight in a flurry of feathers). This is why, in the *Dit de l'Alerion* [the *Dit* of the Alerion], (which certain manuscripts entitle the *Dit des quatre oiseaux* [the *Dit* of the four birds]— though there are, in a sense, five birds, since the alerion will come back to the narrator) the birds of prey endlessly replace each other, the eagle, like the others, being subject to this perpetual displacement.

If, in the beginning, the narrator has some difficulty with this dimension of loss inscribed in the object, he later follows the wise counsel of Reason; he must forget the lost object, he must replace it as soon as possible in order not to suffer *merencolie* [melancholy] which is the inevitable consequence of loss (v. 3802 ff.), or rather, that which he must try to efface by eternal substitution is the knowledge that the object is forever out of reach—a more profound oblivion than oblivion itself:

> Quant j'ameroie
> Un oisel, se je le perdoie
> Et aucuns griés m'en assailloit,
> Qu'autre chose ne me failloit
> Que viser comment j'en raroie

3. One will remember that at the beginning of the *Jugement du Roy de Navarre*, Guillaume-narrator is entirely *abymé* in a desiring quest: . . . J'estoie entendus/Et tous mes engins estendus/A ma queste tout seulement. (vv. 551–53) [I, along with all my instruments, was exclusively devoted to my quest.]

> Un au plus tost que je porroie,
> Pour plus tost mes griés alegier
> Et pour issir hors dou dangier
> De merencolie la fole
> Qui mains amans tue et afole. [*DA*, vv. 3751–60]

If I loose a bird that I love and if this causes me pain, then the only thing for me to do is to try to obtain another one as soon as possible in order to alleviate my grief more quickly and in order to avoid the danger of mad melancholy, which kills and maddens many lovers.

For the bird that flies away gives all its amplitude to the place which institutes it as a symbolic object that is not of the nature of property (*l'avoir*) nor even of that restitution that the poet calls the *ravoir*; it is

> Ce que jamais ne pues ravoir
> Par biau prier, ne par avoir. [*DA*, vv. 3805–06]

That which you can never get back with eloquent prayers nor with property.

This implies, first of all, the poetic work; as Machaut declares, at the beginning of the *Remède de Fortune:* "Mes oeuvres estoient volages" ["My works were flighty," v. 49]. The attribute applies not only to his so-called early works ("oeuvres de jeunesse"), but also to the flight of the pen on any white page. For what remains of the vanished *ucello*? A virgin space, ready to receive other birds, desires, words. A space under the absolute law of substitution, the unbendable law of a reversability within which the prince does not recognize his offspring, for the question has already been resolved, whether it concerns power or love:

> Car le droit estat d'innocence
> Ressamble proprement la table
> Blanche, polie, qui est able
> A recevoir, sans nul contraire,
> Ce qu'on y vuet peindre et pourtraire;
> Et est aussi comme la cire
> Qui sueffre dedens li escrire,
> Ou qui retient fourme ou empreinte,
> Si comme on l'a en li empreinte. [*RF*, vv. 26–34]

For the true state of innocence is exactly like a white smooth plank which can receive anything that one would wish to paint and represent on it, and it is also like wax in which one may write, and which conserves any form or imprint exactly as it has been pressed in.

The white backdrop (which we will see is neither as innocent nor as pure as it seems) is precisely that which makes every place absolutely reversible: that which takes away all assurance regarding the nature or the essence of power. It is that which puts everyone—princes, ladies and poets—on an equal plane where no difference and no hierarchy can reasonably expect to take hold. With one small exception: the alerion will come back to the poet, for he alone can articulate a name that has power over the bird and its flight:

> Lors l'appellay je par un non,
> Le quel non si bien entendi
> Que son bec devers moy tendi
> En signe de recongnoissance. [*DA*, vv. 4588–91]

Then I called it by a name which it knew so well that it turned its beak toward me as a sign of recognition.

No text from Machaut's *corpus* escapes this feigned innocence of the white background. For example, let us take the *Prise d'Alexandrie*, a chronicle of the crusade of Pierre I of Lusignan, where we could expect to find the most refined discourse on power. And indeed, the figure of the prince here seems to border on perfection (cf. v. 7197ff.). However, upon a closer reading, the story of the capture of Alexandria, the capture of a name whose fabulous origins are recalled ("Or parlons des fais d'Alixandre" ["Now we will speak of the feats of Alexander"], v. 7176) seems to completely contradict the panegyric: this capture amounts to a one night occupation of the city. It is nothing but a visit, quickly finished, which subsequently becomes a defeat in negotiations with the *Sarasins* (Saracens). The control of the name will have lasted only an instant, immediately escaping the power of the crusading prince (*du prince croisé*): "*à la tour abolie.*"

In the same manner, the account of the last years of Pierre's reign show the prince slipping toward madness: his instability imperils and finally obliterates the institution of monarchy itself on which he relies and which he represents. The accusation of Florimont de Lesparre, contained in a letter which Machaut cites as if to avoid assuming responsibility for it, is highly significant:

> "Or est einsi que depuis un po de temps en sa, vous avez pris merencolie seur moy, ou par faus rapport, ou par vostre volonté, ne say lequel."
> [*PA*, 228]

Now it is true that you have been ill disposed toward me for a while, either because of a false report or by your choice, I don't know which.

In this way, the dithyrambic project is subjected, between the lines, to its own denial. There is a shrewdness that we find everywhere in Machaut's work, and which is inescapable even for the Lady, the apparently supreme figure of the power of Love (see the definitive promise of the Prologue—"Et des dames blasmer me garderay" ["And I will refrain from criticizing ladies"]—and the alternation of defamation and praise to which they are subjected in the rest of the work). This game of affirmation/denial often seems to center, in Machaut, around the famous anagrams in which he encloses his problematic "signature" and the identity of his addressee (cf. *La Fontaine amoureuse*, le *Dit dou Lyon*, le *Remède de Fortune*, le *Dit de l'Alerion*, *Le Roi de Behaigne*, le *Voir-Dit*).

What does this tell us? First of all, that the poem tends toward the sounding of one or two names, whose echos are multiplied in the textuality through the open secret of the anagram. This displaces the control of the work toward the adventure of reading, the anchoring of the name being determined by the reader rather than the writer.

> Et pour ce qu'il n'apartient mie,
> S'on nel demande, que je die
> Que ce livre ay mis en rime . . . . [*Dit dou Lyon*, vv. 2171–73]

And since it is not at all for me to say, if one should ask, that I wrote this book . . . .

The encoding then, is not only an open secret, it delivers the name (the identity) to the rule and to the play of the letter.

Thus in the *Prise d'Alexandrie* for example, the anagram signifies the simultaneous staging of the prince and the poet. In order to read the name, in order to enter into the space of its resonances, "il convient desassambler / Ses lettres, et puis rassambler" ["one must take apart its letters, then put them back together," vv. 247–48] In this respect, the prince and the poet are of the same *estat* (station): that of the melodious linearity of written language which couples them quite plainly, without hierarchy. It veils them as well, but it can just as well unveil them, which means that the anagrammatical crypt resides not only—or not at all—in its power of decomposition or recomposition. In the *Prise d'Alexandrie*, Machaut with supreme casualness accords himself the right to reveal inside information, as if to demonstrate the absence of the secret for which the anagram is the pretense:

> Pierre, roy de Jherusalem
> Et de Chypre, li nomma l'en
> Et moy, Guillaume de Machaut,
> Qui ne puis trop froit ne trop chaut,
> Si que nos deux noms trouverez,
> Si diligemment les querez
> En ces II vers de grosse lettre. [*PA*, vv. 8874–80]

He was called Peter, king of Jerusalem and of Cyprus, and I, Guillaume de Machaut, who couldn't care less as you will find our two names in these two plainly written verses, if you will look for them diligently.

II

La Fontaine amoureuse is also traversed by the problematic of the power-language relationship; the poem presents a noble from the French court, Jean de Berry, whose name Machaut couples anagrammatically with his own. But here it is the prince who is a poet. At first glance, the narrator seems content with the function of voyeur and hidden transcriber who puts the lament of the Duke to paper:

> Si que je pris mon escriptoire,
> Qui est entaillie d'ivoire
> Et tous mes outils pour escrire
> La complainte qu'il voloit dire. [*FA*, vv. 229–32]

And so I took my writing desk, which was inlaid with ivory, and all my implements in order to write down the lament that he wished to speak.

In assuming the ficticious role of secretary, Machaut seems to wish to confer his own poetic power over language upon the prince-lover, thus reversing the roles. But, if the prince can be a poet, can the poet not be a prince—of language? For we know that the secretary is not only a simple agent of transmission or of transcription, a transparent stenographer for the palinodic voice. And so, in the *Voir-Dit*, when the narrator appoints as secretary the bearer of Péronelle d'Armentières's first letter, he is not simply a scrupulous scribe. He is entrusted with the right (the reserve) of silence and of the secret, which plays on the name of his function:

> Mais vous, serez mon secretaire,
> Pour parler à point et pour taire. [*VD*, 12]

But you will be my secretary, to speak when appropriate and to keep silent.

There is then a reversability between the prince and the poet, between the voice and writing. The *Fontaine amoureuse* prolongs this parity[4] by engaging Jean de Berry and the narrator in the space of the same dream, thus affirming desire's equal sovereignty over both of them, and hiding the fact that Machaut perhaps secretly *wrote* the Duke's lament ("improvisée" [improvised] and yet perfectly versified, without any repetition of rhymes), and that, in any case, he subjected it to the staging of its "own" textuality.

It is in the *Confort d'Ami* that Machaut pushes to its very limits the paradoxical logic that structures the relationship between power and poetry. Written to console Charles de Navarre while he was a prisoner of Jean le Bon, this poem assumes all the characteristics of an occasional poem.

---

4. On this subject, see the excellent chapter "Paternité et parité" in Roger Dragonetti, *La Vie de la lettre au Moyen Age* (Paris: Seuil, 1980), 133ff.

(But what is "occasional" in literature? That which dictates the necessity of writing? Or that which this latter appropriates by whatever means it can, thus submitting the king, the prince—the very emblem of the occasion of writing—and the writer, his biographer, to the equanimity of its endless whiteness?)

Here, as elsewhere, Machaut claims the right to join his name to that of his addressee, by dispersing them in the anagram. But this is not the only element which gives this philosophical consolation its strange appearance. In fact, the biblical *exempla* that Machaut chooses to console Charles de Navarre are all about fallen kings whose power is limited by divine transcendence. The paradigm is Nebuchadnezzar, who turns to the services of an inspired reader, the prophet Daniel, in order to decipher the "Mané, techel, pharès" which "sans nulle fiction" [without any deception], announces the end of his too earthly empire.

The second part of the *Confort d'Ami* is even more radical, for the speaking subject here claims the privilege, not of governing the prince, but even more, of inscribing in his fiction the law according to which the prince must reign:

> Or te dirai que tu feras
> Et comment tu gouverneras
> T'ame, ton corps et ta manière. [*CA*, vv. 1661–63]

Now I will tell you what you will do and how you will govern your soul, your body and your comportment.

The servant thus takes the master's place. He had let this be understood as early as the prologue, treating the powerful as an equal.

> Sire, et se je t'apelle amy,
> N'en aies pieur cuer a my;
> Car bien sçay que tu es mes sires,
> Et je des mieudres ne des pires
> Ne suis, mais sans riens retenir
> Sui tiens, quoy qu'il doie avenir. [*CA*, vv. 21–26]

Sire, and if I call you friend do not hold it against me, for I know well that you are my lord, and I am neither one of the best nor one of the worst, but I am yours without reserve whatever may happen.

There should then be a third term, hidden, which would equalize the knowledge of the hierarchy and level the master-subject relationship. And, in fact, Machaut multiplies the instances in which the prince and the poet are equally subjected. We have already mentioned divine transcendence; but there is also Fortune, the petrified bronze woman with feet of clay (cf. *RF*, v. 1055), of whom Charles de Navarre, like everyone, is a *subjés*:

> Et se tu vues dire que tu ne
> Yès mie subjès de Fortune,
> Et que ta grant attration
> Affranchist ta condition . . . [*CA*, vv. 1871–74]

And if you mean that you are not a subject of Fortune, and that your great power exempts you . . .

And also Desire, that is, at the same time the Lady and Love:[5]

> Aussi m'as tu dit de Desir
> Qu'i te fait durement gesir,
> Avoir lons jours et longues nuis,
> Et dis qu'il te fait trop d'anuis. [*CA*, vv. 2209–12]

Thus you have told me that Desire makes you sleep badly, makes your days and nights seem long and you say that he gives you too many troubles.

All these figures that dominate the prince are emblems of this third secret equalizing term, which names itself only through the detours of representation: language. God is language insofar as it is related to truth and falsehood. Fortune represents its relationship to what Lacan calls *tyché*, the strokes of imagination which traverse the poet's language. Love, of course, sets out the relationship of language to desire.

Consequently, one can better understand the surprising equality between the prince and the poet. They are both subjected to the nature of language, to its felicities, to its desires. This nature permits power to find its names and permits poetry to make and un-make them. Language: that which subverts every appropriation of place by whatever subject, if only in order to there define itself by a fundamental usurpation. If, according to Guillaume, the founders of law—whom Rousseau calls the Legislators— were wise, it is only because of this carefully hidden usurpation:

> On voit et scet tout en appert,
> Que moult furent sage et appert
> Cil qui les sciences trouverent,
> Et aus peuples les lois donnerent.
> Lamech li mauvais fu bigames,
> Et si ot tout premier .II. femmes. [*VD*, 228]

We clearly see and know that those men who founded the sciences and gave the laws to the people were very wise and gifted. The evil Lamech was a bigamist and he was the first to have two wives.

---

5. In the *Dit dou Vergier*, the law of Love is said to be as strict and as inescapable as that of Death: "Je suis comparez a la mort, / Car je pren le foible et le fort / Que nuls ne m'en puet eschaper . . ." (vv. 329–31) [I am comparable to death, for I take the weak and the strong and none can escape me . . .]

The *Confort d'Ami* is thus a mirror in which the prince sees himself fall because language is the Law from which his power abusively originates. "This object in which power is inscribed is language (*le langage*)—or, more precisely, its inevitable expression, speech (*la langue*). Language is a legislature, speech is its code" (R. Barthes). But a doubt remains: this Law to which the prince, the legislator and the poet, by definition, take a second place, confused in a strict parity—the poet could be the most experienced in the tricks of the trade, having practiced them professionally. If this be the case, his position as counselor, as a governor of those who govern (a position which Machaut lays claim to in the *Confort d'Ami*) would not result from a more successful usurpation, but from a true claim to mastery.

III

In the *Voir-Dit* Guillaume de Machaut's dexterity with language codes is at its zenith. First, as a master of styles and rhetorics—letter, poem, versified narration—and in this respect the *Voir-Dit* is one of the most ambitious and most accomplished works of the Middle Ages. In its mastery of intertextuality—courtly literature, mythology, the Bible, the Arthurian novel—the *Voir-Dit* designates a practically limitless *mathesis*. Machaut seems to accord to writing the power to say anything and everything.

This mastery and this confidence are summed up in a single word: *ordenance*, the Law of discourse, the nature of fiction. A master word which at the beginning of the manuscript BN fr 1584 institutes Machaut as a master workman: "Vesci l'ordenance que G. de Machaut wet quil ait en son livre" ["Here is the *ordenance* that G. de Machaut wants his book to have"]. A complete catalogue of the *corpus* follows. To my knowledge this is the first time that the "complete works" of an author are constituted in medieval literature, because they are brought together integrally by the will, the power and the resonance of a proper name. This is the first time that this care of the "complete works" is not left to the good or ill will of a copyist.

This said, the copyist does have an influence: the *corpus* lacks a signature which would confirm the authenticity and the completeness of the poetic utterance and which would conclude it in the truth of a legal act. But only in appearance, because for Machaut, as for Derrida[6] or the thirteenth-century prosateurs,[7] the signature, even if notarized, is irremediably drawn to the space of fiction, ready to lose there its power to designate a presence (that of an author, for example).

In the *Voir-Dit*, the calling into question of mastery, of will and of

6. Cf. *Marges de la philosophy* (Paris: Seuil, 1972) 365ff.

7. Cf. my chapter "Qui parle?" in *Le Graal et la littérature* (Lausanne: L'Age d'homme, 1982), 21–53.

power passes precisely by this word which seems to have to avoid all questioning: *ordenance*. In fact, Machaut seems to abandon it to the Lady who replaces the prince as the text's addressee:

> Ains sera tout à l'ordenance
> De celle en qui gist m'esperance.[8] [*VD*, 17]

Thus everything will be done according to the orders of her in whom lies my hope.

Apparently Machaut radically denies the position of the master (ès arts) that he assumed so well—although a little covertly ("un po couvertement")—when his address was directed to the prince. He thus refuses to accord Péronelle d'Armentières the right to use in his place the feudal metaphors of seigniory, and replaces them with the parity of the names of *ami* ("friend"—masculine) and *amie* ("friend"—feminine):

> "Et, ma tres-chiere dame, je vous suppli que se jamais vous m'escrisiés aucune chose, que vous ne m'apellez pas seigneur; car qui de son serf fait son seigneur, ses ennemis mouteplie. Et, par Dieu, c'est trop biaus nons d'amy ou d'amie; car quant Seignourie saut en place, Amours s'en fuit." [42]

And, my very dear lady, I beg you that if you ever write me anything you will not call me lord, for whoever makes her serf her lord multiplies her enemies. And, by God, friend is a very beautiful name, for when Seigniory appears, Love flees.

Numerous occurences reveal that this denial of the *place* of power, in favor of parity, is linked to the practice of writing: Péronelle writes without fail (268); as his so-called lord, she is the mistress of poetry (153); she has the power to correct (*ordener*) the *Voir-Dit*, and to put her mark upon it in the symbolic form of a sign (*enseigne*) and a seal (*signet*).

But this mistress appointed by the fiction humbles herself in turn, in accordance with the requirement of symmetry and of absolute reversability which is that of textual space:

> S'il vous plaist, vous m'apenrez à mieus faire et dire [dis et chansons]. Car je en apenroie plus de vous en un jour que je ne feroie d'un autre en .I. an. [48]

If it please you, you will teach me to compose and perform better (poems and songs). For I would learn more from you in one day than I would learn from another in one year.

---

8. Also see 265: "Ma mort et ma vie, mon deduit et ma joie, ma douleur et ma santé gist en voz mains et en vostre ordenance. Et en povez ordener come de ce qui est vostre, sanz rien retenir." [My death and my life, my pleasure and my joy, my pain and my health lie in your hands and under your orders. And you can order them as if they were yours, without reserve.] and 113: "Si, met m'ame, mon cuer, ma vie et quanque j'ay en vostre ordenance." [And so I put my soul, my heart, my life, and all that I have under your orders.]

Textual space seems then to come up against the impossibility of articulating the name of the father (of writing)—of anchoring power and of pinning down a master signifier. All are equal there, under the sign of a fraternity or a sorority,[9] an indication of a relentless rivalry. It should be noted that sexual difference is there reduced to a mere nothing: the letter *e* which supplements and differentiates *ami* from *amie*. The secretary reminds Machaut of this in a reply in which paternity disappears in a dizzying succession of familial and feudal relationships:

> Et que diroit vostres bons freres,
> Qui vous est fils, sires et pere,
> Qui si doulcement vous norrit,
> Que chascuns hons de joie en rit. [*VD*, 286]

And what would your good brother say; he who is your son, your lord and your father, who raised you so tenderly that every man rejoiced at it.

Therefore, "souvereinneté se taist et unité parole" ["sovereignty is silenced and unity speaks" *VD*, 113]. More or less. For a letter from Guillaume to Péronelle in which he criticizes two of her poems seems to restore—imperceptibly, surreptitiously—all the distance which separates teacher and student, lord and serf:

Les deux choses que vous m'avez envoiées sont très bien faites à mon gré. Mais se j'estoie un jour avec vous, je vous diroie et apenroie ce que je n'apris onques à créature. Par quoi vous les feriés mieus. [21]

The two pieces that you sent me are very well done, in my opinion. But if I could spend a day with you, I would tell and teach you things that I have never taught anyone: and you could thus make better poems.

Poetic mastery is then of the nature of the secret—of a secret which the secretary (*secre/taire*) may know.

Which secret? That which institutes the secret of poetry, its hidden power, that which perfects the work and saves it from the fraternity's jealousy by placing it out of its reach (*hors pair*), is the effectiveness of fiction:

Ores vient le fort et les belles et subtives fictions dont je . . . pense à parfaire [notre (c'est à dire *mon, ton*) livre] par quoy vous et li autre le voiez volentiers et qu'il en soit bon memoire à tousjours mes. [262]

Now comes the end and the beautiful and subtle fictions with which I intend to finish [our (that is, *my, your*) book] so that you and the others will be pleased with it and so that it will be remembered forever.

The "beautiful and subtle fictions" name first of all a discourse that is true without any reference to fact, that institutes its truth through its structure

9. See the addresses of the letters (189 and 262): "Mon tres-dous cuer, ma chiere suer et ma tres-douce amour." [My very sweet heart, my very dear sister and my very sweet love.]

as speech itself: one thinks immediately of the mythical parable, numerous in the *Voir-Dit* and elsewhere. But not only this: for the pact of truthful discourse, which underlies the framework of the fiction and gives its baptismal name to the entire text,[10] is violently drawn toward a multiple space which contests it and of which it is here appropriate to articulate the names:

—Dissimulation (the secret):

> . . . Dont j'ay mainte pensée éu
> Que chascuns n'a mie scéu. [*VD*, 17]

Of which I have had many thoughts which no one has ever known.

—Truth as a hypothesis rather than an assertion:

> Bien porroie estre voir disans . . . [*VD*, 9]

It could very well be true for me to say . . .

—Truth as an autoassertion, as an aporia which depends only upon its utterance and not upon any exteriority:

> *Le Voir-dit* vueil-je qu'on appelle
> Ce traictié que je fais pour elle,
> Pour ce que jà n'i mentiray. [*VD*, 17]

I want this treatise that I am writing for her to be called the *True Story* because I will not lie in it.

—Counterfeit, which in a deeper reading appears as an indispensable corollary of the truth, the *Voir-Dit* being unable to prove itself as truth unless reserving the possibility of counterfeiting:

> Car cils qui vuet tel chose faire
> Penser li faut au contrefaire. [*VD*, 18]

For he who wants to do such a thing must think of counterfeiting.

This reaches its highest point in the following passage, where truth appears as incomplete (*pas-toute*), impossible to speak:

> Mais, ce n'est pas necessité
> Que quanqu'on dit soit vérité;
> N'en ce qu'on dit n'a pas le quart
> De verité, se Dieus me gart. [*VD*, 326]

But it is not necessary that everything that one says be truth, nor does that which is said have a quarter part of truth, as God is my witness.

---

10. "Et aussi, votre livre avera nom le *Livre dou Voir dit*. Si, ne vueil ne ne doy mentir." [And your book will be entitled the *Book of the True Story*. And thus I should not lie, nor do I want to. *VD*, 263]

In this manner, the truth of literature—which is to prove its truth only in proportion to fiction, and as incomplete—this proportionality, which holds back its part of counterfeit and absence of meaning, covers not only the space of mythology or of dreams, but coincides with the very surface of the book as a whole, and in spite of all the pacts, promises, etc.

However, all things being equal, we will have recourse to mythology. At the same time, we return to a flight of birds, truth's messengers.

Let us frame the parable which itself is about framing and limits. Believing the word of some obscure slanderers (*losangiers*), who describe Péronelle as inconstant, the poet has locked her picture inside two coffers. But the image returns in one of Machaut's dreams, and through prosopopoeia tries to show him that he must not believe the lies of the jealous men. Two *exempla* are used in this aim. The Raven, who, like an innocent page, "jadis plume blanche / avoit plus que la noif sur branche" (formerly had feathers whiter than snow on a branch, 317), see Coronis, Phoebus's lover, committing adultery with a young man.[11] A pure incarnation of one who speaks the truth, he wants to denounce the lovers to Phoebus, his master. On his way to Phoebus he meets the Crow and tells her the story. The Crow dissuades him from playing secretary to the truth (in citing the image of Péronelle and thus breaking the seemingly rigorous frames which spearate truth-telling from mythology, the *mise en abyme* of the first story). For, the Crow says, "Tous voirs ne sont pas biaus à dire." [All truths are not good to tell, 319] The Crow has good reason to know: she was dismissed from Pallas's service for having surprised Erichtonios's secret. This secret is nothing more than a vast metaphor of the births of fiction: Erichtonios was born of Earth and the sperm of Vulcan, who had tried to win Pallas. The son of Onan, in a certain sense (he who did not want sons from his works) and, in addition, having two mothers, since Pallas adopted him. The figure, then, of dubious and impure genealogies of fiction, to which his monstrously equivocal nature bears witness, the top of his body being that of a man, the bottom that of a serpent. Pallas was quick to lock up (to frame) the child in a coffer, but the Crow surprised the guards as they were opening it. She quickly reported the truth of the secret and, as a fee for her services, was dismissed from her functions as secretary and replaced by the Owl. The Owl herself is not without fault:

> Et si coucha avec son pere.
> Et maintenant Pallas s'en pere. [*VD*, 323]

And so she lay with her father. And now Pallas goes around with her.

---

11. See R. Howard Bloch, *Medieval French Literature and Law* (Berkeley: Univ. of California Press, 1977), 56ff., and *Le Graal et la littérature*, 174ff. for adultery as a metaphor of truth.

The incestuous Owl thus permits the goddess to include her in her finery, but we also hear the echo, in the mythological example and the verse, of the parade, all feathers dressed, of the father's absence, the monstrous parity which abolishes generations and makes the daughter the wife of the father.

However, the effectiveness of the parable, for the Raven, is nil: it does not stop him in the least from accomplishing what he believes to be his mission.

(It should be noted as well that at the level of the frame story, that of the relati nship Machaut-Péronelle, the parable has no effect: it does not demonstrate the invalidity of the gossip, but accomplishes exactly the opposite.)

Let us return to the second narrative coffer: Phoebus, learning of the adultery, kills Coronis and then has her embalmed. But Coronis was pregnant: he thus delivers her of her works:

> Mais il la fist ouvrir et fendre
> Avant toute euvre, et l'enfant prendre. [VD, 327]

But before the work began, he had her slashed open and the child taken out.

A fiction of birth which again designates the impure origin of fiction: as if this latter needed the death of the mother, and here, her constitution as a relic, in order to develop.

For the Raven, the white page, will find himself blackened, his feathers will lose their innocence and become as black as ink. Such is the reward for truth that he receives from the shining sun god:

> "En signe de mémoire,
> Sera ta blanche plume noire,
> Et tuit li corbel qui l'ont blanche
> L'aront plus noire que n'est anche,
> A tousjours perpétuelment." [VD, 328]

As a sign for posterity, your white feathers will be black, and all the ravens who have white feathers will have feathers blacker than ink forever.

Such is the black secret in which the writer dips his pen and which Machaut describes elsewhere: "Car toudis leur fis dou blanc noir" ["For I presented white as black to them" RF, v. 3883]. A transformation of the original white into black, this white that is without a doubt a metaphor of this "white writing" ("écriture blanche") of which Dragonetti speaks,[12] and of which the poet tries to fill in and cover the gaping cracks. Such is the

12. See "L'enjeu et l'événement" in L'Esprit créateur 23 (1983), 12.

secret which assures him a matchless superiority over other poets, as Machaut narcissistically has it written to himself by Péronelle:

> Les deux balades que vous m'avez envoies sont si bonnes que on n'y saroit trouver que redire. Mais ce n'est pas comparison, car ce que vous faictes me plaist trop mieus à mon gré que ce que li autre font. [279]

> The two ballads that you sent me are so good that one could not improve upon them. But this is not a comparative judgement, for your work pleases me so much more than what the others do.

IV

It remains to be seen if this mastery of the secret, this engima of power over language and its codes is not overturned if the writer is not in fact mastered by the nature of the secret. The Raven and the Crow demonstrate this reversal, for they pay the price of the secret: it relieves them, not only of their innocence—of their transparence to "communication"—but also of their place of power next to the gods. He who dips his feather in troubled waters has no place—not even that of the secretary of truth.

It could still be that the force of the secret is simply *too great*, whether it be hidden or discovered, whether the coffers of all histories be opened or closed: impossible, as Machaut writes of the medieval Real, that is, of God:

> Par exemples te vueil prouver,
> Qui sont contenu en la Bible
> Et qui sont a nous impossible . . . [CA, vv. 46–48]

> I want to show you by examples contained in the Bible which are impossible for us.

It remains to be seen as well, if the superiority of Machaut over Péronelle is not fleeting, transitory (a question which seems insignificant, but which is, in fact, the condensation of all the "remains—to be seen"): for the Lady is herself the guardian and the formidable figure of a secret which governs and masters writing, which comes before it and remains after the last word.

The Lady is always double:

> "Et si avez double visage,
> Tout ainsi comme avoit l'image
> De Fortune, dont li uns pleure,
> Et li autres rit à toute heure!" [VD, 356]

> And so you have a double face just like the picture of Fortune had, one of them crying and the other always laughing.

On the one hand, she revives the narrator, draws him from melancholy and death by a "Lazarus come out" which is, in the last analysis, of the nature of profanation:

> En moi, où elle ouvra jadis
> Trop plus que sains de paradis.
> Car j'estoie du tout perdus
> Mas, desconfis et esperdus;
> Mais deux fois m'a resuscité. [*VD*, 63]

In me, where she once worked more than heaven's saints; for I was completely lost, unhappy, disheartened, and hopeless. But twice she resurrected me.

But, on the other hand, she is that which turns the writer to stone, which disables and silences him:

> "Mon tres dous cuer et ma tres chiere amour, j'ay grant doubtance que vous ne tenez mains de mi, de ce que, quant je suis en vostre présence, je n'ay sens, maniere, ne advis et suis comme uns homs perdus." [130]

My very sweet heart and my dearest love, I strongly suspect that you are less attached to me, and so when I am in your presence I am senseless, mannerless, and empty-headed, and I am like a lost man.

So when the presence arrives, makes something happen (here we must stop and weigh our words, not only because we do not know *what happens* in the text, but also because we cannot imagine what a happening is which *does not happen*) when the lovers see each other, while the narrator holds himself immobile under the mortal menace of Love:

> Là vi-je d'amour la maistrie:
> Car j'estoie comme une souche,
> Delez ma dame, en ceste couche,
> Ne ne m'osoie remuer
> Nient plus s'on me vosist tuer. [*VD*, 147]

There I saw the mastery of love, for I was rooted beside my lady in this bed, and I would not have dared to move even if threatened with death.

The text here places us before the petrifying irrepresentability of the Other, of the Law, which is also that of the phallic Mother, from which leave and to which return all the birds, all the words, and against which there is no recourse, that which need not usurp power, because it is the seat of power.[13]

13. Cf. Jacques Lacan, *Ecrits* (Paris: Seuil, 1966), 813. *Ecrits*, trans. Alan Sheridan (New York: Norton, 1977), 310–11. "Let us set out from the conception of the Other as the locus of the signifier. Any statement of authority has no other guarantee than its very enunciation, and it is pointless for it to seek it in another signifier, which could not appear outside this

This petrifying mother, the mute exterior of writing, which crosses the group of figures like that which since the beginning dispossessed them of all pretention to power and mastery, finds its parabolic form (never will a metaphor have been more *necessary*, since it is a question of representing the irrepresentable) in the form of the Gorgon:

> Ovides le dit en ses fables,
> En moralitez veritables. [*VD*, 227]

Ovid says it in his fables, in truthful allegories.

It is without a doubt Freud who has drawn the best lesson from the ambivalence of the Gorgon. In fact, for him the myth possesses a double truth. That of castration, certainly, but also that of the phallus's erection: the petrification is not only the sign of death and loss, but also the consolation of a lack. The tension and the effectiveness of the myth stem from the paradoxical simultaneity with which the myth represents castration and carries out the work of its mourning:

> The hair upon Medusa's head is frequently represented in works of art in the form of snakes, and these once again are derived from the castration complex. It is a remarkable fact that, however frightening they may be in themselves, they nevertheless serve actually as a mitigation of the horror, for they replace the penis, the absence of which is the cause of the horror. . . .
>
> The sight of Medusa's head makes the spectator stiff with terror, turns him to stone. Observe that we have here once again the same origin from the castration complex and the same transformation of affect! For becoming stiff means an erection. Thus in the original situation it offers consolation to the spectator: he is still in possession of a penis, and the stiffening reassures him of the fact.[14]

Péronelle is thus a consoling figure of the horror, facing which the *Voir-Dit* is written in an alternation of avoidance (of denial) and of fascina-

---

locus in any way. Which is what I mean when I say that no metalanguage can be spoken, or, more aphoristically, that there is no Other of the Other. And when the Legislator (he who claims to lay down the Law) presents himself to fill the gap, he does so as an impostor.

But there is nothing false about the Law itself, or about him who assumes its authority.

The fact that the Father may be regarded as the original representative of this authority of the Law requires us to specify by what privileged mode of presence he is sustained beyond the subject who is actually led to occupy the place of the Other, namely, the Mother." And, although it may seem paradoxical, Jacques Derrida, *Glas* (Paris: Galilée, 1974), 134: "I am the mother. The text. The mother is *behind*—all that I am, do, seem—the mother follows. Since she follows absolutely, she always survives, future which will have never been presentable, that which she will have engendered, witnessing, impassive, fascinating and provocative, the burial of that whose death she forsaw."

14. Sigmund Freud, "The Medusa's Head," *Standard Edition of the Complete Works of Sigmund Freud*, trans. James Strachey (London: Hogarth Press and the Institute of Psychoanalysis, 1955), vol. 18, 273.

tion. The unity of the writing strategy here aims to bypass the unbreakable law of castration whose powers the king, in the *Dit de l'Alerion*, had usurped a little too quickly.

Hence, for example, the multitude of secretaries, messangers and copyists between the Lady and the narrator: the proliferation of obstacles (bandits, disorders, epidemics, any pseudohistorical reference is valid) which make the union of the lover and the Lady difficult, if not impossible.

The *Voir-Dit* is, in fact, horrified by presence: there is throughout a vast strategy of *delaying*, destined to guarantee that the happening of presence—petrification—does not *happen*.

> "Car vous me faites vivre en paix et en joie, loing de vous; et se je estoie en vostre presence, je porroie bien querir ce que je ne vorroie mie avoir." [19]

> "For you make me live peacefully and happily far from you; and if I were in your presence, I might well seek that which I would not want to have."

For whoever would give Machaut presence in its entirety, in its truth and in its totality would rob him of everything at a single stroke: when Péronelle offers to give him her treasure (that secret to which both possess the key, about which the text remains mute, implying a sexual rapport, but we cannot wholly reduce it to this) the poet refuses, in an ambiguous "no" which avoids saying "no" definitively:

> "De mon tresor que tant prisiés,
> Qui ne porroit estre prisiés,
> Amis, je le vous abandoing,
> Prenés-le, tout je le vous doing."
> Et je li respondi tantost:
> "Qui tout me donne, tout me r'ost." [*VD*, 106]

> "Friend, I yield to you my priceless treasure which you prize so highly. Take it, I give it all to you." And I then answered, "Whoever gives me all takes everything from me."

The gift of the Other, an impossible poisoned present, gains its worth only when refused: to accept it is to enter into the ruses of the imaginary, to find oneself radically deprived. It is thus necessary to indefinitely suspend its possession under the veils of a "miraculous" obscurity which Venus happily accords to the poet at the moment of union:

> Si, qu'ainsi, de la nue obscure
> Eusmes ciel et couverture,
> Et tous .II. en fumes couvert
> Si qu'il n'i ot rien descouvert.
> Et ce durement me séoit
> Qu'adont riens goute n'i véoit. [*VD*, 158]

So thus from the obscure cloud we had sky and cover and both of us were covered with it so that nothing was uncovered. And it suited me very well that nothing could be seen.

It is better, in fact, to see nothing, to understand nothing. We will never know more than Machaut wishes to tell us: like Polyphemus of the legend (292)—he is also a figure of the one-eyed poet who becomes blind—we are stupefied by the writing which veils that which happens in the detours of its fiction.

The scene of the dispossession is then the very theater of writing which *makes a scene:* to the impossible, to the absence of the sexual rapport "qui ne s'écrit pas" ["which is not written"—Lacan]. The word of unity replacing sovereignty's silence is thus in the nature of fiction. Machaut's greatness is to have related this infinite, delightful conversation which he calls the *soufisance* (self-sufficiency) of writing,[15] with that which unveils it as a *lack*, making it by definition fragmentary: this hole which makes truth incomplete (*pas-toute*) and thus makes it true. In passing, mastery and *ordenance* have themselves become fiction, all the names of power are returned to their inarticulation—except to give proof of a fundamental usurpation.

Is it necessary to emphasize that in this manner the authenticity of the amorous demand and of writing is guaranteed and that, paradoxically, the title *Voir-Dit* is entirely justified by the very structure of the fiction?

The truth of the demand, of the word and of writing is in fact this syncope which interrupts the overly slick and overly elegant flow of the rhetoric—ready to be recovered immediately by the noise of articulation in the textual space, of the word "silence," of the word "syncope":

> . . . Et qu'il li couvient recoper
> Ses paroles et sincoper
> Par souspirs puisiez en parfont. [*RF*, vv. 1762–64]

And when he must break off speaking and syncopate his words with deep sighs.

The paradox here is that writing is only syncopated when prolonged in confession of fissure. The marks of division (burned letters, 250, missing letters, 263, missing "material" ["*matière*"], 342) signal a continuation of the infinite conversation. On the other hand, linearity becomes the symbol of the detour by which writing masks its fragmentary essence, that by which the book must "be in pieces" ("soit par pièces," 69).

---

15. Cf. the *Voir-Dit*, 53 and 279: "Quant je commence, je n'i say faire fin, pour la tresgrant plaisance que je pren en penser, en parler et en escrire." ["Once I begin, I don't know how to stop because of the great pleasure I find in thinking, in speaking and writing."]

V

And the prince, in all this? It would seem that he has been somewhat lost to view. But how could he dare pretend to escape the Law of the Other, the ascendancy of the Mother and that of the Gorgon, if it is not in the trinkets which are the sign of his power?

Let us return to the *Prise d'Alexandrie:* what does Machaut tell us about the origin of power, of the law which founds it? Not everything that one would expect in this text which participates in a dythyrambic aim: that the monarchy would be, for example, of a divine essence and right. For Pierre de Lusignan draws the (il)legitimacy of his power from a mythological origin, which opens the text and completely effaces the terrestrial ascendance (and, at the same time, the legitimation that this latter could draw from transcendence). The king of Cyprus is the son of Mars—hence his bellicose tendencies—and of Venus, the symbol of grace and courtliness.

The Christian God exists only to give life (although his primacy is affirmed), *after* the decision of the counsel of the ancient gods. It is hardly necessary to point out the theologically unorthodox character of this cohabitation, in an improbable Elysium, of mythology and the biblical canon—a cohabitation which, however, characterizes all of Machaut's works.

The conclusion of the *Prise* is itself paradigmatic. One sees the confrontation of two ideologies of power, that of an absolute monarchy represented by Pierre de Lusignan, and that of the feudal system, emblematized by the great lords who surround him.

These vassals, seeing their rights exceeded by their capricious king, decide to kill him. The assassination accomplished, they burn the kingdom's charters and replace them with an ordinance which institutes them as governors. (What is easier to break than the Tablets of the law, what is easier to replace when the Law is confused with its inscription?)

And the prince? If he had, by his death, legitimized the takeover of power by loyal supporters, his body would have been embalmed and preserved as a relic founding the natural origin of this power. But such was not the case: his burial must not make life difficult for the usurpers and their descendants.

The entombment must then become a parodic staging of the fall of Pierre: the corpse, disfigured by the wounds inflicted by the conspirators, is hidden. It is crowned with a parchment crown, and the other signs of power are equally inverted in derision:

> Couronne avoit de parchemin
> Painte, et tele que par chemin
> N'est nul homme, s'il la trouvast,
> Tant fust povres, qui la levast;

> Et aussi le sestre et la pomme
> Estoient aussi povre comme
> La couronne et de tel peinture. [PA, vv 8780–86]

He had a crown of painted parchment and it was such that no man, no matter how poor, would pick it up should he find it by the roadside. And the scepter and the orb were just as poor as the crown and painted in the same way.

Under the cover of a "historical" relationship, Machaut here amasses all that makes the improper of the operation of writing, when it is applied to the prince. He becomes an illuminated figure, a figure disfigured by fiction, this fiction of which we have just remarked the fragility, but also the power—be it a power of avoidance.[16]

Translated by Peggy McCracken

JOHN D. LYONS

The *Heptaméron* and the Foundation of Critical Narrative

The *Heptaméron* marks the end of a tradition, and Marguerite de Navarre explicitly establishes herself as closing the generic adventure that began with Boccaccio's *Decameron*. After the *Heptaméron*, narrative prose flows into another tradition, the novel, and leaves behind the great collections of novellas. Incorporating into her work the tension between claims to represent history "objectively" and claims to derive ethical norms from such representation, Marguerite brilliantly adumbrates the conceptual issues that lead not only to a change in literary fashion but to a crisis in philosophy. At stake in the *Heptaméron* is the role of literature in an era that is increasingly confronted by a withdrawal of the divine order from the observable world. In attempting to establish order without abandoning the divine, narrative can only displace the transcendant function onto some human agency.[1] How that displacement is made and who assumes responsibility for an order is a problem that concerns the poetics of prose as well as its politics.

Important recent criticism emphasizes the "ambiguity" of the *Heptaméron*.[2] This ambiguity can be described, I believe, more systematically by considering it as the direct product of a privileged theme—the opposition between external or "objective" truth and internal or "subjective" truth—and of the basic structural characteristic of the novella collection, the alternation between story and commentary. Marguerite de

---

1. Philippe de Lajarte, "L'*Heptaméron* et la naissance du récit moderne: Essai de lecture épistémologique d'un discours narratif," *Littérature* 17 (1975), 31–42, and "Le Prologue de l'*Heptaméron* et le processus de production de l'oeuvre," in *La Nouvelle française à la Renaissance*, ed. Lionello Sozzi (Geneva: Slatkine, 1981), 397–423.

2. Marcel Tétel, "Ambiguité chez Boccace et Marguerite de Navarre," in *Il Boccaccio nella Cultura Francese*, ed. Carlo Pellegrini (Florence: Olschki, 1971), 557–65, and *Marguerite de Navarre's Heptaméron: Themes, Language and Structure* (Durham, N.C.: Duke Univ. Press, 1973).

Navarre has pushed the novella collection to an extreme such that difficulties or tensions in the genre cannot be passed over or ignored. First, in the celebrated claim of the prologue that the court of Francis I was elaborating a set of novellas similar to those of Boccaccio in all respects except the veracity of the stories ("different from Boccaccio in one respect: to write no novella that is not true history"), Marguerite has established a criterion limiting what can be told, exposed the problem of learning something from actual event, and divided the text into two fields of language which differ not only formally (objective narrative versus discussion) but also cognitively (actuality versus potentiality).[3] Secondly, accentuating these contrasts, Marguerite has further expanded the frame narrative in such a way that apparent inconsistencies or contradictions between the stories and the discussions can no longer be taken lightly. Third, Marguerite has stressed the latent problems of the novella collection by harkening to its traditional origin in the *exemplum*. In many collections this relationship is merely implicit, but in the *Heptaméron* the word *exemple* and the declared intention of each frame narrator appears frequently and rather heavy-handedly (e.g., "There, my ladies, is a story that I gladly give you as an example . . . " 27). This reminder forces the listeners, within the frame narrative, and the readers of the *Heptaméron*, to lend some attention to the relationship between the general discussion with its adoption of ethical positions and the narrative "reality" that seems intended to lend weight to these positions.

The pretension to "veritable history" may be a pose, as has been suggested, but the question remains: what does Marguerite force us to do to cope with this "pose"?[4] How can the couple history/example be guiding lines towards understanding the creation of the ambiguity of the *Heptaméron* and of its place in the culmination of the novella tradition in France?

The answer may lie in the complex of cognitive and discursive concepts that cluster around the term "history." Cognitively, history, as fact or recognized event, differs from fiction, or plausible but nonrealized event. This contrast between history and fiction is, however, complicated by the fact that both must appear in language and in so appearing are subject to discursive classifications that do not break into the same neat pair. Discursively, history (*récit d'histoire*) finds itself in contrast not with fiction but with discourse (*discours*) according to the indications of who is speaking and in what concrete, usually dialogic, situation. Other state-

---

3. Here the formal distinction between *récit d'histoire* and *discours*, familiar from the work of Emile Benveniste, parallels Aristotle's cognitive distinction between "what has happened" and "the kind of thing that *can* happen." *Poetics* 51b1 trans. Gerald Else (Ann Arbor: Univ. of Michigan Press, 1967), 32.

4. Tétel, *Marguerite de Navarre's Heptaméron*, 195–96.

ments appear without trace of this situation; they appear to be transcendent, timeless, and "objective." Yet a text bearing the marks of this "objective" history (*récit d'histoire*) may be either fiction or history in the cognitive sense.[5] Discourse can, on the other hand, be narrative, but it does not pretend to objectivity. Instead it is the vehicle for a personal, subjective expression of belief, experience, and judgment. Discourse is the mode in which ethical judgments are made and in which alternative action is described. The *Heptaméron*, like many novella collections, is divided into a domain that is enunciated objectively as actual event (the novellas) and a domain that is enunciated subjectively, dialogically, as judgment and statement of alternative or potential event (the discussions within the frame narrative). However, the *Heptaméron* claims that *all* of the internal narratives that are enunciated "objectively" are history in the cognitive as well as discursive sense.

Despite a tendency in *Heptaméron* criticism to concentrate on the frame narrative—at least one whole book has been written without particular reference to the novellas but with detailed accounts of the relationships between the characters of the external narrative—I will argue that the discussions of the frame narrative are not privileged vehicles of truth and that only an understanding of the relationship between history and discourse in both novellas and discussion can help us understand the way in which the *Heptaméron* challenges the didactic possibilities of both modes of enunciation.[6] Furthermore, the history/discourse opposition as structural feature of the novella collection seems to be exploited by Marguerite with a view towards exposing (and perhaps expounding, though that is less sure) the theme of the struggle between objective truth as it is taught in history and subjective truth as it wells up in the discursive behavior of individuals.

This argument can only be carried out with attention to the detail of novellas and discussions, and Marguerite has offered us a splendidly provocative story pair that raises acute questions about all I have mentioned. The celebrated novellas concerning "Rolandine" and her aunt are among the tales that have been most confidently and securely described as fully historical. These novellas, the first story of the third day and the last story of the fourth day (numbers 21 and 40), both narrated by Parlamente, are apparently based on the lives of Anne de Rohan and Catherine de Rohan, daughter and sister respectively of Jean II, vicomte de Rohan.[7] The narratives are are linked in a way that is unique in the *Heptaméron*, for

5. Jenny Simonin-Grumbach, "Pour une typologie des discours," in *Langue, discours, société*, ed. J. Kristeva, J.-C. Milner, N. Ruwet (Paris: Seuil, 1975), 85–121.

6. Betty J. Davis, *The Storytellers in Marguerite de Navarre's Heptaméron* (Lexington, Ky.: French Forum Publishers, 1978).

7. Marguerite de Navarre, *Nouvelles*, ed. Yves Le Hir, (Paris: P.U.F., 1967), 369–72.

they have a character in common, Jossebelin, Rolandine's father (in novella 21) and her aunt's brother (in novella 40). In the first story Parlamente announces the later one and in the second story she recalls the first. The heroines' sufferings are in many ways parallel—both are forbidden to marry, both contract a secret marriage that is destroyed, and both are imprisoned in the same castle. The two novellas raise the problem of a repetition in history that is manifested by a repetition in storytelling. But more important is the fact that both stories concern the creation of history and the suppression of discourse.

Rolandine's story is worth recalling in some detail. She is presented as a kinswoman of the queen, at whose court she serves. Her father's neglect and the queen's antipathy cause her to pass her youth without marrying. Resigning herself to this state, she spends her time praying and living in an honest and saintly way. Finally she meets another unfortunate, whose state has prevented him from marrying, a bastard. The two of them see one another first openly, then, after the queen forbids it, they meet under the pretext of an illness of Rolandine's. When this ruse is discovered, they meet during mealtimes when Rolandine excuses herself on the grounds of fasting. Thereafter the bastard disguises himself as her confessor. After their secret marriage, they can speak together only through two neighboring windows of a castle. Having been discovered, they resort to writing letters carried by a young page. When the page is trapped and saves their secret only by burning the letters, the bastard employs an old servant, who refuses to testify against his master even under torture. Rolandine's story is clearly an account of royal attempts to regulate discourse, both by silencing Rolandine and blocking every channel conceivable to her communication with her husband, and by extracting words from those who want to remain silent. "If you are willing to speak the truth, you will be saved," the soldiers cry to the old servant before throwing him bound into the water. But Rolandine and the bastard are still ahead. Only the king's confessor, cleverly reassembling the fragments of a letter, is able to bring the proof of the marriage.

When the queen confronts Rolandine, the heroine erupts in an open challenge to royal and parental authority. Her marriage, which threatens the royal control over history through the succession of family power, also threatens the discursive control of the court. Rolandine defends her action, setting forth individual right and sentiment against the constraint of institutions (her husband would be of the same rank as she "if the love of two persons were valued as much as the ring" 168) and claims that she will remain married: "I am decided to sustain this purpose *(propos)*. . . . "

Rolandine's crime is clearly a crime of speech. The *propos* is not merely a "plan" or "intention" but, closer both to the Latin and the modern usage, something which is *set forth (pro-ponere)* or exposed. The disclosure, the revelation of a fissure in the royal control, is clearly the primordial crime:

> The queen, seeing her so determined and her speech so truthful, could not reply with reasoned argument. Instead, continuing to rebuke her and to scold her angrily, she began to weep, saying, "Wretch that you are, rather than humbling yourself before me and repenting of such a great fault, you speak brazenly, without a tear. . . . But if the King and your father listen to me, they will put you in a place where you will be forced to speak differently [*parler autre langage*]." [169–70, italics mine]

Rolandine's speech in response to the queen's attempt to control and limit her subject is not a defense so much of her marriage as it is of the right to speak the truth:

> since I have none to speak for me, except truth itself, which I alone know, I must declare that truth fearlessly, hoping that, if it is known to you, you will not believe me to be such as you have called me. I have no fear of any mortal hearing how I have behaved. [169–70]

What Rolandine says may be intolerable, but the fact that she says it herself is even more outrageous. It is true that she does not have an advocate (this is simply the choice made by the narrator of the story), but as witness to her own marriage, only Rolandine and her bastard husband could establish its occurrence. Furthermore, she establishes a difference between her knowledge of the truth and the possible recognition of that truth by the queen or others after Rolandine has broken the silence. Rolandine is setting herself up as a privileged vessel of truth. No advocate could speak for her in the same way, so that even though she proposes herself as a substitute for her advocate (who would be a substitute for herself), no substitution is possible. The truth is established by Rolandine's speaking. Even though one may argue that the narrator shows sympathy for Rolandine's position, within the world of the novella itself Rolandine speaks alone in defense of the individual word. Essentially she argues for an individualist subjective transcendence of the social authority incarnated in the queen, king and father, who are the historically dominant authorities. On her side, Rolandine alleges a divine Father, who is not here but who is the exact inverse of the earthly, real (historical) father: "but I have a Father in heaven, who, I am sure, will give me much patience in proportion to the evils you inflict, and in Him alone I have perfect confidence" (170). The *I* is the safeguard of law and divine right. In speaking the truth, Rolandine does not fear God and need not fear any human person. The symmetry is clear. Rolandine is the substitute of her substitute (the advocate); the Father in heaven is the substitute of the father on earth. The earthly father should have spoken out to permit her marriage (he had, on the contrary, given a "cold response" to proposals); she should not have had to marry herself. In a certain way Rolandine is therefore the substitute for her father, but, more radically, she is also the substitute for her Father. God may be on Rolandine's side, but He cannot speak for her; she must speak for Him. God is within her word, not external to it. He was the witness to her marriage ("they kissed in the church before God, whom they took as witness to their promise" 162). But she alone in the novella gives witness to Him. God is not one of her listeners but rather the very truth that she is speaking, a truth known to her: "I know that God and my honor are in no way offended. And that this is what makes me speak without fear, being sure that He who sees my heart is with me . . . " (170). This defense of the word (Word) itself runs head-on into the institutional refusal and deprecation of the word, as expressed in the struggle between Rolandine and the churchmen and lawyers over the status of her marriage. These spokesmen,

> arguing with her, *since her marriage existed only in words*, it could be easily set aside, and that they leave one another, according to the King's wish that she do so in order to preserve the honor of her family [*maison*]. She replied that in all things she was ready to obey the King, unless it were a thing against her conscience. But what God has put together, men cannot separate. She asked them not to tempt her with such an unreasonable request, for if love and good will founded on the fear of God are the true bonds of matrimony, she was so firmly bound that neither iron, nor fire, nor water, could break her bonds. [171; italics mine]

Here the identification of Rolandine's discourse with the divine reaches its apogee, for Rolandine has by her pledge not only bound herself but, in a sense, God as well. She could have married another, but once she has given her word, that act is fully guaranteed by God.

The punishment that Rolandine suffers—being shut up in a castle in a forest—is a last attempt to prevent her from speaking, an attempt therefore to exclude her from the world of discourse and to reject her into the world of history (the castle itself comes from the world of history, from the history of her aunt). By shutting her out of the city, out of the court, beyond any human society, the forces against Rolandine prevent her from being a subject of discourse and convert her into the "non-person," as Benveniste defines the third person of grammar.[8] Within the world of the novella, people will hear *about* Rolandine, but they will not hear Rolandine:

> And however much she had erred, the punishment was so great and her constancy such, that she made her fault seem virtue. Her father, learning this piteous story [*nouvelle*], would not see her, but sent her to a castle in a forest, which he had built long before in circumstances worth telling. [172]

8. Emile Benveniste, "Les Relations des temps dans le verbe français," *Problèmes de linguistique générale*, (Paris: Gallimard, 1966), 237–57.

Already Rolandine is, within the novella, the subject of third-person narrative. Her story is told her father as a *nouvelle*, with the full ambiguity of that term: not only a piece of news but, in a collection of stories that cites its model in "Boccaccio's novellas," also a novella, within which Rolandine is a character. While Rolandine's words were and remain dangerous—so dangerous that her father's refusal to see her may not only be a punishment for her but also a defense for himself—her *nouvelle*, her history, turns out to be equally dangerous and achieves the opposite result from that intended by her enemies. Now it is not Rolandine's speech but the reports about her, her story, that changes the perception of what she did. This transformation, by which *fault* becomes *virtue*, is not due to a voluntary gesture by Rolandine but to the action of her enemies ("the punishment was so great") and is therefore one of Rolandine's characteristics as *persona* within a story.

From this moment on, Rolandine disappears from the novella as speaker and appears only as character. We are fully within the story—and indeed within the *histoire* of Rolandine, whose discourse is now redeemed and guaranteed, as she said it would be, by the story of what God does next. For instance, the husband is unfaithful: "Therefore, the Divine Goodness, which is perfect charity and true love, had pity on her sorrow and saw her patience, so that, after a few days, the bastard died while courting another woman" (173). Likewise this loving and deadly God acts to rid Rolandine of her troublesome brother: "God saw to this matter, for the brother, who wished to possess everything, gave up in one day, by a sudden death, his own estate and his sister's . . . " (174).

To recapitulate quickly the relationship between history and discourse in the story of Rolandine, we can identify three allied concepts that are all grouped under the term history: the historical narrative (*récit d'histoire*), the actual occurrence, and those institutions that are traditionally the subjects of historical narrative and which frequently attempt to control that narrative (kings and aristocratic houses). In another contrast to these historical instances, the concept of discourse, as the speech of a subject of enunciation (a speaking I) is chiefly represented by Rolandine as an act opposed to the silence mandated by the historical institutions. Moreover, the subject of this discourse, once silenced, becomes the subject of history.

Rolandine's aunt ended up in the same castle. In the act of narrating, the castle serves therefore as the first-mentioned and principal link between the two stories and the two women. Within the world of both narratives the castle serves the same function, keeping the woman from talking, and represents the authority of the same person in two roles (as brother and as father). The castle can be understood as the metaphor of a metonym, as the figure for one aspect of the historical institution earlier referred to as the *maison*. Just as Rolandine's marrying a bastard without her father's consent was a threat to his *maison* (171), so the castle is that form of a *maison* which can prevent further injury to its name. The figure of the castle thus unites historical institution with historical narrative, because it marks the moment in novella 21 when the heroine stops speaking and becomes a historical character and also because it marks the conjunction between two historical narratives. Moreover, the castle serves as the figure for historical occurrence, for what has preceded something in time, since the castle is what remains from a previous event, the incarceration of a nameless woman.

This woman, the sister of the comte de Jossebelin, is beautiful and loved by her brother so much that "he preferred her to his wife and children." From a combination of love and avarice, Jossebelin does not let his sister accept any of the worthy proposals of marriage made to her. When her youth has passed, she and a young gentleman who lives as a servant in Jossebelin's household fall in love. Having heard her brother say that there is no one he would prefer as brother-in-law, she and her lover marry, before a priest and witnesses, and pass several years of clandestine wedlock before Jossebelin discovers the arrangement. Thereupon he has the husband killed before the wife's eyes and then has a castle constructed in a forest for the specific purpose of keeping his sister from talking because "the fear that his sister might ask for justice or revenge led him to build a castle in the middle of a forest, where he shut her up and forbade anyone to talk to her" (277). The castle does not stop people from talking about the brother's crime. The tale does not give any indication of steps taken to prevent report of his action. But the castle does prevent his sister from executing a specific discursive act with judicial effect, the act of accusal. Jossebelin forbids people to talk to her, not about her. The consequence of this silencing is remarkably similar to what happened in Rolandine's case. The aunt's prison makes her a saint. Refusing to consider another marriage proposed to her by her brother, she finishes her life in her prison in patience and austerity so that after her death "all ran to her as if to a saint" (277). The culmination of her fame occurs when she will never speak again.

The historical institution of the family or *maison* in both instances functions to repress the heroine's dangerous speech, but by doing so causes her to reappear as a dangerous character within a story. In the long run the heroine—who is thus both heroine of the novella and heroine of a certain fabulation occurring within the novella—triumphs over the authorities who have persecuted her. But it would be difficult to say that one instance of language wins out over the other. The heroine of the word does win, but not through the word itself. Rolandine is right. God did strike her enemies. But this is evident only within the novella as narrative, as *histoire*, for her discourse alone did not prevail.

Until this point I have considered primarily the content of the novellas themselves, rather than the more commonly discussed alternation between the novellas as narrative and their accompanying discussion. Having seen the struggle between history and discourse in the primary diegetic level of the *Heptaméron* permits us to see the discussions themselves in a new light. One might even go so far as to say that in a certain way the stories comment on the discussions.

The discussions are, like Rolandine's angry statement to the queen, discourse that represents the values and judgments of individuals. These opinions do not grow out of the stories that are told; instead, the opinion precedes and motivates the story. Each storyteller chooses to counter the position of an interlocutor in the discussion by an appeal to history as example. This notion of "history as example" is a neat way of referring to a very confused concept, for the exact relationship between potentiality and actuality that underlies example can never logically be resolved except in a purely atemporal, deductive way. There can only be an ever expanding universe of occurrences that translates into reality a configuration that had previously only belonged to the world of possibility, but the latter can never be entirely drained into the former. Therefore, to give an example of a clever merchant only proves the existence of clever merchants and cannot exclude the possibility that a foolish merchant will soon appear. Or in terms of degree, to give an example of a man who has been much crueller than any woman previously mentioned in the earlier examples cannot prevent someone from finding an example of a still more heinously cruel woman, and so on. By setting the rule that all the novellas must be actual events, Marguerite has merely sharpened the horns of this dilemma of the genre. In a novella collection which does not set forth that restriction, the passage from discussion to narrative is merely enunciatory, not cognitive. Anything you can think of can immediately become a story—all you have to do is tell it. This explosive potential of the novella is clearly recognized as both an opportunity for formal perfection and as a threat, for novella collections are repeatedly submitted to the external constraints of fixed arithmetic units. Boccaccio set the classic model of ten days and ten storytellers which Marguerite apparently followed, but even a noncanonical collection like *Les Quinze Joies de Mariage* fixes a specific limit to the miseries of the misogamistic imagination rather than lose all form in an attempt to embrace the infinite sufferings of marriage.[9]

Marguerite has chosen to set a second condition to limit the proliferation of her narratives, the requirement of historical actuality. But even this, without the arithmetic limit, would be endlessly productive. The first words of the first day of the *Heptaméron* are Simontault's:

9. Unless one considers Longarine's general comment about "faiz si pesant" (174) as an allusion to Rolandine's sufferings.

My ladies, I have been so badly repaid for my long service that, to avenge myself on her who is so cruel to me, I will try my hardest to make a collection of all the bad tricks women have played on poor men, and yet I will say nothing but the honest truth. [11]

This desire to be exhaustive and to make a complete enumeration, *ung recueil*, is the great weakness of the novella as didactic tool. Remaining in the pure realm of historical narrative, it cannot rise into the realm of judgment and value.

This, the ethical side of a novella collection, must come from outside of event itself, from the discursive commentary applied to the narrative. If this seems circular, that is because it is circular and, once more, risks running on forever. The discussion elicits stories to back up positions in the discussion which then produces more stories to back up contrary positions. Another way to put this is to say that the discussions are not really interpretative but polemical, and the goal of the examples is not to extract truth from them but to use them to establish one's authority within a discursive situation.

With this brief glance at the general problem of the status of example in the text, let us return to a more detailed view of how the story-pair earlier described is fitted into the discussion. The story of Rolandine is followed by a very brief discussion oriented strictly along the lines of Rolandine's fidelity and her lover/husband's infidelity. All the rest—the antagonism and persecution inflicted on Rolandine (and to a lesser extent her lover), their stratagems to overcome the obstacles created by the queen, the loyalty and cleverness of their intermediaries, Rolandine's eloquent and courageous defense of her rights—all this is simply not mentioned. In designating the story as an example, the frame narrator, Parlamente, says of Rolandine, "Now, ladies, I pray you that men, who want to portray us as fickle, come and show me an example of a husband as good as this woman was a wife . . . " (174). The only villain in the story seems to be the bastard, and, moreover, only one phase of the bastard's career is taken into account, his infidelity, something that is mentioned nine-tenths of the way through the text of the story, during most of which he is described as a patient, enduring, and resourceful lover.[10] One could, in fact, easily read the comments of the discussants as praising only Rolandine's fidelity after her arrest, thus setting aside more than half of a long and extremely detailed story in this rather brief discussion.

In the case of the nameless aunt, Parlamente points the discussion in a direction exactly opposed to the action of the tale's heroine:

10. The lover's betrayal is necessary for the triumph of Rolandine. As Oisille comments, invoking a kind of literary *felix culpa:* "what gives such luster to her perseverance is the disloyalty of her husband, who wanted to leave her for another" (174).

> I pray God, my ladies, that this example may be so profitable that none of you be tempted to marry for pleasure, without the consent of those whom one must obey. For marriage is such a long-lasting state that it should not be undertaken lightly nor without the advice of our closest kin and friends. And still one cannot act so prudently that there is not at least as much pain as pleasure. [277]

The irony of this "interpretive" statement is hard to ignore if one considers that the heroine's "closest kin" is precisely the person who destroys her every hope of marriage out of motives that the narrative itself indicates are based on his own good and not that of his sister; that the marriage was not long-lasting because of the action of the kinsman whose function should be (in Parlamente's reasoning) to increase its duration; and that the only pain associated with this particular marriage is its termination, not its internal strivings. Parlamente's comment would apply as well, if not better, to Rolandine's story, for the aunt was guided in her choice of a husband by her brother's opinion and did not openly defy authority, whereas Rolandine disobeyed her father, the queen, and the king. Rolandine, furthermore, married without a priest or human witness. It seems almost as if the "lessons" of the two stories had been scrambled. One could easily imagine assigning to Rolandine's aunt praise for fidelity to a husband. After all, she married only once, and after her husband's death she refused to marry again, preferring to live out her days in saintly widowhood. Conversely, the blame that the aunt receives for having married without permission could easily be given to Rolandine. The cross-reference of the two stories is such that the commentary on one is bound to affect our reading of the other.

The comments in the discussion of story 21 are largely in agreement in praise of Rolandine. The second discussion is much more specifically addressed to the events of the narrative and shows much less agreement. In other words, the first story precedes a discussion which either trivializes the narrative by ignoring most of it or by swerving away from the narrative altogether, while the second story produces considerable disagreement about the behavior of the characters. This is an extremely interesting outcome in view of the second comment on the second story, Oisille's affirmation of the efficacy of the example of the aunt: "In all truth, said Oisille, even if there were neither God nor law to teach girls to be good, this example is sufficient to give them more reverence for their parents than to think of marrying according to their own wishes" (277). Oisille, the most scripturally oriented of the frame characters, is the least likely to argue a position in the hypothetical absence of God or law. Yet here she declares that this utterly secular history would be sufficient to teach women their "place." This is strong affirmation not only of the correctness of a certain conduct but of the convincing didacticism of the "history as example." In other words, we have a test case for the efficacy of the *exemplum* as genre, at least insofar as the extreme claim to complete efficacy is concerned, the claim to constitute a new "secular scripture" that could function outside the older Scripture. Perhaps we should take Oisille's claim as hyperbole, but at least it is clear that she is saying that the example works. But it doesn't. The story of the aunt was the second of the two only in the order of narration, but the story of the aunt took place before the story of Rolandine. If anyone knew the aunt's story, Rolandine must have. Yet her conduct was not affected by it in any apparent way, unless one assumes that the accumulation of injustices can be considered an implicit motivation for Rolandine's protest. Not only does the effect of the aunt's example on Rolandine run against the interpretation given by Parlamente and Oisille, but the second story runs into a strong rebuttal from several of the other frame characters.

Nomerfide most strongly attacks the center of Oisille's contention that the outcome of history, the evolution and conclusion of actual event, can itself teach a value.[11] Even the misery of this widow is not decisive, in Nomerfide's view, for history as source of meaning can only be actualized by a subjective decision, one that appears in language as discourse. Nomerfide's demonstration of this principle involves a combination of personal commentary and a restatement of the story of the aunt in concise historical terms:

> She who has a good day in the year is not unhappy for her whole life. She had the pleasure of seeing and speaking for a long time with the man she loved more than herself; and then she had marital pleasure with him without any pangs of conscience. I consider this happiness so great that it seems to me to surpass the ill that she suffered. [277–78]

What Nomerfide says here seems perfectly to agree with the values of Rolandine and her aunt. Yet this statement has vaster implications than a simple criticism of a given interpretation of an example. Nomerfide is showing that any story, any historical account, can be simultaneously respected in its detail and called to support widely varying subjective values. Thus she underscores the lability of history, which awaits the imposition of meaning through the discursive statement either of an external commentator—a frame character of the *Heptaméron*—or of an internal commentator like Rolandine herself. We might even say that history (as the actual) and histories (as the linguistic statement of the actual) await the discourse of a subject who alone can select values and a pattern of conduct from among the paradigms offered.

11. For a different interpretation of the character of Oisille, as representing a specifically "feminine" form of authority, see Paula Sommers, "Feminine Authority in the *Heptaméron:* A Reading of Oysille," *Modern Language Studies* 13, 2 (Spring, 1983), 52–59.

In terms of the overall structure of the *Heptaméron* we can see that there is a parallel between the internal history/discourse dichotomy and the external or frame-narrative dichotomy of the same sort. First of all, the most evident, there is the alignment of certain frame characters with certain of the novella characters. Nomerfide and Geburon side with Rolandine's aunt, while Parlamente and Oisille side with the brother—or at least with the general notion of the authority of (males of) the family over the individual (woman). Through the general principles expounded in the discussion of the aunt, moreover, one can say that some of the frame characters seem to endorse the position of Rolandine and others seem to side with the social authorities.

Secondly, beyond this choosing of sides and sympathies in the specific matter of the repression of individual desire, this dichotomy in the frame characters points to a strange symmetry in regard to the mode of language on which these sympathies are based. This second parallel of novella and frame involves the preference of some characters for discursive statement and of others for historical statement. Parlamente and Oisille emphasize the didactic properties of the history as example, while Nomerfide and Geburon place themselves on the level of an individual ethical declaration that both transcends and yet utilizes the historical givens. What is at stake, in short, is the authority of history and the limitation of discourse. Within the two novellas the figures of historical authority silence the heroine, cutting off her discourse. In doing so, they make of her the subject of a story. This process, within the novella, works against the intentions of those who thus inaugurate the historical existence of the heroine. Curiously, in the frame narrative, Parlamente, the narrator, and Oisille, the most enthusiastic exponent of the total efficacy of historical example, are not only on the side of those who limit the freedom of the heroine, but also on the side of the *process* of historical narrative. Yet in the case of these two frame characters as well, that process escapes their control: Oisille is wrong in her assertion that even without God or law one must accept the lesson of submission taught by the history of Rolandine's aunt.

Rolandine, within the novella, and Nomerfide, outside it, speak on the side of a subjective right which is within that very discourse. Rolandine speaks in the name of the eternal truth of God, whose invisible presence compensates for the actual deficiencies of queen and father. This God is not part of her experience, but precisely absent from that experience, outside of time and present only to faith. He is the Word within Rolandine's word. In taking the side of the aunt, Nomerfide underlines the way in which moments can be measured in subjective terms having nothing to do with the way a third party would see the passage of time. To exalt "one good day a year" is to refuse both the teleology of history (always oriented towards consequences) and the tendency of exemplary narrative to deny individual, internal values in favor of external, institutional ones (apparent in the actions of the makers of history—the queen, the brother, the narrator). Yet Nomerfide accepts history as occurrence and uses it to authorize her own discursive statement of value.

A third parallel between the novellas and the discussions concerns precisely this use of history to authorize discourse. Yet it would be difficult to draw any clear conclusions from the *Heptaméron* about the relationship between history and the truth of discourse except to say that the relationship is problematic and in a state of flux. Truth is not merely "extracted" from history as content from a container, nor does discourse necessarily follow history to interpret and validate it. Oisille says that history should teach something, but she is wrong about what it taught (at least as far as what it teaches Rolandine, Nomerfide, Geburon, and Simontault). Rolandine's triumph in novella 21, in which she survives the death of faithless husband, avaricious father, and cruel brother to marry again and live happily, is a way in which history seems to give *a posteriori* support of her discourse to the queen. We are confronted here neither with an allegorical history within which truth can be read as preexistent message nor with an empirical history systematically used to validate or invalidate hypotheses. Instead, the *Heptaméron* marks the grave crisis of history—in all the senses of the term—which strikes the sixteenth and seventeenth centuries.

In a world in which observation replaces textual learning in the sciences and in which the epic gradually wanes in favor of other forms of historical narrative (*mémoires, nouvelle historique*), it is not surprising that a "realistic" but traditional genre like the novella should find itself torn between fidelity to a concept of multiform experience and a concept of recurrent pattern.[12] Marguerite de Navarre, however, by stressing (more than most of her precursors) the exemplary pretension of her novellas, points to something more than a textual/empirical frontier in intellectual history. She participates in a splitting between inductive and deductive knowledge—or rather, between collective assessment of truth and individual apprehension of a transcendent reality. Similarly, Pascalian apologetics wrestles with the problem of using revealed sacred history as well as profane political history to bring about a conversion that is ultimately purely interior, or at the very most, dialogic ("j'ai versé telle goutte de sang pour toi"). The polyphony of interpretations provided by the frame characters in the *Heptaméron* points to the struggle to recuperate history to lend weight to individual discourse, a struggle which leads only to other individual utilizations of the same history. This proliferation is explosive, held in check only by the formal limitations of the novella collection. It is perhaps not an accident that the *Heptaméron* remains unfinished.

---

12. H. R. Jauss, "Theory of Genres and Medieval Literature," in *Toward an Aesthetic of Reception*, trans. T. Bahti (Minneapolis: Univ. of Minnesota Press, 1982), 86–109.

III. Allegories of Discourse

KEVIN BROWNLEE

Discourse as *Proueces* in *Aucassin et Nicolette*

The Prologue to *Aucassin et Nicolette* is purposefully and strategically duplicitous: it is not what it appears to be. This duplicity only becomes clear, however, by means of a reading of the entire text, which programmatically undermines its own proleptic presentation in the Prologue. This process continues up to and including the last lines of the concluding verse section (41), which function as Epilogue and serve to make the reader (or the audience) aware that only at this point (that is, in the context of the work as a whole) can the Prologue be fully understood.

I would like to examine several interrelated issues raised by the Prologue and elaborated by the text that follows: (1) the "identity" of the author figure and the way in which his authority—his power—is established and guaranteed by the text; (2) the subject matter of the work as a whole, as revealed by its two protagonists and their "authentic" identities; (3) the status and function of "discourse" with regard to the questions both of identity and authority; (4) the highly suggestive redefinition of *proueces* in terms of discourse. In this context, I shall be employing the term "discourse" in a general, though somewhat technical, sense: to designate "signifying activity"—the systematic deployment of communicative and/or aesthetic codes.[1]

The Prologue opens with a formulaic address to the audience reminiscent of a *chanson de geste,* then goes on (in vv. 2–7) to present the subject matter of the story to follow in terms of a combination of epic and romance generic conventions:

1. I would like to acknowledge at the outset my intellectual debt to Eugene Vance, who first demonstrated the necessity of "discourse analysis" to an understanding of this text. See Eugene Vance, "The Word at Heart: *Aucassin et Nicolette* as a Medieval Comedy of Language," *Yale French Studies* 45 (1970), 33–51 and "*Aucassin et Nicolette* as a Medieval Comedy of Signification and Exchange" in *The Nature of Medieval Narrative,* ed. Minette Grundmann-Gaudet and Robin F. Jones (Lexington: French Forum, 1980), 57–76.

> Qui vauroit bons vers oïr
> del depart du viel antif
> de deus biax enfans petis,
> Nicholete et Aucassins,
> des grans paines qu'il soufri
> et des proueces qu'il fist
> por s'amie o le cler vis? [I, vv. 1–7][2]

Who would like to hear a good poem about how an old man separated two beautiful young children, Nicolette and Aucassin; about the torments that this latter suffered and the exploits he accomplished for his beloved with the radiant face?

There is thus no explicit self-presentation on the part of the author figure in the first part of the Prologue.[3] The two protagonists are, on the contrary, both named and characterized: Nicolette is presented as love object and Aucassin as active subject, motivated by his beloved to endure *grans paines* and to perform *proueces*.

The Prologue then shifts from a thematic to a *formal* (and aesthetically judgmental) presentation of the text to follow: "Dox est li cans, biax li dis / et cortois et bien asis" (1, vv. 8–9) [The song is sweet and the story beautiful, courtly, and well-made]. Implicitly then, the presence of the author figure in his work is identified with the visible (and audible) traces of his preeminent artistic craft.

This suggestion is elaborated in the Prologue's conclusion, where the work's effect on its audience is described by means of an elegant (even, it might seem, precious) rhetorical figure:

> Nus hom n'est si esbahis,
> tant dolans ni entrepris,
> de grant mal amaladis,
> se il l'oit, ne soit garis
> et de joie resbaudis,
> tant par est douce. [I, vv. 10–15]

---

2. All quotations are from Mario Roques, ed., *Aucassin et Nicolette: Chantefable du XIIIᵉ siècle*, CFMA, 41 (Paris: Champion, 1955). The excellent edition-translation by Jean Dufournet (Paris: Garnier-Flammarion, 1973) has been repeatedly consulted with great profit.

3. I adopt Margaret Pelan's emendation of *depart* for *deport* in v. 2. See Pelan, "'Le deport du viel antif,'" *Neuphilologische Mitteilungen* 60 (1959), 180–85. Other readings scarcely change this overall impression—not even that of Alfred Schultze in *Archiv für das Studium der neueren Sprachen und Literaturen* 102 (1899), 224 (followed by Dufournet, ed., 45) in which *le viel antif* would in some sense represent the author and/or the *jongleur*. G. Paris (in *Romania* 29 [1900], 287–92), suggests "del ten antif," which would thus be an example of the medieval literary commonplace whereby the authoritative antiquity of a given subject matter is evoked. Mario Roques suggestively proposes another topos: "on pourrait encore songer à voir dans le *viel antif* non pas l'auteur, mais le modèle ancien auquel celui-ci aurait emprunté le thème initial de son oeuvre" (ed., 42).

There is no one so dejected, so distressed, so badly off, so seriously ill that he would not be healed and filled with joy as soon as he heard it/her, because it/she is so sweet.

The audience's reception of the work (the act of interpreting—of "reading" in the broadest sense) is made analogous to the act of healing. The text is like a relic, whose interpretation constitutes a kind of miraculous "exposure" or contact, with the power to cure "illness."

In this context the controversy over the precise referent of the feminine adjective *douce*, which concludes the Prologue, is significant. R. Piccoli considers the referent to be the *cantefable* itself.[4] While I basically agree with this interpretation, I think that the referential ambiguity built into the syntax is both purposefully suggestive and poetically functional. Thus Kurt Rogger's insistence on Nicolette as referent,[5] as the locus of healing *douceur* is far from irrelevant. Indeed, I hope to give detailed consideration, in the pages that follow, to the fundamental and highly nuanced relationship between the character Nicolette and the poetic text that "contains" her even as she serves to emblematize it.

Having examined, in summary fashion, the salient features of the Prologue, let us turn to a selective consideration of the work's narrative structure in order to analyze the progressive development of the two protagonists in light of—in contradistinction to—the initial adumbration of their respective identities. In the context of the present study, my point of departure will be the highly charged term *proueces* used to introduce Aucassin in v. 6 of the Prologue.

On two separate occasions in the course of the story, Aucassin engages in acts of chivalric prowess. The first (and more elaborate) occurs in section 10, when Aucassin battles the enemies of his father. Aucassin's entry into battle is prepared in section 9 as he is carefully armed in accord with epic convention.[6] His initial performance on the battlefield is somewhat comic, however, as he inadvertently allows himself to be captured as the result of his complete absorption by the thought of his beloved (10, vv. 7–17).[7] When Aucassin comes to himself and realizes the gravity of the situation, his behavior changes completely as he is temporarily transformed into a successful epic hero (10, vv. 25–32). The culmination of his chivalric prowess is his capture of Bougar de Valence, the leader of his father's enemies.

4. Piccoli in *Zeitschrift für romanische Philologie* 32 (1908), 600–06 followed by Dufournet, ed., 164.

5. Rogger, "Etude descriptive de la chantefable *Aucassin et Nicolette*," *Zeitschrift für romanische Philologie* 70 (1954), 6.

6. See Dufournet, ed., 172.

7. Lancelot's behavior in Chrétien de Troyes's *Chevalier de la Charrette* seems to function as model here.

This seeming success is, however, immediately undercut: the code of chivalric behavior simply does not function efficaciously in the poetic world of *Aucassin et Nicolette*. Thus, Aucassin's battlefield success fails to win him the amorous reward that had motivated it. Further, Aucassin reacts by carefully "undoing" his chivalric success as such by freeing his prisoner after making him swear to continue the war. Not only is Aucassin's first act of prowess ineffective in that it fails to bring about its explicit goal of reuniting the separated lovers, it renders that separation yet more extreme by leading directly to Aucassin's imprisonment by his outraged father (11, vv. 1–7).

Aucassin's second (and final) act of chivalric prowess occurs in section 32, where he battles the enemies of the King of Torelore. Aucassin's entry into battle this time is prepared by the twice-repeated description of its comically nonchivalric nature. At the end of section 30, Aucassin arrives at the battlefield and sees that the weapons employed are overripe fruit, eggs and soft cheese (30, vv. 17–18). He is astonished ("s'en esmevella molt durement," 30, v. 19). In section 31, Aucassin contemplates the vigorous exchange of these weapons by the opposing forces and we learn that— according to the code of Torelore—victory is obtained by maximum disturbance of the ford on the battlefield: "Cil qui mix torble les gués / est li plus sire clamés" (vv. 9–10). Aucassin's reaction as well as his designation by the author figure is highly significant: "Aucassins, li prex, li ber" (31, v. 11) [the valiant, the noble Aucassin] breaks out in laughter. This is the only time in the entire work that Aucassin is explicitly called *prex* and his claim to the term (indeed, the positively marked chivalric sense of the term itself) is undercut not only by the character's own laughter but by his ensuing behavior. Thinking to "avenge" the king, Aucassin reenacts in miniature his chivalric "feat" (against his father's enemies) in section 10, the link between the two scenes being stressed by verbal parallels. Again, Aucassin obtains a nominal victory: the king's enemies flee. But his chivalric prowess is radically and comically incongruous in the context of Torelore and the king himself begs him to stop.

Furthermore, Aucassin's behavior seems almost to provoke a second separation of the lovers. When the king and Aucassin return from battle, the inhabitants of the country request that Aucassin be expelled from Torelore and that Nicolette remain as the companion of the local prince (32, vv. 16–21). It is only the direct intervention of Nicolette (in section 33) that forestalls this result.

There is thus a series of parallels between Aucassin's two acts of chivalric *proueces*. They are both incongruous (rather than heroic) within the world of the poem. They both have comic overtones. They are both ineffective. As is so often the case in *Aucassin et Nicolette*, a pattern of structural doubling obtains, in which the second element is at once more abbreviated and more explicit than the first. When Aucassin is finally (and uniquely) designated as *preux* by the poet in section 31, v. 11, the effect is simultaneously to recall and negate the ostensibly chivalric semantic field of the term *proueces* as applied to Aucassin in the Prologue (v. 6). At the same time, Aucassin's fundamental inadequacy as locus of *proueces* in the poem is underscored.

Before going on to consider Nicolette in this context, certain preliminary remarks concerning the work's global narrative structure are necessary.[8] The lovers are twice separated and twice reunited. Again, a kind of telescoping is evident: the second cycle involves a faster narrative pace and a correspondingly abbreviated articulation. At the same time, however, a heightened explicitness is very much in evidence. In quantitative terms, the first separation of the lovers occupies sections 2 through 29, when their first reunion is effected. This reunion lasts until section 34, when the lovers are separated for the second time. The second period of separation is, textually speaking, substantially shorter than the first, comprising sections 34 through 39. The second reunion of the lovers begins in section 39 and is definitively and permanently effected in the work's final section, 41.

Within the context of this narrative structure, it is Nicolette who effects both reunions, who successfully overcomes the obstacles presented by the two externally imposed separations. Let us now turn to an examination of *how* she succeeds in these two cases, keeping in mind both the methods she employs and the way in which she is depicted by the author figure.

The first reunion of the lovers involves a two-tiered effort on the part of Nicolette. In each case what is foregrounded is her extraordinary efficacy in manipulating discourse in ways which are simultaneously communicative and aesthetic.

Having escaped from Beaucaire, Nicolette acts to bring Aucassin to her hiding place in the forest outside the city. In section 18 she gives a message to a group of shepherds (*li pastorel*) who are to transmit it to Aucassin. This message is as follows: (1) there is a *beste en ceste forest* (18) [beast in this forest] that Aucassin should hunt (*cacier*, v. 18); (2) the value of this beast cannot be quantified, i.e., expressed in financial terms: "s'il l'i puet prendre, il n'en donroit mie un menbre por cent mars d'or, non por cinc cens, ne por nul avoir" (vv. 18–20) [if he can catch it he would not part with a single one of its limbs for one hundred gold marks, not for five hundred, nor for any amount of wealth]; (3) the beast has such curative power (*mecine*, v. 30) that it will heal Aucassin's wound (*son mehaing*, v.

---

8. For the narrative structure of *Aucassin et Nicolette* cf. Kurt Rogger, "Etude descriptive de la chantefable *Aucassin et Nicolette*," *Zeitschrift für romanische Philologie* 67 (1951), 409–57 and 70 (1954), 1–58.

31); (4) Aucassin must capture it within three days or he will never be cured of his wound.

Nicolette has, of course, deployed the figure of metaphor to describe herself, her situation and her love for Aucassin. Several aspects of this metaphoric discourse should be noted. First, metaphorically speaking, it is Nicolette who is acting as hunter, as she sets her lure for Aucassin, by means of discourse. A suggestively ironic opposition thus emerges not simply between Aucassin and Nicolette as hunter and hunted but between literal and metaphoric discourse as such. Second, while the curing of the wound of love is certainly a standard topos, it is remotivated within the context of *Aucassin et Nicolette* by the claim made in the Prologue with regard to the effect of the text on the reader. Finally, the metaphoric status of Nicolette's discourse is further emphasized by the fact that the shepherds interpret it literally and therefore refuse to believe that it is "true," most specifically in the context of quantifiable financial value. They know all the various beasts in the forest, and the maximum value for a single *menbre* of even the most prestigious of these is "dex deniers u . . . trois au plus, et vos parlés de si grant avoir!" (18, vv. 26–27) [two deniers or at most three—and you speak of such a great sum!] The literal interpretation of metaphoric discourse produces nonsense: "c'est *fantosmes* que vos dites" (vv. 24–25) [what you say is pure fantasy.] The shepherds accuse the enunciator of this discourse of being a *fee* (v. 28) [fairy]. At the same time, however, comprehension is in no way a precondition for effective transmission. Indeed, the literal interpretation of this diegetic audience guarantees the "safety" of the metaphoric message, which is thus "protected" by its status as metaphor. Similarly, the diegetic transmission of the message is effected by means of money: simple transmission *is* an act whose value can be quantified in precisely the register the shepherds understand. Nicolette thus gives them five sous to repeat her words to Aucassin, should they see him.

To summarize, then, Nicolette has encoded *herself* by means of metaphor in a message destined for Aucassin who (unlike the neutral transmitters) will correctly decode it.

The second "tier" of Nicolette's "strategy of entrapment" leading to the lovers' reunion involves a similar kind of reciprocal encoding/decoding, but with two significant differences: the transmitters, the mediators, are suppressed, and the dominant rhetorical figure is no longer metaphor but metonymy.

In section 19, Nicolette decides to "test" Aucassin's love by, in effect, constructing a text which he must correctly interpret. This is the *bele loge* (19, v. 15) [beautiful hut] which she herself builds out of material that she herself has gathered: "des flors de lis / et de l'erbe du garris / et de la foille"

(19, vv. 12–14)[9] [lilies, moor grass and leaves]. To make use of Jakobson's now classic distinction, the *bele loge* is a metonym for Nicolette.[10] The transpositional relationship between the two is based on contiguity not, as in metaphor, on comparison. More particularly, this is an example of the metonymic subcategory in which the effect signifies the cause. The figure is, as it were, dramatized as Nicolette is described in the act of constructing the hut, in a process of "metonymic contagion." Nicolette makes clear that only Aucassin's competence as a "reader," his capacity to understand that the *loge* signifies his beloved, will show him to be worthy of her love (19, vv. 17–22).

In the ensuing narrative sequence, Aucassin successfully decodes Nicolette's two encoded messages. First, in section 22 (prose), Aucassin encounters the shepherds who repeat with great accuracy the four elements of Nicolette's metaphoric text (22, vv. 32–42). The message is effectively transmitted from sender to receiver, the process of transmission being entirely motivated by money. Nicolette as sender, we remember, had paid five sous. Aucassin, as receiver, pays ten.[11] In section 23 (verse), Aucassin correctly interprets Nicolette's message and responds accordingly by riding deep into the forest in search of his beloved. While riding, Aucassin articulates his understanding in a passage of direct discourse (vv. 9–18) which is a structured response to each of the various components of Nicolette's message. Metaphoric and literal discourse are programmatically mixed. Nicolette is, of course, identified as the object of his search and it is her beauty and her speech (*vos dox mos*, v. 14) which "ont men cuer navré a mort" (v. 15) [have mortally wounded my heart.] The hunt, which is literally on horseback, in a forest teeming with "real animals," is of course a metaphoric hunt (though a literal search): "je ne cac ne cerf ne porc / mais por vos siu les *esclos*," (vv. 11–12, emphasis added.) [I am hunting neither stag nor boar; rather, I am following your tracks.] In the context of

9. Flowers in general and the "fleur de lis" in particular are repeatedly associated with Nicolette at various points in the text.

10. See Roman Jakobson, "Two Aspects of Language and Two Types of Aphasic Disturbances" in Roman Jakobson and Morris Halle, *Fundamentals of Language*, 2nd ed. (The Hague: Mouton, 1975), 67–96 (esp. 90–96).

11. It is interesting to note, in addition, that the shepherds, after having been paid by Aucassin, explicitly state that they had earlier been paid by Nicolette. Furthermore, Aucassin offers his "receiver's fee" for what is in effect the wrong message—the song the shepherds had been singing in section 21 on the subject of Nicolette's payment to them. Aucassin wants the *pastoriax* to repeat this song and it is only their impolite refusal to function in any capacity other than the one for which they have been paid that leads to successful communication between the lovers. Significantly (in part because of the formal organization of the work explicitly remarked on in the Prologue), the shepherds' spokesman refuses to *canter* but agrees to *conter*. Nicolette's original message, of course, had been *conté*, i.e., delivered in one of the prose sections (18).

the drama of interpretation and discourse that is here unfolding (even, it would seem, becoming thematized) I would suggest that the tracks, the *traces (esclos)* that Aucassin follows are verbal traces, those left by Nicolette's deft deployment of metaphoric discourse. In section 24 Aucassin comes across the other *esclos*, the other trace of Nicolette's discourse left in the forest: the *bele loge.*[12]

The efficacy of this sign is immediately manifest: Aucassin's correct interpretation is well nigh instantaneous: "E! Dix, fait Aucassins, ci fu Nicolete me douce amie, et ce fist ele a ses beles mains; por le douçour de li et por s'amor me descenderai je ore ci et m'i reposerai anuit mais" (24, vv. 78–81) ["In God's name," said Aucassin, "my sweet friend Nicolette has been here and she has made this hut with her beautiful hands. For the sake of her sweetness and her love I will dismount right now and spend the whole night here.] Aucassin enters the *loge* and proceeds (in section 25) to sing a love song. At the beginning of section 26, Nicolette, waiting hidden nearby "en un espés buison" (vv. 3–4) [in a thick bush] hears Aucassin's song and enters the *loge* herself.[13] The first reunion of the lovers has thus been effected by Nicolette's deft manipulation of figurative discourse; first metaphoric (the *beste* message), then metonymic (the *loge*). An implicit displacement of chivalric *prouesse* is thus suggested. Indeed, it is Aucassin's capacity as reader of texts, as decoder of messages (*not* his feats of arms) that leads him to his beloved. Interestingly, this reunion also involves a healing that is at once literal and metaphorical. As Aucassin dismounts to enter the *loge* in 24, 82–85, he is so absorbed by thoughts of Nicolette that he falls and dislocates his shoulder: "Il se senti molt blecié," (v. 85) [he felt he was seriously wounded]. The literal wound, which is simultaneously a metaphor for the wound of love (the *mehaing* of 18 and 22, the *cuer navré* of 23) is then literally cured by Nicolette in section 26, even as the metaphoric wound is being cured. An artful and highly self-conscious structure of *dédoublement* is thus created: a kind of reciprocal specularity in which metaphoric and literal discourse simultaneously "reflect" and reinforce each other. Indeed, each becomes necessary to the other's functioning: each, paradoxically, "guarantees" the other. Furthermore, Nicolete's act of healing recalls and duplicates the process of metonymic contagion by which she had constructed the *loge*. Emphasis is placed upon her *blances mains* (26, v. 11) [fair hands], already foregrounded

12. Aucassin's arrival at the *bele loge* is preceded (in 24) by his gratuitous and ineffective use of metaphoric discourse with the *bouvier*. This latter's situation, it should be noted, is a *literal* version of Aucassin's metaphoric hunt, to which it is implicitly (and contrastively) compared by a series of verbal and situational parallels (e.g., the three-day search motif). Of particular importance in this regard is Aucassin's payment of twenty sous to end the *bouvier*'s literal search for a literal animal which *does* have a financially quantifiable value.

13. Cf. 13, where Nicolette heard Aucassin's crying and lamentations but could *not* enter into his prison.

as the privileged "instrument" in the construction of the *loge* by Aucassin's initial exclamation of recognition (24, v. 79: "ce fist ele a ses *beles mains*," [emphasis added]). These same hands now touch and manipulate Aucassin's dislocated shoulder so efficaciously as to reset it. As if to make sure we get the point, Nicolette then applies to the wound a dressing which is comprised of the same (highly stylized) materials she had used to construct the *loge:* "des flors et de l'erbe fresce et des fuelles verdes" (26, v. 13) [flowers, fresh grass, and green leaves.] Both the literal and the figurative wound are thus healed simultaneously by means of Nicolette's artful "manipulation" of discourse. In addition, the metaphoric *beste* (with the miraculous power to heal) and the metonymic *loge* are now brilliantly conflated. This first reunion scene thus concludes with the statement that Aucassin "fu tox garis" (26, v. 14) [was completely healed]. In this context, it is highly significant to recall the promise made at the end of the Prologue. Nicolette, at the diegetic level, has produced the same effect on Aucassin (who is, we remember, a successful lover by virtue of being a successful reader) that the Prologue promised would be produced, at the extradiegetic level, on the "readers" of the text as a whole.[14] Nicolette has thus become (by section 26) an emblem of the very text in which she is embedded, that "contains" her. The ambiguity of the referent for the feminine adjective *douce* in the final line of the Prologue now seems, in retrospect, to be both intentional and poetically functional.

But if Nicolette has come to emblematize the text, it is because she functions qua character by means of the same signifying processes and rhetorical strategies (metaphor, metonymy, etc.) that have generated the text. Her diegetic activity implicitly parallels that of the extradiegetic poet-author.

In accord with the work's narrative structure of telescoping and *dé-doublement*, all these matters become explicit in connection with the lovers' second (and final) reunion. For if Nicolette functions as an *index of the author* as she effects the first reunion, she transforms herself into an *icon of the author* in order to effect the second reunion.[15] As such, she is revealed as the authentic locus of a radically redefined *prouesse*.

The lovers' first separation had been the work of Garin de Beaucaire, Aucassin's father, who wanted him to marry not Nicolette, but a woman worthy of his social and familial status. Nicolette ultimately nullifies the separation by making Aucassin come to her.

14. The story of Nicolette's miraculous healing of a seriously ill Limousin pilgrim (narrated by the imprisoned Aucassin in section 11) is also relevant here. The words used to describe the *pelerin*'s illness (11, vv. 20–21) duplicate those used to describe the hypothetical illness of the reader in Prologue vv. 11–12.

15. For the distinction between index and icon see Charles S. Peirce, *Collected Papers II: Elements of Logic*, ed. Charles Hartshorne and Paul Weiss (Cambridge, MA: Harvard Univ. Press, 1932), 156–73.

The lovers' second separation results from their capture by a Sarassin fleet which places them in different ships.[16] Aucassin thus becomes a *caitis* (34, v. 6) [captive] of the Sarassins, assuming the status that had been Nicolette's at the beginning of the work.[17] This reversal initiates a series of inversions operative throughout the second separation/reunion sequence as compared to the first.

Aucassin's ship swiftly and miraculously runs aground near Beaucaire, whose inhabitants instantly recognize him and install him as count, his father and mother having conveniently died in his absence. Aucassin's position is thus a kind of positive reversal of his situation at the opening of the work. Not only does his father have no power over him, he has replaced his father. Not only is he out of prison, but he possesses—qua count—a kind of maximum freedom to act. Yet Aucassin appears in section 35 just as incapable of joining his beloved as he was in section 11, when Garin had imprisoned him.

At this point (section 36) the text explicitly turns away from Aucassin to begin a progressive and multileveled revelation of Nicolette's "true" identity. This "drama of identity" will continue right up to the end of the work and will exploit repeatedly the difference between the extradiegetic speech situation (author as sender/audience as receiver) and the various diegetic speech situations (in which characters function both as senders and receivers). The process begins in section 36, as the poet-author reveals to the audience that Nicolette is the daughter of the king of "Cartage" (=Cartagena, in Spain). Nicolette herself remains explicitly unaware of her familial identity when questioned by the sailors who are taking her to her birthplace. It is only when she actually sees the walls of Cartagena that Nicolette "se reconut" (36, vv 9–10): realizing both that this city is her birthplace[18] and that its king is her father. She is thus returning to a social and familial status equal to or even more prestigious than that of Aucassin in Beaucaire at the beginning of the text.

It is at the very moment of her physical arrival at the place that confers this prestigious "public" identity that Nicolette is presented by the poet-author as what Nathaniel Smith has called a combination of "a Roland and an Olivier"[19] in the first verse of section 37: "Nichole li preus, li sage, / est

16. It is interesting to note the complete absence of chivalric *proueces* on the part of Aucassin in this scene, where it would have been "generically" appropriate. The suppression of chivalric *proueces* at this crucial narrative juncture works to underscore once again its progressive and definitive exclusion from the poetic system of *Aucassin et Nicolette*. The additional detail that Aucassin was tied up hand and foot by the Sarassins ("si loierent Aucassin les mains et les piés," 34, v. 7) further emphasizes this point.

17. See 2, vv. 28–30, where Garin describes Nicolette as "une caitive" whom "li visquens de ceste vile [acata] as Sarassins"; this description is repeated by the viscount himself in 6, vv. 14–16.

18. A fact first revealed to the reader in 3, v. 9, by Aucassin's mother, denigrating Nicolette to Aucassin.

19. Smith, *Kentucky Romance Quarterly*, 26 (1979), 480.

arivee a rivage" [the valiant and wise Nicolette has arrived at the shore.]

Several observations must be made in this connection. First, the nominalized adjectives *preus* and *sage* which are here applied to Nicolette for the first time in the text are both epicene, while the Picard dialect allows a similar status for the definite articles. Morphologically then Nicolette is treated like a male hero.[20] Second, this application of a formulaic binome of epic identity represents the beginning of a programmatic redefinition of the term *preux* in the context of *Aucassin et Nicolette* considered as a whole. Third, the point of departure for this redefinition is the (now discredited) claim made in the Prologue regarding the ostensibly chivalric deeds of *proueces* done by Aucassin. Finally, a fundamental component of Nicolette's identity is involved—but its full meaning will only emerge progressively, over the course of the work's concluding five sections.

The privileged and seemingly proleptic revelation of Nicolette's identity as *preus* occurs on the level of the extradiegetic speech situation. It is intimately linked to Nicolette's diegetic *rejection* of her newly recovered social and familial status as "noble." What is at issue is the *authentic* source of Nicolette's identity and her "power," i.e., her diegetically functional "nobility" and its manifestations. In this context, it is highly significant that (in section 37) Nicolette's realization of her noble birth is coterminous with her explicit rejection of this "natural" identity. In its place, she substitutes her "self-created" identity as Aucassin's lover/beloved. It is interesting to note that in the direct discourse (37, vv. 6–18) in which Nicolette explicitly affirms this identity, she characterizes Aucassin as "gentix et sages" (v. 10) [noble and wise], thus making Aucassin's *gentillesse* correspond and contrast with her own *prouesse*.

It is in section 38 that Nicolette's "true" identity is most explicitly (and ironically) revealed. Having simply articulated her status as the daughter of the king of Cartagena, Nicolette receives instantaneous public confirmation of this status. She thus places herself in an inverted version of Aucassin's constraining "noble" identity at the beginning of the text. Now *Nicolette's* father wants to marry *her* to someone of suitable social status. This "honorable" public identity thus becomes a metaphorical prison for Nicolette, who finds herself, like Aucassin (in sections 2–20), obliged to marry against her will, in accord with the dictates of her class.[21]

20. There is thus a contrastive recall of the presentation of Aucassin in 31, v. 11, as Charles Méla remarks, noting how "par un glissement de langue que tolère le dialecte picard, le chanteur ne distingue plus le genre féminin du masculin: sur le modèle de 'Aucassins, li prex, li ber' on retrouve 'Nichole li preus, li sage'" (*Blanchefleur et le saint homme ou la semblance des reliques* [Paris: Seuil, 1979], 61–62). It is interesting to note that the first time the epicene adj. *preus* appears in the work, it is used to characterize the male watchman as he helps Nicolette evade capture by Garin's men: "li gaite fu mout . . . / preus . . ." (15, vv. 1–2).

21. For Nicolette the social level is higher though the religious context is inferior. She is to marry "un roi de paiiens," (38, v. 10).

Unlike Aucassin, however, Nicolette will, in accord with her behavior throughout the work, take *active* steps to remedy her situation. She simultaneously rejects the constraining "prison" of an unwanted "public" identity and invents a strategem (an *engien*, 38, v. 11: a *hapax* in the text) which will effect her escape, insure her (definitive) reunion with her lover and reveal in the most explicit manner possible her "true" identity.

She learns how to play the *viele* and, having effortlessly escaped from the palace, disguises herself as a *jogleor*. This involves a physical self-transformation that recalls Nicolette's construction of the *loge* and her subsequent "healing" of Aucassin. In section 38, Nicolette "prist une herbe, si en oinst son cief et son visage, si qu'ele fu tote noire et tainte," (vv. 15–16) [took an herb and smeared her head and face with it until her complexion became quite dark and dull.] It is only after this neatly symmetrical inversion of her "normal" appearance ("o le cler vis") that Nicolette dons the masculine clothing that completes her disguise.[22] Disguised then as a *jongleur*, Nicolette obtains passage on a ship which takes her to Provence.[23] Here she disembarks "si prist se viele, si ala vielant par le païs tant qu'ele vint au castel de Biaucaire, la u Aucassins estoit" (38, vv. 21–23) [with her *viele* and travels through the country playing it until she comes to the castle of Beaucaire where Aucassin resides.] On the diegetic level, Nicolette has thus arrived at Aucassin by doing exactly what the poet-author figure does at the extradiegetic level, also "arriving" at Aucassin. Space within the text thus parallels the text as space, as Nicolette the character parallels the author/performer.

In section 39, these parallels are elaborated with extraordinary explicitness, and the progressive redefinition of *prouesse* is definitively effected. First we have the setting. Aucassin seated on a stone bench, surrounded by his courtiers ("si franc baron," v. 4) dreaming of the absent Nicolette to whom the poet-author now applies (for the second time) the epithet *preux*—but, as it were, more emphatically than in 37, v. 1, for the word is no longer part of a binomial formula and it is placed in the final assonanced position: She is (in 39, v. 8) "Nicholete le prox."

At this point (39, v. 11), the disguised Nicolette arrives on the scene, takes out her *viele* and bow,[24] and begins to sing her own song, the story

22. The motif of hero/heroine disguised as *jongleur* was a veritable topos in medieval French literature. See in particular (1) the *Folies Tristan*; (2) *Beuve de Hantone* (esp. as treated by Dufournet, ed., 26–27 and 190); (3) *Le Roman de Silence* (see R. Howard Bloch, "Silence and Holes: The *Roman de Silence* and the Art of the Trouvère," *Yale French Studies* 70, 81–99 and *Etymologies and Geneologies* [Chicago & London: University of Chicago Press, 1983], 195–97, 205).

23. Cf. Aucassin in 28, where he obtains passage on a ship that lands them in Torelore and in 34, where the Sarassin ships separate the two lovers.

24. There seems to be a purposeful exploitation of "epic syntax" here: "Es vous Nichole au peron,/ trait vïele, trait arçon" (39, vv. 11–12). Is there perhaps the implicit suggestion that these instruments of art have displaced instruments of war in terms of the "artistic" *prouces* that is at issue in *Aucassin et Nicolette?*

of the love and deeds of Nicolette. She is thus doubling in miniature and within the context of the story line the signifying activity of the poet-*jongleor* with respect to the text as a whole. This *mise en abyme* functions diegetically to advance the narrative. At the same time, it involves a corrective rewriting of the duplicitous Prologue, a rewriting sanctioned by the author figure himself.

Nicolette's song (vv. 14–36), is tripartite. It begins with a *chanson de geste* style prologue which simultaneously recalls and transforms the Prologue of the work as a whole:

> Escoutés moi, franc baron
> cil d'aval et cil d'amont:
> plairoit vos oïr un son
> d'Aucassin, un franc baron
> de *Nicholete la prous!* [39, vv. 14–18, emphasis added]

> Hear me, noble lords, whether seated low or high: Would you like to hear a song about Aucassin, a noble lord, and about the valiant Nicolette?

Nicolette as disguised *jongleur* thus presents Nicolette as character in a way that makes *her* the locus of *prouesse* in the story.[25] On the one hand, this substitutes Nicolette for Aucassin who, we remember, had been proleptically designated as doer of *proueces* in the Prologue to the work as a whole (I, v. 6). Secondly, Nicolette's self-designation here (within the diegetic speech situation) has been authorized in advance by the poet-author's use of the same designation in the extradiegetic speech situation ten verses earlier. In this context it is worth noting the shift to the Francien form of the feminine definite article.[26] The second part of Nicolette's song

---

25. Nicolette's use of *baron* (v. 17) to designate Aucassin is also worth noting. This is the last time in the work that *ber/baron* is used in the singular with the meaning "homme noble" (Roques, ed., 57). (It appears in the plural with this meaning twice in section 39: in v. 4 the poet-author uses it to designate Aucassin's courtiers; in v. 14 Nicolette-*jongleur* uses it to designate her audience.) On the three earlier occasions where the term appears in the singular with this sense, Aucassin is also the referent (of the nominative, *ber*). In 13, v. 6, it is applied to Aucassin for the first time by Nicolette in a passage of direct discourse aimed at comforting Aucassin, who is crying helplessly in prison. The contrast between the situation and behavior of Aucassin and the standard semantic content of the term is of prime importance and serves to color the poet-author's use of the epithet to designate Aucassin as he picks up the lock of hair Nicolette has thrown to him, before he returns to weeping ("Aucassins les prist, li ber" 13, v. 17). The final use of the term is also by the poet-author as part of a binomial epithet in the already discussed passage in 31, where Aucassin is referred to as *prex* for the only time in the entire work: "Aucassins, li prex, li ber, / les coumence a regarder, / s'en prist a rire" (31, vv. 11–13).

26. It is of course impossible to draw definitive interpretive conclusions from this kind of evidence in a single surviving manuscript. It is nonetheless suggestive that in the two cases where the narrator designates Nicolette as *preus* and *prox* he uses *li/le* (37, v. 1 and 39, v. 8) while in the two cases where Nicolette designates herself as *prous* she uses *la* (39, vv. 18 and 24). Charles Gossen notes that in *Aucassin et Nicolette* as a whole "*le, li* [are] plus fréquents que *la*" (*Grammaire de l'ancien picard*, Paris: Klincksieck, 1970, 122), as they are in the majority of Picard texts in Gossen's corpus.

involves a four-line summary of the lovers' first reunion and second separation (vv. 19–22). The third and final part (vv. 23–36) treats Nicolette's situation and behavior during the second separation. Within the context of the song, Aucassin as character is dismissed and attention is focused exclusively on Nicolette. At the same time, she is again presented as embodying *prouesse* for the last time and in the most "particular" context of the work: that of her threatening situation in Cartagena: "D'Aucassin rien ne savons, / mais Nicolete la prous / est a Cartage el donjon" (39, vv. 23–25) [We know nothing of Aucassin, but the valiant Nicolette is in the castle-keep at Cartegena.] Nicolette's retelling stresses the parallels with Aucassin's situation at the beginning of the work (already alluded to) and ends with a statement (in the present tense) of her resolve not to marry the "roi de paiiens" (v. 29) chosen by her father and her oath to remain faithful to Aucassin, the only man she will ever marry. The progressive redefinition and relocation of *prouesse* is now nearly complete. On the level of the plot, Nicolette's *prouesse* has already enabled her to effect her second escape and her second reunion with Aucassin, just as it had done the first time around. And this characteristic is now explicitly associated not with chivalric excellence but with the ability artfully to manipulate signifying codes. Nicolette's disguise and performance as *jongleur* involves her third and final "self-encoding": as poet-figure to the extradiegetic audience, as heroine to the diegetic audience. In both cases she is *preux* and in both cases the manifestation of her *prouesse* is in the realm of discourse, programmatically and repeatedly privileged by the text.

This final time, however, the duplicitous nature of Nicolette's discursive power is underscored by a significant shift: a sharp differentiation between diegetic and extradiegetic audiences as interpreters. A configuration of interpretive solidarity had obtained—with regard to the metaphoric *beste* and the metonymic *loge*—between Aucassin within the text and the reader outside the text. Now, this configuration is undone. Only the extradiegetic audience fully understands, correctly decodes Nicolette's final self-encoding. Aucassin is deceived and manipulated; unable correctly to interpret this final message from Nicolette.

But he is not intended to "read" correctly here: that is our task. Nicolette's audience and that of the poet-author have now become coterminous. Aucassin as privileged member of the diegetic audience is intended simply to react in a way which signifies simultaneously his love and his inadequacy. Ironically, Aucassin designates (in section 40) Nicolette-*jongleur* as his emissary, to go seek out Nicolette-lover in Cartagena and bring her back to Beaucaire.[27] It is thus the figure of the *jongleur*—

27. Furthermore, Aucassin quantifies the financial value of this "transaction" by paying Nicolette-*jongleur* (n advance) "vint livres" (40, v. 22). Here (as in 24, v. 67, where he pays twenty sous to the *bouvier*) Aucassin spends money gratuitously with regard to the reunion of

rather than the "disembodied" discourse of the *jongleur*—that now serves as the mediator of desire.

Once again, the metaphoric and the literal become conflated, and mutually illuminating. Nicolette's metaphoric journey back to Beaucaire (which is also a function of the successfully deceived perspective of Aucassin) is literally an undoing of the *jongleur* disguise—a reversal of this linguistic and physical transformation. In a final ritual of "self-healing," Nicolette anoints herself with "une herbe qui avoit non esclaire" (40, v. 34)[28] and regains her previous physical identity. After a final change of clothes which symmetrically completes the undoing of her disguise, she sends for Aucassin and the two lovers are reunited as such in the last section of the work (41). Marriage follows immediately and they live happily ever after.

The last four lines of this section constitute an Epilogue:

> Or a sa joie Aucassins
> et Nicholete autresi:
> no cantefable prent fin,
> n'en sai plus dire. [41, vv. 22–25]

Now Aucassin has found happiness and so has Nicolette. Our *chantefable* is at an end. I have nothing more to say.

The author figure remains anonymous as in the Prologue. And the work remains anonymous as well, receiving nothing more than a neutral and descriptive generic (or pseudogeneric) designation that simply recombines the elements of the proleptic formal description contained in v. 8 of the Prologue. By the conclusion of *Aucassin et Nicolette* we have come full circle. The author figure remains an absence rather than a presence in the text: the Prologue and the Epilogue are in this sense complementary. At the same time, the progammatically repressed first-person presence of the author figure has been "represented," figured with increasing explicitness by the third-person female hero: Nicolette. The process of representation has involved the entire work—beginning with the Prologue and *culminating* in section 38: Nicolette's inscribed performance and rewriting of the work in minature, disguised as a *jongleur*. But the process of disguise—artful, duplicitous, efficacious—is not unidirectional. For Nicolette the character is in a very real sense the "disguise" adopted by the author figure for himself in his own text. At the same time, the very duplicitousness of

---

the lovers, because he acts on his own, outside the context of Nicolette's plans. This recalls contrastively the effective use of money in the transmission of Nicolette's metaphoric message (five sous in 18, 31 and ten sous in 22, vv. 24–25) which brought about the first reunion of the lovers.

28. This entire sequence thus recalls Nicolette's healing of Aucassin in section 31 with its play between the literal and the figurative levels, involving both metaphor and metonymy.

the Prologue now appears to function as part of the author's identity, which necessarily involves "disguise" at the level of discourse. The necessarily duplicitous yet highly artful poetic discourse of *Aucassin et Nicolette* is the source and the guarantee of the author's *prouesse.* For in redefining the term vis-à-vis Nicolette—indeed by means of the very process of this redefinition—the author is implicitly valorizing his own identity— his own signifying activity as the source of *his* power. Thus the authentic locus of *prouesse* in the text is double—though in both cases determined by artful manipulation of discourse. Diegetically it is Nicolette who finally is revealed as an explicitly inscribed poet figure and whose power, whose efficaciousness—derived from her discourse—is demonstrated on the level of plot by the way in which she successfully effects the two reunions.At the extradiegetic level the locus of *prouesse* is the author figure, whose power and efficaciousness are demonstrated by the poetic functioning of the text itself.[29]

29. I would like to thank Peter Dembowski and Mary Speer for their careful reading of this essay and for their helpful comments.

BERNARD CERQUIGLINI

The Syntax of Discursive Authority: The Example of Feminine Discourse

Mikhail Bakhtin has frequently pointed out the fascination inherent in the way human discourse, as represented in the literary text, insinuates itself into the reader's consciousness.[1] This literary mimesis of discourse is of crucial importance for anyone wishing to ally history and literature. But to succeed, one must first become a linguist. For we must not forget that the literary code simply exemplifies phenomena proper to human language; historical or esthetic interpretation take as their primary object of study language procedures which, technically speaking, are the province of the grammarian.

Of what do our conversations consist, notes the Soviet linguist, if not of previous conversations that we reproduce, quote, and manipulate? Speaking consists largely of circulating, along with our own words, snatches of other people's conversation: half-remembered replies, felicitous expressions and turns of phrase. Words e-voked, borrowed from other voices. Or, more clandestinely, within the very web of language, to speak is to assign one's own discourse to other speakers (e.g., the witness [*témoin*], the formal speaker [*allocutaire*], the authority [*autorité*]. In short, a constant discursive drift, a strategy of feigning, which makes linguistic exchange less a kind of social commerce than, as Anglo-Saxon philosophy has so well demonstrated, a kind of warfare. One may thus explain the number and diversity of speech processes designed to master the discourse of others: from the explicit to the surreptitious, from the narrative to the stategem.[2]

---

1. Bahktin, Mikhail, *Esthétique et théorie du roman* (Paris: Gallimard, 1978), 122–52; M. B. *Le Marxisme et la philosophie du langage* (Paris: Minuit, 1977), 153ff.

2. The enumeration and description of these processes seems to constitute a priority, in the same way as the definition of contemporary linguistics—whether pragmatic, enunciatory, etc.—may be said to be.

And it *is* a matter of mastery. Extremely polyphonic, discourse is nonetheless linked to a unique enunciatory instance which takes charge of the reference-markings and controls and thus bears, according to the point of view of the Oxford School, the responsibility for illocutionary acts. This enunciatory instance, at times masked (argumentation), indeed in a ritual absence (novelistic fiction), always at the risk of its own defects (lapsus), directs the innumerable enunciatory operations that constitute what we have called, placing it at the heart of speech activity, "evocation."

The clearest example, one for which grammarians and linguists—including Bakhtin himself[3]—have shown a great interest, is reported discourse. The most obvious aspects of reported discourse are the manipulations to which the speaker, master of the game, gives himself over, to represent and form at will the discourse he attributes to others. The modes of appropriation are well known in the case of "indirect discourse": temporal, aspectual, personal, and the other indicators that originate with the speaking subject who takes control of them. The indirect style is thus a form of annexation.

"Free indirect discourse," more subtle in its processes, is no less efficient an enunciatory technique, mixing the voice of the speaker with echoes of the evoked discourse. It constitutes a kind of "softcore" annexation, a veiled discourse (*verschleierte Rede*), whose riches have inspired many a gamble.[4]

The general perspective adopted here, which situates evocation among the primary linguistic acts, should not lead to a neglect of direct discourse, whose seeming transparency has often bothered grammarians. Again it is a question of a discourse technique or signifying activity whose range, often imperfectly perceived, justifies the privilege we grant it. On the one hand, even in cases where the speaker strives to report faithfully the words of another, those words appear as they were heard and perceived. Moreover, they belong to the setting (*mise en scène*) that the speaker continually directs. Direct discourse is always a representation; to quote someone, as one must, is to convoke him by evoking him.

On the other hand, it is part of the game to present this reported discourse in its original markers; it is important, then, above all orally, to indicate explicitly that a rupture has taken place in the midst of the narrative, and to place forthrightly on stage a second speaker. In sum, direct discourse is a gesture that designates speech as other. And this gesture, a necessary condition and paradoxical definition of direct discourse (to the point of having misled the grammatical tradition), possesses many linguistic manifestations. To name but two, we find diverse kinds of ante-

3. *Le Marxisme et la philosophie du langage,* 173ff.
4. See my forthcoming article, "Le Style indirect libre et la Modernité," in *Langages* 73 (March 1984), 7–16.

posed structures which we shall call "prolepses"; and a multifaceted play of interpolated clauses or "analepses." Although declared a "faithful" representation by grammar books, which generally have no more to say about it, direct discourse is a speech activity whose study has only just begun.

The first insight was offered by Mikhail Bakhtin, chiefly attentive, as his period was, to the obvious forms of reported discourse (indirect and free indirect). His approach, however, can be extended to the analysis of direct discourse. The polyphonic nature of discourse necessarily involves social dimensions, to paraphrase Bakhtin. On the one hand, to represent the words of another, whether or not one intends to quote that person, implies an acceptance of his or her alterity, not in a pure form, but assimilated and reformulated through the twin filters of the unconscious and of ideology. On the other hand, the linguistic materials available to the speaking subject, and that he deploys freely by implementing the discursive techniques (control and manipulation) that we have just drawn attention to, are, by their diversity and dependence (*mouvance*), a socializing force in language. The speaker, mastering the discourse of others, designates what supports and qualifies this mastery: sociological status, human relations, cultural legitimation, etc.[5] The polyphonic nature of discourse rehabilitates the forgotten Saussurian axiom that makes of language inescapably a social object.

One can readily see the use that the history and meaning of literary forms can derive from this perspective. Whatever the particular status of its narrator, novelistic fiction grounds itself in illustrating and extending the polyphonic nature of everyday language. But it's a question, on the one hand, of an inverse extension, since by representing fictive discourse, the novel plays a trick by authenticating its speaker. On the other, it's a coded extension, marked by conventions and constraints, which formalizes a speech activity at the very heart of the formalized linguistic exchange we call literary communication. The modes of representation, of control and manipulation of discourse manifested in the literary work, as well as the particular language segments that it deploys, are all highly meaningful.

From an internal perspective, the specifics of this mimesis invoke typology of forms, genres, and modes of writing. Viewed from without, they provide clues that, from the choices made by the speaker, reveal individual tastes, social preferences, and ideological configurations. The discourse proposed by a literary work, the particular morphology and syntax it attributes to this enunciation, thus constitute a sensitive locus for meaningful reading. Finally, we see that grammatical investigation takes for its goal the history of esthetic experimentation.

5. See the pioneering remarks of Henri Bauche on interpolated clauses of the type: "Alors?" *qu'y m'fait;*—"Ça va," *que je lui fais,* etc. Henri Bauche, *Le Langage populaire* Paris: Payot, 1920).

This line of research can prove singularly fruitful for medieval studies for reasons that are at once general and specific. For one thing, there's the stylization, formalism, and forceful repetitiveness so characteristic of Old French; then again, the requisite grounding of medieval studies in language and historical grammar. The literary works of the French Middle Ages manifest a conventional language which the developing vernacular literature had to adopt both for geographical reasons (*scripta* transcending the dialects) and for historical reasons (the diffusion and legitimation of clerical knowledge). The conventional language, in exchange, helped to establish the young literature as an institution.

This literature innovates models which it tests, plays with, and rejects in a kind of inventive euphoria that results in a diversity of codes, multiple constraints, and local interests. A literature incessantly haunted by the formula, recurrence, and reprise, it obeys laws as rigorous as they are partial, laws that are precarious rituals. Medieval writing refers less to the stylistics of an author than to the typology of forms governed by an inventive tradition. One may rightly suppose that the grammar of discourse acquired by the medieval literary work is valorized by the particularities of its mode of writing: modes at once explicit, rigorous, and diverse, and thus all the more worthy of interest and rich in meaning.

Furthermore, to attach oneself solely to direct discourse results from a gamble and a paradox. Does it not show a surreptitious desire to seek out the living, to perceive beneath ponderous codes, at whatever cost, what is still vital? In brief, to reach by means of direct discourse spoken language itself? This point of view is shared by a large number of studies, not all of them outdated, many of them masterful, for which *oratio recta* is the ideal outpost from which to observe language in its truth, free from the constraints of literary style.

It is precisely this viewpoint that one must attack to discredit the idea of a restful and reassuring elsewhere (*ailleurs*), of a vernacular intact from esthetic formalization, and thus sheltering studies of syntax from literary interpretation, thereby separating the linguist from the philologist. Much is at stake here as regards the orientation of medieval studies. Accordingly, it is of great importance to show that the distribution of linguistic elements between narrative and discourse is controlled by esthetic formalization. Conscious usage of syntactic formulas and speech processes serve to distinguish discourse from nondiscourse, to designate it as such and to represent it. The medieval text is not porous, allowing some authentic statement or other to pass through to us by accident: its texture is just varied. We shall see how this corroborates the general perceptions stated above, and attributed to Bakhtin, and which holds that the status of discourse in a work of fiction is one of the most sensitive aspects of literary writing.

That the unfolding of language becomes the medium of esthetic con-figuration, indeed of social representation, may happily be illustrated by medieval literature. The primacy of language and its distribution in these texts depends on precise reasons which reinforce the tendency towards formalization mentioned above. From the viewpoint of literary analysis, the mimesis of discourse may be regarded as a doubly signifying activity: of verification, in the first instance, indicating that there is or will be dis-course and indicating its source; and then, of mime, playing out the dis-course, exhibiting it. Both activities pose problems for medieval texts.

The first activity depends of necessity on the material of language. Old French uses no material sign to indicate discourse; it is only in its language that the medieval manuscript must find the means to signal discourse. What this implies is a grouping of linguistic elements (linking adverbs, declarative verbs, etc.)—in other words, a proper syntax. This grouping operates according to the esthetics of the text, of the genre, of the mode of writing on which it depends: it constitutes an *écriture*. Linguistic mate-rial, in its most technical reality, is the empirical projection, and thus verifiable, of an ordered sequence of signifying configurations at work, in a general way, in the literary text. It is thus that we may follow the ideal path from linguistics to semiotics, and from semiotics to history.

Along these lines, we have shown elsewhere that of all the means by which lyric introduced discourse, the emergent prose of the thirteenth century retained only one: the anteposed and strongly articulated se-quence.[6] The primacy thus accorded to prolepsis animates a linguistic formation whose rigor and regularity are sometimes astounding. Such a grammar of discourse seems consistent, on the one hand, with the stylistic characteristics of prose already mentioned and contributes to this mode of writing; it reveals, on the other hand, elements that determine the genesis of such a form.

A new method for representing discourse, at once authoritative and dogmatic, makes its appearance at the beginning of the thirteenth century. This new status of discourse within the literary text—a status we may call "prose"—arises and develops in narratives that, borrowing the vehicle (*voie*) and voice (*voix*) of the sacred, narrate along with the history of the grail, the Gospel of Revelation and its exegesis. It is hardly without signifi-cance that such *summae* of revealed knowledge should be attributed to that minority of the clergy (Cistercian monks) who encountered serious rivalry, at the beginning of the thirteenth century, both from the mendi-cant orders, on the spiritual level, and from the University, on the practical level of the dissemination of legitimate knowledge.

Mime is the second aspect of this new representation of discourse.

6. Bernard Cerquiglini, *La Parole médiévale* (Paris: Minuit, 1981), 17–123.

Enunciations bearing discourse markers are attributed to the fictional speaker. These markers do not refer to a locutionary truth, but to a literary code that, as such, has its own laws, forms and figures. Medieval discourse may be said to be less represented than figured. And this figuration is one of the major and most risky tasks of literature in the Middle Ages, for two principal reasons.

First, discourse in medieval society is the guarantor, the memory, and the everyday hub of social relations; the text, this hum of humanity, only recently launched on the path of the written, must provide the image of this discourse. The second reason also relates to the youth of this literature, engaged in inventing its models and establishing the canons of its writing: it learns, by groping its way, to make discourse heard and understood. This explains the experimental and formulaic character of discourse that narrative often pushes towards bombast. This figured utterance, solemn, conventional even in its violence, is the magnified echo of the muffled hum of human relations.

We can thus see that medieval mimesis of discourse serves to link language forms, esthetic practice, and collective representations. This all-encompassing activity which constructs discourse and makes it heard and understood is, in reality, that ancient and venerable discipline: rhetoric.

By evoking the old rhetorical machinery of Aristotle, which we know to work so well with medieval texts, we wanted to summarize our thoughts.[7] The meaning of discourse lies in the modalities of its representation. This mastery lays bare its supporting elements, and signifies more by the marks of its domination than by that for which it seeks to be a surrogate. In an important way, it's a kind of grammatical "wiretap" tuned to the plots and strands of fictional discourse which it knows how to sort out and make sense of.

We now have a methodology, an analytical system, replete with a safeguard, which can enable us to study, without being seduced or resorting to reductionism, the exact forms that the medieval work gives to its culturally specific discourses. By way of advancing the hypothesis that ideological configurations are at issue, and apparently bound up with certain segments of language, let us take the example of feminine discourse.

This literature reflects the thousand facets of the dominant culture, which is obviously masculine. For a woman to take up writing at the end of the Middle Ages, prior to the example of Christine de Pisan, would have little import other than the obvious audacity of the act. The moral and

---

7. We can thus enumerate the tropes, such as anadiplosis, used to signify discourse. The scholarly tradition for studying proper "discursive figures" may be seen in the thesis of A. Hilka, *Die direkte Rede als Kunstmittel in den Romanen des Kristian von Troyes* (Halle: Niemeyer Verlag, 1903).

political concepts expressed by Marie de France, for example, hardly differ from those of her contemporary, Chrétien de Troyes; and only the ruffling of courtly language by certain of the women troubadours (*trobairitz*) betrays the violence of an otherwise inaudible desire. The fact that women in love and mothers speak freely in Old French texts does not mean that they voice the discordant demands of an alienated individuality: male authors control their speech. We cannot fail to take an interest in such discourses, however. The strongly marked mimesis that conveys this speech portrays with broad strokes a female image which the dominant masculine community finds comforting and reassuring. It allows these audible forms of feminine discourse to be heard, or more precisely it allows us to hear the code and the signs by which we may recognize this sheltered alterity. We should hardly be surprised to encounter, among such markers, the major sign of medieval discourse, the adverb *mar*, of which certain uses are so directly mingled with the feminine voice as to constitute a genuine figure for this evocation.

It behooves us, as already observed, to take syntax as our guide, since it leads directly into the subject. The syntactic richness of the Old French adverb *mar* is such that an exhaustive description calls into question many aspects of Old French.[8] We will mention here only those of importance for the analysis to follow.

1. *Mar*, above all, is the remnant of a complex enunciatory process. It expresses a discordant mode in conjunction with a predicative pairing, within the framework of a discourse couplet. For example, this couplet from the *Chanson de Roland:*

E_1: Felun paien mar i vindrent as porz
E_2: Jo vos plevis, tuz sunt jugez a mort. [Vv. 1057–58]

[The wretched pagans shall rue the day they came to the pass,
I swear to you, all are condemned to death.]

Mar, in the middle of E_1, attributes a discordant signification to the predictive pairing (*Felun paien . . . vindrent as porz*) of the variety, "contrary to what I, the speaker, rightly suppose to be the intentions of the subject(s)." The discourse predication of E_2—such statements frequently underline causal relationships—simultaneously justifies and delineates this discordant mode. To be exact, the subject is taken to have attributed to its actions a minimal implication: either that this action will have some effect (an implied operational value), or, at the very least, that it will not be prejudicial to the subject (an implied nondetrimental value). *Mar* then

8. Cerquiglini, *La Parole médiévale*, 128ff.

enunciates an inoperative discordance, e.g., "in vain," or, more frequently, a discordance of detrimentality: "to one's harm or misfortune."

Let's stop here. The connotation of inoperance ("in vain," "for nothing," "a total waste") is so minimal (*minoritaire*) in the texts (and apparently so badly linked to the notion of detriment), that editors and philologists had the greatest of difficulty in isolating it; and they did not explain it.[9] It signifies, as we have said, that the subject was wrong in thinking (first discordance connoted by *mar*) that the predicate (an action undertaken by him or an attribute associated with him) would have some effect.

Now, if one looks closely at the corpus of incontrovertible attestations of inoperance, one will see that the subject, most frequently, is feminine, and the predicate, in such cases, is formed with *être*, an existential qualification. It is thus about a woman that one says that something in her being exists as total waste, thereby presupposing, without any justification beyond ideological evidence, the ends of that existence.

Thus the physical beauty with which a man may be endowed is not supposed to help him. Only once does such a predicate constructed with *mar* signify that, contrary to expectation, the beauty of a knight is useless to him, and in this case, we note that he is also not endowed with that foremost of masculine attributes, courage:

> Car moult a poi el cors vertu,
> Sa grans beauté tant mar i fu. [*Partenopeus de Blois*, v. 5458]

> Since he has so little courage in his being,
> his great beauty is good for nothing.

Ordinarily, it is a woman's beauty that one evokes, but not as an autonomous qualifying value. The frequency of the predicate "beauty" in a *mar* proposition attributed to a woman reveals a definite semantic configuration in which the enunciated discordance presupposes that this beauty cannot be vain. We see here an ideological complicity sought by the speaker and shared through the fiction by the author and his public. Feminine beauty must be useful, serving, first of all, the greater glory of God. So for example, the oxymoronic theme of the "belle paienne" ["beautiful pagan woman"] that may be set against the example just quoted:

> Tant mar fui la seue grant beauté,
> Quant Deu ne croit et la seue bonté! [*La Prise d'Orange*, AB, 258]

> What a waste of so beautiful a woman,
> Since she does not believe in God and his goodness.

9. See my study, "Le Romanisme dans sa pratique," ed. A. M. Dessaux-Berthonneau, *Théories linguistigues et traditions grammaticales* (Lille: Presse Universitaire de Lille, 1980), 55–88.

But the feminine body is above all given over to the service of man, intended to respond to his desire, masked or not by courtly language. Thus the following difficult passage. The king, who has dined as a guest of his seneschal, finds himself dreaming of the seneschal's wife; he is somewhat troubled and tries to justify his guilty desire:

> Si bele dame tant mar fust,
> S'ele n'amast e dru n'eust! [Marie de France, *Equitan*, vv. 83–84]

> What a waste of so beautiful a woman,
> If she's not in love and has no lover!

We must understand this to mean: "Contrary to what she may think, it would be a waste for this woman to be as beautiful as she is if she were not in love and had no lover." This enthymeme absolves the royal desire, which pretends to reestablish the harmony of the courtly world where the female body is defined and realized by masculine lust.

Women also serve to perpetuate lineage and the values associated with it.[10] In the following instance, Félice expresses her surprise that Gui, a vassal of her father's, should declare his love for her:

> Se ore amasse un garçun
> Que mis hom est e estre dreit,
> Ma belté tant mar serreit.
> [*Gui de Warewic*, mss. FHMC, vv. 350–52]

> If now I love a young man
> Who is and must be my man,
> My beauty would be vain.

"My beauty would be labor lost." Lover and mother, such are the operative connotations of women, so obviously that they supply the great majority of the uses of *mar* signifying "in vain." The first attestation of our adverb in Old French provides the archetype of an extensive paradigm of female laments over a dead son, laments by beings suddenly empty and without purpose, wretched things no longer of use to anyone:

> Sempres regrete: "Mar te portai, bels fils! . . . "
> [*La vie de Saint Alexis* v. 437.]

> She mourns incessantly: "What a waste that I bore you, my handsome son!" . . .

2. The syntactic construction semanticized by ideological recurrence can assume the value of a commonplace. A second figure based upon the

---

10. From here on, we will give examples of feminine discourse properly speaking, i.e., first-person discourse spoken by a woman. The ideological configurations that we have begun to elucidate here represent only the articulation of subordinated discourse.

second, detrimental connotation of *mar* structures feminine discourse. To understand it, we have to backtrack slightly. The predicate to which *mar* imparts a discordant connotation, and which will thus be detrimental to its subject, in contrast to his or her expectation, may be reduced to an existential predicate. In this event, one conveys the idea that the very fact of existing is fatal and pernicious; an urgently dramatic perception generally expressed, for obvious reasons, in the first person.

And yet we never encounter, except in a corrupt reading proposed by Francisque Michel, *mar sui* ["What a waste I am (= my life is)."] For an unexpectedly rigorous aspectual constraint comes into play that requires the predicate to be expressed in the aorist tense, thereby marking a rupture between the speaker and the predicative statement (the whole operation is of a thetic order). The aoristic valence will generally be conveyed by the simple past, giving *mar fui* ["What a waste I was (= my life has been)."] The sense of misfortune is nonetheless immediate, current, as either the narrative clearly shows, or, on the level of language, certain parasynonymic pairings:

> "Las, fait il, hé las, com je sui
> Maraurox et com mar fui." [*La Folie Tristan* de Berne, vv. 64–65]

> "Alas," he says, "alas, how I am
> Unfortunate; what a waste my life has been!"

Clearly, *mar fui* expresses an almost biological sense of misfortune. What might be taken as on the order of a scream, of existence radically endangered, the decompensation of the subject in its very nakedness, is uttered by a *mar fui* [*mar* + *je* + *être* + aorist tense] which focuses the constraints. This obligatory discourse pairing contains the seeds of a commonplace by which extreme misfortune may be conventionally expressed.

If one examines the distribution of such a commonplace in the discourses found in a medieval work, one quickly becomes convinced of its very strong formulaic vocation. *Mar fui* is the very essence of the feminine utterance: preceded by *lasse* or *dolente*, in conjunction with an intensifier, it initiates her discourse. She assigns it to the register of the lament, a privileged speech-act for the female voice; its signature, in fact, by which it may be heard and identified. One thinks of the famous lament of Enide:

> "Lasse, fet ele, con mar fui!"
> [Chrétien de Troyes, *Erec et Enide*, v. 2492]

> "Alas," she says, "how miserable I am!"

Examples abound; under the masculine gaze, heroines go through medieval texts incessantly crying out: *"com mar fui!"* The haunting grandeur of the few words spoken by Aude as she dies on learning of the death of her fiancé, Roland, undoubtedly spring from the fact that they avoid this formula. On the other hand, some lines eariler, Bramimonde has cried out on cue:

> Si li ad dit: "Dolente, si mar fui!
> A itel hunte, sire, mon seignur ai perdut!"
> [*La Chanson de Roland*, v. 2823]

She says to him: "Wretched, how miserable I am!
I have lost my lord, sire, so disgracefully!"

This lyrical figure of female discourse is pure lament. It is a predication of existence, and the minimum presupposition of nondetrimentality that one may associate with it—to live should not be, at the very least, harmful to life—which the *mar* clause calls into question. That such a construction should be one of the signs of feminine discourse is revealing. In masculine discourse, for example, the detrimental sense of *mar* is conveyed with a wide variety of action verbs, mainly verbs of motion. In this way, it complies a list of the risk-specific acts through which the virile ideology manifests itself. But what kinds of acts are left for the woman besides pleasing and reproducing, acting for another, and being?[11] The consequence is an astounding solitude for women, reduced to an endlessly imperiled existence, by the very topos that symbolizes her painful speech.

3. The expression of the existential predicate in the aorist tense often takes another form. To understand fully the success of this type, we need to understand how it works. The past participle or the past anterior of the verb *naître* connotes existence in Old French. In its nominal form, *nus nez, rien née*, it frequently means "living person"; in its verbal form, a compound tense of *naître* [to be born] is the equivalent of a simple form of the verb *être* [to be.] To be born is thus to be. Consequently, we have no difficulty understanding the use the constructions based on *mar* make of this equivalence. The past anterior, *mar fui né(e)*, is a compound aorist connoting a situation at once distinct from that of the enunciation and completed. This turn of phrase succeeds, then, in expressing the predicate of existence as a form of accomplishment; whence its success with *mar*. It's the crowning triumph of the aoristic.

We seriously doubt that the expression *mar fui né(e)* refers to a fatal birth or destiny, the sense translations usually accord to it. It's really a question of syntax. Comparing a large number of these expressions, one finds that the lamented misfortune is not linked to an old problem, either

---

11. When the woman brings about the man's misfortune, it is less by a voluntary act than by her presence itself which has aroused an unfortunate love. To this fact may be ascribed the masculine lyric commonplace, *mar vous vi* [For my undoing I saw you]. When a female utters the same lament, it becomes, significantly, passive: "Lasse, dist ele, mar fui oncques veue!" (*Ami et Amile*, v. 1522). ["Alas," she says, "what misfortune that I was ever seen!"]

congenital or permanent, but to something in the immediate present. That's what proposition E_2 expressly states when, in feminine discourse, the misfortune consists of rape or incest:

> E_1: Je suis cele qui mar fui née
> E_2: Quant del tot sui a mort livrée.
> [*Partenopeus de Blois*, vv. 4753–54]

> I am the one whom fate strikes down
> Since I am irrevocably condemned to die.

> E_1: "Lasse, dist ele, mar fui née,
> E_2: Quant je suis or a ce menée
> Que mes peres m'espouse . . . "
> [Philippe de Beaumanoir, *Manekine*, vv. 595–97]

> "Unfortunate wretch, she says, miserable life,
> To be forced to become my father's wife.

Once again, the syntactic structure bears the germ of a commonplace, if only the recurrent ideology in the form of the dominant (male) perspective of feminine discourse fully semantizes the construction. According to the principle of this construction, the verb *naître* is semantically transparent, or at least it signifies only one aspect of the existential predicate. It carries with it, however, the idea of a natural vocation for misfortune, and reinforces perfectly the image of an anguished solitude constituting feminine existence.[12] As we see in this famous lament which inspired Guillaume Apollinaire:

> "Laise, fait Oriour, com mar fui née!
> J'ai laxiet ma serour an la vallée . . . "
> [Bartsch, *Altfranzosische Romanzen und Pastourellen*, I,5, vv. 21–22]

> "Unfortunate wretch," says Oriour, miserable life!
> I left my sister in the valley . . . "

Lasse, com mar fui (née), a stereotyped formula, a lyrical inflection of the voice, a painful exclamation—at the heart of the literary code, it becomes the very mark of feminine discourse, as the following scribal error confirms. In the *Chanson de Guillaume*, the fierce, but unorthodox Rainouart exclaims, according to the standard edition:[13]

---

12. As may be seen in such a legitimate variation as: "Ha! fet elle, lasse, dolente, / Mar fui oncques *de mere* née, / Quant a tel honte sui livrée. . ." / (Jehan Maillart, *Roman du comte d'Anjou*, vv. 718–20). ["Ah!" she says, "miserable, wretched, / To be born of a mother only / To be delivered into such shame!"]

13. We should note in passing that Rainouart, a burlesque character, is also socially *displaced*.

"Allas, dolent, cum mar fui unques nez!"
[*La Chanson de Guillaume*, v. 3355]

"Alas, wretched, that ever I was born!"

But the manuscript gives a different lesson:

Allas dolent cum mar fui unques ne*e*

This suggests possibilities for parody. Trubert, a gross and obscene character, disguises himself in woman's clothing; mistaken for a young girl, he is abducted and cries out:

"Lasse, dit, com mar onques fui!
Ou m'en porte on? Que devenrai?"
[Douin de Lavesne, *Trubert*, vv. 2332–33]

"Unfortunate wretch," [he] says, "miserable that ever I was!
Where am I being taken? What will become of me?"

Trubert expresses himself precisely in the expected literary formula for feminine distress, thereby reinforcing his disguise. A paradigmatic situation in which a man expresses what feminine discourse, wholly in the power of men, ought to express. A tricky situation in many ways of identification with the dominated sex and which secretly manipulates the text.

Let us once again be guided by the syntax. The exclamation quoted above: "Lasse, dit, com mar unques fui!" contains two anomalies. The first is the unusual position of the adverb *onques*, unusual because *mar* can only be separated from the verb by a conjoined pronoun. The second was noted by T. Franzen in his study on the pronoun subject: we have here one of the very rare cases of an interpolated clause constituted solely by the verb *dire* without a pronoun.[14] Now, precisely who is speaking here? Trubert, made up as a young girl. From this point on, when he speaks, should one say he (*il*) or she (*elle*)? The first time the text has the "young woman" speak, it does not commit itself, using instead a prolepsis whose subject is the name of the hero:

Estrubert respont maintenant,
A basse voiz, tout simplement:
"Par foi, sire, il s'en est alez. . . ." [*Trubert*, vv. 2307–09]

Estrubert answers now,
   With a low voice, quite simply:
   By my faith, sire, he has gone his way."

14. "These examples are so rare that one is forced to doubt their authenticity." T. Franzen, *Etude sur la syntaxe des pronoms personnels sujets en ancien français* (Uppsala: Almqvist, 1939), 116.

The second time, there's no prolepsis, hence the use of the interpolated clause:

> Trubert ne laissierent il mie,
> Portent l'en a grant seignorie,
> Un des chevaliers devant lui.
> "Lasse, *dit*, com mar oncques fui! . . . [*Trubert*, vv. 2329–32]

> They would not let Trubert alone,
> They convey him with great pomp,
> One of the knights going before him.
> "Unfortunate wretch," says, "miserable that ever I was!"

The pronoun is avoided, while the speaker is obviously feminine: all the elements of the formulaic feminine lament appear, *mar fui* and *lasse*, and the morphology of the adjective is clearly feminine.[15] In fact, the text is quite subtle, for the adverb *onques*, interpolated in defiance of the syntax, and acting as a sign of the manipulation, has two syllables, exactly like the medieval pronoun *ele*, but unlike *il*. So one may conclude that this adverb functions as an ostensible mask, concealing the feminine pronoun: "Lasse, dit *ele*, com mar fui!" [Unfortunate wretch, *she* says, miserable life!] Both the syntax (of *mar*, and of the interpolated clause) and the formulaic feminine lament proclaim this a canonical expression. But it is one that the text, prevented by the values it must uphold and which deprecate the total sexual inversion of its masculine hero, cannot express.

We have focused on a narrowly circumscribed area: the expression of the feminine lament in medieval texts—where women *do* seem to weep a good deal. We have also chosen a particular viewpoint that privileges syntactic formalization. We needed to show, from a general perspective, how syntax, in handling dense ideological material, can create a commonplace that disseminates and authorizes dominant cultural values. This close contact between language and cultural expression, and which constitutes the phenomenon of evocation, as we understand it, seemed fruitful for the study of *mentalités*. It should doubtless prove equally so for the analysis of language itself.

Let us conclude on this point. The adverb *mar* disappears from the French language in the course of the fourteenth century. One may certainly cite internal linguistic reasons for this disappearance (e.g., competition with *mal*, with negation, etc.), and the linguist is at home here. To leave it at that, however, would be to overlook the formulaic vocation of our adverb. Analysis of a prose romance of the fourteenth century reveals

---

15. Moreover, the listener may still hear echoes of this feminine lament uttered sometime previously: "Deus, dit ele, com mar fui née!" (*Trubert*, v. 369). ["My God," she says, "miserable life!"]

feminine discourses which, a century earlier, would certainly have begun with *mar fui (née)*. The context is the same, and certain signs remain in place, as well as the dual structure in paired utterances (E_1 and E_2). And we recognize a certain rhythm [*musique*]:

> "Hemy! lasse, comme je sui perdue et mal baillie,
> quant mon corps fu onques livrez a vous! . . .
> [*Roman de Berinus*, para. 32]

> "Ah me! Unfortunate wretch, how lost and mistreated I am, since my body has been given over to you! . . .

The melody, however, has become much fuller. The austere speech-act of the twelfth and thirteenth centuries is paraphrased quite accurately, but at greater length:

> "Lasse, que pourray je devenir quant par mon occasion est mon seigneur occiz et livré a mort? Hemy! comme je suis meschante, quand ce que je cuidoie fere pour bien m'est tourné a si grant contraire. . . ."
> [*Roman de Berinus*, Mss. BCF, para. 505]

> "Unfortunate wretch, what will become of me when on my account my lord has been killed and delivered up to death? Alas! how wicked I am when what I intended to do for good has turned out so much the opposite. . . ."

This painful lament takes time to provide an exact definition of the notion of the discordance of detrimentality: "What I imagined doing in a beneficial way has proved prejudicial to me." It paraphrases, sorts out constraints, expresses them. The old lament adopts the rhythm of the era, feminine misery expresses and explains itself. It loads itself with words, entering of its own accord, significantly enough, a new verbal register:

> "Lasse, fait elle, que j'ay mal esploitié quant celui a qui j'ay tout mon cuer donné ay mis en peril de mort recevoir!" [*Roman de Berinus*, para. 188]

> "Unfortunate wretch," she says, how badly I have acted in jeopardizing the life of him to whom I have given my whole heart!"

Com mar fui (née) expressed a misfortune that characterized feminine existence; *que j'ay mal esploitié* links a pejorative judgment to a (certainly minimal) action, ascribed to an affective subject. Something has changed in the mastery of feminine discourse, for something has clearly penetrated the forms that constitute it. Language caught in the play of the literary code, even while maintaining its proper historicity (paraphrase tries, in a way, to protect the old formula), makes of itself a sounding board for ideological change. Let feminine discourse assume another inflexion, and the old adverb, *mar*, has had its day.

If such be the case, this procession of weeping heroines must be honored. They remind us that the arid diachrony of linguistic change is not unrelated to the history of human societies.

Translated by Cynthia Hoffman,
David Pelizzari,
and Stephen G. Nichols

SUZANNE FLEISCHMAN

Evaluation in Narrative: The Present Tense in Medieval "Performed Stories"

INTRODUCTION

> Li quens Bougars de Valence *oï* dire c'on penderoit
> Aucassin son anemi, si venoit cele part;
> et Aucassins ne le *mescoisi* mie:
> il *tint* l'espee en la main, se le **fiert** par mi le hiaume
> si qu'i li **enbare** el cief. Il *fu* si estonés
> qu'il *caï* a terre; et Aucassins **tent** le main,
> si le **prent** et l'en **mainne** pris par le nasel del hiame
> et le **rent** a son pere.

Count Bougar of Valence *heard* / that they would hang Aucassin his enemy / if he came their way. / And Aucassin *did not fail to spot* him:/ He *took* his sword in hand,/ **strikes** through his helmet,/ and **bashes** him in the head./ He [Bougar] *was* so stunned / that he *fell* to the ground./ And Aucassin **takes** his hand,/**holds** it,/ and **leads** him off / by the nose piece of his helmet,/ and **surrenders** him to his [A's] father.

Among the notable linguistic features of this passage from the thirteenth-century *Aucassin et Nicolette* is a seemingly gratuitous alternation of past and present verb forms.[1] "Confusion des temps"—as this alternation has

---

1. The laisse where this passage occurs is given in the Appendix as Text 1. The four texts of the Appendix will be abbreviated, respectively, *Aucassin*, Villehardouin, Weinrich, and Schiffrin. All translations are my own, except where otherwise indicated. The following typographic conventions are observed throughout: *italics* for *past tense* (preterit, or, in French, *passé simple*) verbs (including subjunctive forms and anterior pasts which function as simple preterits); **bold** for **Narrative Presents** (presents referring to past events); SMALL CAPITALS for SPEECH-EVENT PRESENTS (*présents de la parole*); and *ITALICIZED SMALL CAPITALS* for *GENERAL PRESENTS*, unmarked for time. These categories will be defined more precisely in our discussion. The present perfect, a verb form infrequent in narrative (cf. Labov & Waletzky 1967: 29), will be highlighted only where relevant; its typographic representation PRES. AUX + *p.ptc.* (I'VE *seen*, J'AI *vu*) reflects its constituent morphological structure, which in turn

199

come to be known in the French tradition,[2] turns out to be a widespread phenomenon in the early Romance literatures. The sheer abundance of studies—stylistic, literary, philological—devoted over the years to this phenomenon only points to the absence of a definitive explanation.[3] In view of this volume of scholarship, one might wonder whether anything more could be said on the issue that is not simply 'old wine' in new, more fashionable terminology. I believe there is. The approach taken here involves a radical shift in the premises and direction of inquiry, away from exclusive enclosure within the problematics of medieval textuality—or literary textuality in general—to a domain of modern linguistics which has of late drawn considerable attention: the analysis of everyday conversational storytelling—what has been referred to as "natural narrative"—, as developed in the tradition of American sociolinguistics associated with William Labov.

The intrusion of present-tense verbs into conversational narrations of past experience has long been recognized, occurring as it does in a broad spectrum of languages. But only recently have the mechanics of this tense switching phenomenon (henceforth TS) been studied in any rigorous way, notably by investigators into the structure and organizational strategies of natural narrative, whose research has focused almost exclusively on con-

---

reflects formally its connection to the moment of speech. Imperfective pasts are not marked, nor are verbs in direct speech, for reasons which will become apparent. The texts are arranged with one clause per line of transcript. Where a clause exceeds a single line, the remaining lines of that clause are indented. Clauses preceded by a letter represent narrative events (defined below) in the complicating action. The letter indicates only the clause on that line, except in the case of *verba dicendi* followed by direct quotes, which together constitute single units of complicating action, but which often overrun a single line of transcript. Clauses of 'embedded material' (e.g. evaluation embedded into complicating action) are enclosed in square brackets. In the translations, parentheses are used for material not contained in the original texts and inserted to facilitate the translation.

2. The term has become an umbrella for sundry departures from expected tense usage. In addition to switches between P(ast) and PR(esent), it has been used to refer to "irregular" usage within the past system, notably involving *P(assé) S(imple)* and P(assé) C(omposé). This latter issue falls outside the purview of the present investigation, and is of interest here only obliquely, to the extent that the meaning of every tense-aspect form is relative to those of all other forms in the system. As used here, "PS" and "PC" are *formal* labels referring exclusively to morphological structure; "preterit" and "(present) perfect" are tense-aspect *functions.*

3. Considering just medieval French, the phenomenon has been discussed most often with respect to the epic: cf. Sandmann 1957, 1960, Blanc 1964, Paden 1977; on *Roland* specifically: Hatcher 1942, Blanc 1965, Ruelle 1976; on hagiographic/religious literature: Uitti 1973: 50f, (*Alexis*) Perry 1981: 54ff. (*Passion des Jongleurs*); historical narrative: Dembowski 1963: 48–56 (Robert de Clari), Beer 1968: 54ff (Villehardouin); the lais of Marie de France: Worthington 1966; verse and prose romances: Sutherland 1939, Fotitch 1950 (Chrétien), Blanc 1961, Ollier 1978; *Aucassin et Nicolette*: Foulet 1919, 1920, Schøsler 1973, Stewart 1977. Across genres: Buffin 1925, Blanc 1964, Paden 1977. This list is not exhaustive.

temporary American English.[4] Texts 3 and 4 in the Appendix are conversational narratives recounted by speakers of French and English respectively. While investigators of TS in informal storytelling are not fully in agreement on the function of present tense in narrative diegesis—a state of affairs not unlike that prevailing among medieval Romanists who have grappled with the issue—, the alternation patterns they describe sufficiently parallel those observed in early Romance to warrant reexamining the medieval material in light of their findings, notwithstanding obvious cultural, formal, and sociolinguistic differences between the two types of discourse, to be discussed below.

The goal of my research, of which this article reports on one aspect as documented in older Gallo-Romance, is a reevaluation of this longstanding problem in Romance philology from the perspectives of current work in several intersecting areas of text analysis: (1) pragmatics, specifically the situational pragmatics of performed narrative, (2) discourse analysis, (3) the structure and organization of improvisational or 'natural' narrative; as well as (4) research into performance literature as a textual genre with its own *sui generis* conventions.[5] The results of recent explorations in these areas may open new perspectives on what has long been viewed as an aberrant linguistic feature of medieval vernacular literature.

BACKGROUND OF THE QUESTION

It is not my intention to retrace the peripatetics of critical discussion on tense mixture in early Romance, only to indicate major directions of inquiry. Philologists have tended to account for TS as a characteristic mark of archaizing *literary* styles. Thus Foulet (1920) ascribed the alternation to a consciously *poetic* discourse whose syntax, he observed, differed from that of prose.[6] Along similar lines, it was observed early on that the specifically narrative (diegetic) portions of OFr. texts seemed to show a "freer" use of

4. The foundation of much of this research is laid in Labov 1972 and Labov and Waletzky 1967. Specific issues of tense-aspect and narrative temporality are addressed in Wolfson 1978, 1979, 1982, Schiffrin 1981, Tannen 1982a, and Silva-Corvalán 1983—the last dealing with modern Spanish.

5. A useful introduction to this last area of inquiry, spanning linguistics, anthropology, and literary theory, is the collection of essays *Verbal Art as Performance* (Bauman 1978).

6. Foulet was conceivably the first to posit a double stylistic tradition for medieval French: a "poetic style" for verse narrative in contrast to a "literary style" for prose and drama, the latter ostensibly providing a window onto the spoken language. This notion of two grammars has been taken up by a number of subsequent investigators, most recently by Bernard Cerquiglini (1981) in a study on the representation of direct speech in twelfth-century verse romances and later prosifications. Regrettably, for our purpose, Cerquiglini does not broach the question of TS, nor comment on differences in tense usage between the two varieties of romance discourse.

tenses than did direct speech passages. Manfred Sandmann is credited with the observation that "idiosyncratic" tense usage occurs exclusively in diegesis and never in direct speech. From this he proceeded to argue that the tense usage of dialogue must be taken as a faithful reflection of the spoken language,[7] while the "aberrant" tense patterns of narrative proper, he consigned—like others before and after him—to an archaic, literary style,[8] suggesting further a probable connection to musical recitation, given that most of the genres in which TS occurs are known to have been recited or chanted, presumably with some musical accompaniment.[9]

Investigators with a more literary bias have constructed a variety of esthetic-stylistic or symbolic-ideological hypotheses to account for the medieval variation of tenses: "Temporal connections often seem confused and the choice of tenses illogical, precisely because profane time is intimately linked with sacred time" (Grunmann-Gaudet 1980: 95); "the symbolic aspect of events is underlined by the historical present which divests them of their temporal contingencies" (id., 90). In one of the most nuanced of such analyses—which anticipates in a tentative way the direction taken here—Anna Granville Hatcher (1942) likens the narrator's movements within the verbal system to the movements of a video camera: shifting into PR to cover action in the foreground, then back to P as actors and events emerge from or recede into the background.

7. Foulet, somewhat earlier (1920: 283), had expressed a similar view, if less categorically: "It is in dialogue represented in its original form, whether real or constructed, that we are most likely to encounter the popular usage of the time." Interestingly, Lakoff and Tannen point out that the constructed dialogue of fiction, drama, or film generally strikes readers as more "real" than transcripts of actual conversations, which are filled with disconcerting disjunctions, false starts, repair mechanisms, etc. (cited in Tannen 1982a: 13). While novelists and playwrights often use PR to "lend realism" to their dialogue, we cannot assume that their use of this technique *as authors* is the same as if they were spontaneously recounting a narrative in an informal setting (Wolfson 1982: 8). Thus Beer (1968: 91f.) notes that Villehardouin's potential for "literary contrivance" is more visible in his direct speech passages than in diegetic text, though one wonders on what empirical evidence this judgement can be based.

8. Bauman (1978:18) notes that people often attribute archaism to the special language of verbal art—a natural consequence of the traditionality and esotericism of many performance systems.

9. Sandmann 1953: 267, 1968: 573, 1973 [=1957]: 171f. Cf. also Sutherland 1939: 331, Ruelle 1976: 792. This hint at a connection between TS and performance finds support in Rupert Pickens's statistically based observation that texts with a high density of primary-sequence tenses (mainly presents) in diegesis are in general associated with the French oral traditions (1979: 173). With quite another purpose in mind, Pickens looks at tense usage in a generically heterogeneous corpus of OFr. narratives. Specifically, he calculates relative proportions of "diegetic," "mimetic," and "commentative" discourse, and, within diegesis, the ratio of present (=primary-sequence) to historical (=secondary-sequence) tenses. The emerging tense profiles are presumed to correlate with the degree of historicity of a text and the emergence of a historical consciousness in the narrator. Regrettably, the validity of Pickens's analysis is vitiated by a (not-uncommon) failure to discriminate among different *functions* of particular verb *forms*. See Beck forthcoming.

As is evident from this limited selection of viewpoints, the tendency has been to view TS as variation that was essentially ungrammatical and tolerated for *esthetic* ("the vicarious present must have produced an effect of stylistic elegance signalling the ritual dignity of art," Paden 1977: 557), or other, often linguistically questionable, reasons ("in order to avoid the monotony of a single temporal tonality," Ollier 1978: 102),—in short, as a rhetorical device associated with the stylized poetic language of older genres. And the explanation offered for it is usually that traditionally put forth also to explain the Historical Present (HP) found in narrative writing of many languages, namely that the use of present tense is a technique for reporting events that are vivid and exciting, or for enhancing the dramatic effect of a story by making the audience feel as if they were present at the time of the experience, witnessing events as they occurred. Various grammarians have suggested that the narrator becomes so involved in the story that he recounts the action as if it were being relived, simultaneous with its retelling. He experiences events subjectively rather than viewing them objectively distanced in the past. Such descriptions all assume that the HP renders the past more vivid by shifting events out of their original time frame and into that of the act of narration.[10] Past events "come alive" with HP because it is formally equivalent to a tense whose reference time is not that of *énoncé* but of *énonciation*.[11]

I must acknowledge from the outset that it is not my intent to demolish this consecrated view, but rather to refine it in what I believe to be significant ways. In particular, one would like to be able to identify the specific textual environments in which PRs occur—they do not occur randomly—and to explain why they occur where they do. To say simply

10. Underlying this interpretation is a particular view of the relationship between man and objects in his (spatial) environment, and, by extension, between a speaker and events in time, which has been referred to as the "moving-world" or "moving-event" perspective. According to this view, it is man that remains the fixed deictic center, while objects/events move toward or away from him. The opposite perspective, "moving-ego," sees time/objects as the fixed parameter which man moves to encounter. Ultimately, both systems alternate in our use of spatial metaphors for expressions of temporality (see Fleischman 1982b).

11. For a terminologically updated version of the traditional argument, see Ollier 1978. The question has been debated whether these temporally displaced PRs constitute true present tenses. Advocates of the "past more vivid" view in general assume that they do. However, it has been variously argued (e.g. Paden 1977 and Wolfson 1982, following Kiparsky 1968) that these are really "neutral" or achronistic tenses, whose (past) time reference is established by other elements in the sentence or larger discourse. Kiparsky's interpretation of the Indo-European HP as an underlying P, converted to a surface PR by a syntactic rule, appears to be but a reformulation, within a paradigm of generative grammar, of the view put forth over a century ago by Brugmann that the ability of HP to refer to past events derives from the *timeless* character of the present tense, which can therefore be used to refer to events not only contemporaneous with the speaker's present but also past and future with respect thereto (for details see Emery 1897: 3ff.). According to this view, the narrator does not draw events forward into his own temporal sphere (moving-event), but rather displaces himself back in time to the scenario of narrated events (moving-ego).

that they function to highlight the "most dramatic" events of a story would seem to suggest that past experience offers itself to us 'prepackaged' in narrative episodes and events, some of which are inherently more salient than others, and that the narrator's task is to render as accurate a verbal account of these as possible. The fallacy of this 'bias of objectivity' (endemic particularly among historians, cf. White 1980) is aptly articulated in Walter Ong's essay "Oral Remembering and Narrative Structures":

> Reality never occurs in narrative form. The totality of what happened to and in and around me since I got up this morning is not organized as narrative, and as a totality cannot be expressed as narrative. To make a narrative, I have to isolate certain elements out of the unbroken seamless web of history with a view fitting them into a particular construct which I have more or less consciously in mind. [Ong 1981: 12]

To make a narrative, then, is to structure experience *from the viewpoint of a speaker/writer,* no two of which will organize that experience nor evaluate its component elements in precisely the same way.[12] As we shall see, what transforms a straight chronicle of events into a narrative is, in part, *evaluation.* It distinguishes, for example, the type of historical record characteristic of medieval annals from a truly *narrative* (hi)story of the type found in certain chronicles (Villehardouin, Robert de Clari), and most transparently in the 'popular' historiographic genre of the epic.[13] We will return to this notion of narrative evaluation, which provides one of the cornerstones of our interpretation of the medieval diegetic present.

Much of the work on TS in Romance carries an implicit assumption that the present tense phenomenon of medieval epics, romances, saints' lives, historical narratives, etc., which we shall refer to as the **Narrative Present** or **NP,** is essentially the same animal as the HP of modern novels and historiography. Although there is doubtless an ancestral relationship,[14] the HP of later narrative writing must be recognized as a deliberate *effet de style,*[15] which, with respect to distribution, involves sustained sequences of PR verbs (i.e. no switching), while its medieval counterpart was by all indications a spontaneous phenomenon in which PR alternated with P according to patterns which, if research on natural

12. Obviously this applies more to narratives of personal experience than of vicarious experience.

13. In Fleischman 1983b I discuss the role of evaluation, and of narrativity in general, as parameters for contrasting the 'historical' and the 'fictional' in the Middle Ages.

14. The development of HP from its medieval antecedent lies beyond the scope of this essay. I refer the reader to discussions in Buffin 1925, Sutherland 1939, Blanc 1964, Paden 1977, and Ollier 1978. Most investigators trace the HP ultimately back to a spoken register, cf. Foulet 1920: 280, Buffin 1925: 53, 70f., et passim.

15. According to Buffin (1925: 105f.) the HP only comes into its own in the eighteenth century.

narrative may serve as a guide, can now be described on the basis of linguistically informed criteria rather than impressions and intuitions.

The distinction we are insisting upon here between the HP and the medieval NP points to a basic hermeneutical principle—in this instance a principle of linguistic hermeneutics, although each discipline has its analogue—, which it is appropriate at this juncture to state. The meaning of a tense form—of any linguistic form—is to a large degree context dependent. The category 'present tense' has, in addition to a core meaning (a variable temporal span which must include the moment of speech), a number of peripheral meanings (+past, +future, +temporally unbounded) actualized in different discourse- and situational-pragmatic contexts. Even temporally dislocated presents with a feature of [+past] have no single rhetorical or stylistic value universally valid for all *états de langue*. Their meaning is "a product of the interaction of the form and other factors involved in the communication"—linguistic and extralinguistic (Bull 1960: 82). The 'meaning' of a tense form, i.e. the sum total of its core and contextually actualized values, must therefore derive in part from the pragmatics of the communicative situation, or, in broader terms, from the pragmatics of the genre.[16] For this reason I would insist that the distinctive features of the OFr. NP, specifically those which distinguish it from other varieties of HP, are pragmatic in nature: they emerge from its use in formalized situations of *oral performance*. This point is an important one to which we will return. Wolfson (1979) legitimately criticizes certain investigators of HP for ignoring distinctions of genre. In particular, "a distinction is nowhere made between use of the device in literary as opposed to spoken language" (68). My own probings into the matter, however, suggest that the crucial opposition is not between 'spoken' and 'literary' language[17] (the latter an ambiguous label at best—where does oral literature fit in?), but between narrative actualized in writing and narrative actualized through oral performance. A major focus of our analysis will be to demonstrate parallels between the dislocated present phenomenon of medieval performed narrative and that of everyday conversational stories.

16. This point is cogently argued by Silva-Corvalán (1983) with respect to HP in spoken Mexican Spanish.

17. 'Literature'/'literary' are here understood as defined by Bright (1982: 171) as "that body of discourses or texts which, within any society, are considered worthy of dissemination, transmission, and preservation in essentially constant form." Many oralists however reject the term 'oral literature' because of our traditional association of literature with writing. Several of the papers in *Spoken and Written Language* (Tannen 1982b) make clear that features of discourse traditionally regarded as 'literary' often obtain in spoken discourse, and vice versa. Polanyi in particular cautions: "Literary theorists would do well to examine the devices and problems which they see as defining 'literariness' to make sure that mundane, everyday texts do not exhibit exactly the same features which they would agree separate the literary sheep from the down to earth, everyday goats" (1982: 169).

PERFORMED STORIES

Examination of a substantial corpus of OFr. texts reveals TS to be almost always a mark of oral narratives of the type Nessa Wolfson has labeled PERFORMED STORIES, on grounds that such narratives share a number of defining features with a theatrical presentation: direct speech, asides, repetition, expressive sounds and sound effects, motions and gestures (Wolfson 1978: 216, 1982: 25ff.). Not all, but at least some of these features must be in evidence for a narrative to constitute a 'performed story' and not merely a report of past events. The more fully a story is performed, Wolfson claims, the more likely it is to exhibit TS.[18] Wolfson's research deals with unplanned narratives occurring in contemporary everyday speech; she finds TS to occur only in those narratives in which the speaker "breaks through" into performance.[19]

In the extensive literature on tense usage in older Romance, insufficient account, I feel, has been taken of the performance factor. Not that medievalists have ignored the performance dimension of the texts; but their awareness of it usually does not carry forward into critical analysis. These texts are often dissected as one would modern novels, which are composed, transmitted, and received according to radically different conventions. Ongoing research into oral vs. written strategies in narrative suggests that in oral situations "the meaning is in the context," in literate traditions "the meaning is in the text" (Olson 1977); listeners attend more to what is *meant* and readers to what is *written* (the actual words in the text). Thus to knowingly analyze performance literature as if it were *écriture* is, in a sense, to engage in methodological counterfeiting. Though the present investigation focuses on a single syntactic idiosyncrasy documented in a range of narrative genres, other—to our modern sensibility— disconcerting features of the early texts may also find explanations in the incontrovertible orality of medieval vernacular culture.[20] We are only now

---

18. While such performance features as dialogue, repetition, asides, and expressive sounds can usually be documented from a written text, nonverbal and paralinguistic features (sound effects, intonation, movement, gesture) are harder to identify in the case of performances of which we have only a written transcript. For a thought-provoking analysis of the nonverbal dimensions of narrative performance, see Scheub 1977.

19. On the sociolinguistic and contextual (pragmatic) conditions favoring or inhibiting a "breakthrough into performance," see Hymes 1974, Wolfson 1982: chapter 4. The terms *performance* and *performed story* are to be understood as defined by Wolfson, and not simply as synonymous with oral narration, as, e.g., in Zumthor's characterization of performance: a situation in which the operations of transmission, reception, and, for improvisational texts, also production, are all carried out (aural-)orally (1983: 32f.).

20. Current research is tending more and more to back off from the dichotomous view of 'oral' vs. 'literate' in favor of a continuum. In the *Introduction à la poésie orale* (1983),— which excludes oral literature of the European Middle Ages—Zumthor proposes a four-part typology of oral situations: the purest form, *primary* orality, assumes no intervention of a writing system. The two subsequent stages, *mixed* and secondary orality, both involve the

beginning to recognize the linguistic implications of textual performance and to articulate significant differences between narrative composed by literate writers for a literate readership and narrative composed for performance by accomplished professional storytellers. As Walter Ong notes, "bringing to mind and representing the past is quite different in oral cultures from what it is in cultures such as our own where writing and print, and now electronic processes, have been interiorized so deeply that without great learning, skill, or labor we cannot identify what in our thought processes depends on our appropriation of writing, and what does not" (1981: 13).

The point at issue here is that of the many texts in which TS appears to any meaningful degree, all—or virtually all—conform to the definition of performed stories proposed by Wolfson. Virtually all, since vestiges of the oral switching phenomenon may be found in some later OFr. texts assumed to have been composed in writing for private reading. Blanc (1964: 119) sees this as a "carryover" from epic usage, which I interpret to mean a conscious resuscitation of distinctive markers of the earlier oral style, much like Villon's stylistic use of case markers, long departed from the language, in his "Ballade en vieil langage françoys." Blanc views the thirteenth century as a turning point at which some written (prose) texts still look back to earlier oral epic techniques of composition, while others look forward to "modern" tense relationships. He graphs the relative frequencies of tenses in OFr. texts from ca. 1100 (*Roland*) through the fourteenth century. PR and PC ("primary-sequence" or "discourse" tenses) appear to follow a development in inverse proportion to that of PS and Imperfect ("secondary-sequence" or "historical" tenses). The gradual decline in the use of discourse tenses and concomitant rise in the use of historical tenses produces an X on the graph (100), particularly salient with respect to PR and PS. What this linguistic pattern reflects is a shift from the orally performed texts of the earlier period to the later texts composed in writing, and, to an increasing degree, for a reader. Blanc's analysis (also Pickens

---

coexistence of orality with writing: the secondary variety presupposes a fully literate culture (one in which all experience is marked by the presence of writing), hence the oral text is (re)composed from a written base in a culture in which writing predominates over the voice. In the mixed variety, although the culture is in possession of a writing system, the influence of writing remains external, partial, or for some reason deferred. Lastly Zumthor speaks of *orality diffused by the media*, i.e. mediated by technology, hence subject to displacement in time and space. The OFr. "oral" genres seem to come closest to the mixed variety, though many would argue for tipping the scale toward primary orality in the case of the *chansons de geste*. On the complex issue of defining "literacy" for the Middle Ages, see Baüml (1980), also Brian Stock's monograph (1983) discussing the role of *the text* in the twelfth century in creating a new type of interdependency between orality and writing. The final group of papers in Tannen 1982b explore from various vantages the human as well as linguistic effects of changing oral and literate traditions.

1979, cf. n. 9) is particularly valuable in providing statistical support for our claim that the medieval NP, or more precisely, the P/PR alternation, is a feature of *performance* narration.

In light of our claim that TS is linked to performance, one might wonder at its appearance in chronicles, traditionally viewed as a non-improvised genre composed for private consumption. Yet certain chronistic narratives were obviously designed as "oral persuasion" (Beer 1981: 55), a case in point being Villehardouin, whose oral style has received much attention (see Beer 1968). His account of the Fourth Crusade, "composed in the vernacular by an illiterate" (Beer 1981: 55), was an orally dictated text: "Jouffrois li mareschaus de Champaigne . . . ceste ouvre *dita* . . . " [Geoffrey, marshal of Champagne . . . *dictated* this work] (§120). Also dictated was the crusade narrative of Villehardouin's contemporary Robert de Clari ("qui i fu et qui le vit et qui l'oi le tesmongne . . . et *a fait metre en escrit* le verité" [who was there and who saw it and heard the testimony . . . and had the true account of it committed to writing], 120: 4–6). And these are not isolated cases. Thus while chronistic narrative may well be regarded as a 'literate' genre, literacy need not preclude oral composition and recitation. This is not to deny differences between dictated and fully oral (improvisationally composed) texts, a contrast brought home by Ong's observation on the distances separating traditional oral poets from the blind Milton sitting down to dictate *Paradise Lost*.[21]

TS AND PERFORMANCE NARRATIVE

The connection between TS and techniques of oral narration that forms the cornerstone of our analysis has not passed unnoticed; but neither has it been given the prominence it deserves. A half-century ago Kuen (1934: 493) observed that in Old French the switching phenomenon was characteristic of the older poems which were still sung, but tended to disappear in poems intended for a reader and in prose. Along similar lines Wartburg observed that "Old French narrative frequently mixes the present, the simple tenses, and the compound tenses in a way similar to modern conversation, which often alternates, audaciously, the present and past indefinite" (1937: 83 [=1971:94]). Uitti (1973) likewise includes TS within a repertoire of "highly sophisticated oral techniques" (51), adding that the direction of the shift (P-→ PR or PR-→ P) is usually unimportant.[22] Investi-

---

21. On differences between an orally composed (and performed) text and a reading/recitation of a prepared written text, see Baüml 1977, especially with regard to the roles of, and relationships between, author, narrator, audience, and text.

22. Among conversational narratologists, this same view is taken by Wolfson, but rejected by Schiffrin, who sees only the shift from PR to P as a discourse device marking narrative event boundaries.

gators who have acknowledged a connection between TS and performance nonetheless assume, on the whole, a relatively fixed, written text along the lines of a dramatic script, which was memorized and performed, presumably with some improvisation. Blanc (1964) links TS directly to techniques of oral composition and recitation. The universally recognized parataxis of epic narrative he ascribes, rightly, to the orality of the poetry: epic meter precludes a complex syntactic structure; logical subordination is thus expressed in part by intonation and gesture, in part by shifts involving categories of the verb (110)—features identified above as being distinctive of performance. He sees tense variation specifically as:

> both a result of and a corrective to parataxis, . . . a device which allows to make up for the lack of grammatical and chronological connections.[23] It can be seen to arise from the contradiction between the necessarily linear nature of recitation (in oral recitation events are necessarily placed one after another in time sequence)[24] and the discontinuous character of epic narrative. In a world of disconnected events reported in the present, relationships and continuity are rendered to a large extent by the change of . . . [categories] of the verb. [110]

To paraphrase Blanc's argument, TS is what text linguistics would now call a discourse device, necessitated by epic parataxis, for sequencing and subordinating events in a story. As we move from the chiefly oral genres of the twelfth century to the written genres of the thirteenth, sequencing and subordination come to be transferred increasingly from performance devices to grammar, specifically to tense and temporal conjunctions.[25]

In view of our insistence that the meaning of the NP is context-bound, one might question the legitimacy of applying to medieval literary texts an analytical framework developed for modern conversational stories. Clearly there are significant differences between these two varieties of discourse—the one being what Zumthor refers to as a "document," the other a "monument."

To begin with, the medieval texts are significantly longer than the conversational texts, which often have but a single point to make. But

---

23. Wolfson (1982: 41) sees the absence of explicit subordinators ('before,' 'after,' 'because') as an additional earmark of performed stories.

24. This is also true *a fortiori* of written narrative, which shares with its oral counterpart the condition of unfolding through (reading) time. The 'constraints of linearity' may be relaxed only in cinematic, or certain other forms of *visual* narrative, in which stories unfold in both space and time, thus permitting violations or fragmentation of the linearity of logical time. Much has been written on this subject: for a synoptic overview, see Segre 1979 [=1974], also Sternberg 1978.

25. Cf. also Antoine 1959: 589. The discourse function of TS as a device for narrative subordination is a complex issue which goes beyond the boundaries of the present discussion, but will be taken up in a forthcoming article "Discourse Functions of Tense-Aspect Oppositions in Narrative: Toward a Theory of Grounding."

medieval narrative is typically episodic. Epics, romances, and chronicles tend to be organized like a series of shorter narratives: individual episodes exhibit an internal structuration similar to that of whole conversational texts.[26] Thus laisse 10 of *Aucassin* offers a complete narrative—Aucassin engages in combat and defeats Count Bougar—albeit part of a larger, complex narrative. The Villehardouin passage similarly might be subdivided into three mini-narratives: vv. 1–27, 28–41, and 42—, all subsumed within the larger episode "The taking of the tower of Galatha" (§§155–61 in Faral's edition),[27] in its turn part of a global narrative of the Fourth Crusade.

Another significant difference is that conversational stories as a rule constitute fully improvisational, "unplanned" (Ochs 1979) discourse; medieval performance genres do not. Furthermore, the syntax of many of the medieval texts is subject to formal constraints imposed by meter, rhyme or assonance, and formulaic language, and it seems clear that these factors did influence choice of verb forms. Yet we know that skilled professional storytellers can work comfortably within these formal limitations to construct a discourse that will not strike listeners as deviant, given the horizon of linguistic expectation set up by performance literature. In any event, it appears that the crucial factor with regard to TS is not that the texts must be spontaneous and fully improvisational, but that they must be *acts of performance* as defined by the distinctive features listed above. All the texts under survey in which TS occurs to any meaningful degree are assumed to have been performed, and match the definition developed by Wolfson to contrast *performed stories* from other types of oral representing of past experience. Thus the two types of narrative discourse under investigation here are not as far apart as they might seem. From research compar-

26. This raises indirectly the thorny question of defining a narrative. Labov and Waletzky (1967: 28) define a minimal narrative as any sequence of clauses that contains at least one temporal juncture (two clauses temporally ordered with respect to one another). All narratives included in this study are considerably more elaborate.

27. Note that the mininarrative divisions proposed here do not coincide consistently with the paragraph numbers at the far left (in parentheses) of the text. These paragraphs *do not*, however, reflect the MSS—which differ among themselves in this regard—, but were introduced by Natalis de Wailly in the nineteenth century and have been adhered to by subsequent editors. From a comparison of the actual paragraph divisions of MSS *A* and *B*, representative of the two major MS families, Poirion (1978) concludes that modern editors have segmented Villenhardouin's material according to a principle of chronology which was not the author's own organizational principle: the division into paragraphs by copyists and editors "threatens to camouflage the thinking and artistry of the author" (51). Poirion argues for a fundamentally spatial rather than chronological organization (composition according to *scenes* built up around a nucleus of direct speech), which derives from the structure of Villehardouin's compositional enterprise: the forging of a narrative out of a collage of diverse documentary materials. The passage cited in the Appendix comprises §§85–87 in MS *A*, 109–10 in MS *B*. For *A*, 85 = 155 mid–157, 86 = 158–161, 87 begins with 162 and continues on; for *B*, 109 = 155–58, 110 = 159-162 mid.

ing 'literary' and 'nonliterary' storytelling, Livia Polanyi (1982: 155) concludes that narratives spontaneously produced in natural conversation
contain "the same complexities in manipulating point of view, identity of
reference, and multiplicity of meaning that have hitherto been treated as
special qualities of literary language." Nor are these the only features the
two have in common.

NARRATIVE TEMPORALITY

All narrative is intrinsically structured with two time frames: the time of
the telling of the story and the time during which the events of the story
took place. We will refer to these respectively as "speech-event time" and
"narrated-event time." Each of these time frames has a set of tense functions typically associated with it: primary sequence tenses (present, perfect, future) with speech-event time, secondary sequence tenses (imperfect, preterit, anterior tenses of the past, future-of-the-past—the so-called
conditional [see n. 28]) with diegetic time, although it is well known that
tenses are often "displaced"—synchronically or diachronically—from
their basic temporal meanings for grammatical, expressive, and, we must
now add, pragmatic purposes. Thus in the history of Gallo-Romance the
imperfective past (je faisais) and future-of-the-past (je ferais),[28] along with
their respective compound formations (j'avais fait, j'aurais fait) have all
been pressed into service to express, in addition to temporal values, varying degrees of epistemic modality (hypotheticality) in the context of conditional utterances (si j'avais su, je ne l'aurais pas fait). The "imparfait
pittoresque," "futur historique," and, most important here, "présent historique" represent synchronic dislocations of the basic values of the respective tense-aspect forms.

THE PRESENT TENSE IN NARRATIVE: A TYPOLOGY OF FUNCTIONS[29]

Present-tense forms may refer to speech-event time or to narrated-event
time, or to neither specifically, as in the case of general or timeless presents frequent in narrator asides. The contracted *is* of Schiffrin, 20–21 and
EST of Weinrich, 66–68 illustrate this general, or 'gnomic' present, through
which the temporal boundaries of a verb are extended to include all logically relevant moments in time.

28. Traditional grammar labels *je ferais* 'conditional' even when functionally it is not a
conditional, but rather expresses its (ontogenetically primary) value of future-of-the-past (*Il a
dit qu'il le FERAIT plus tard*). The diachronic relationship of these two functions is explored
in Fleischman 1982a: 55–66.

29. One is here encouraged to read through the texts in the Appendix so as to have the
narrative development of each story in mind.

Narratives (excluding certain experimental genres) are normally related in past time. Thus presents oriented toward speech-event time do not
have a referential function with respect to narrated events, but respond in
general to discourse-pragmatic or situational pragmatic needs. Such PRs
often fulfill a *phatic* function of calling attention to the channel of communication—in the case of our medieval texts, reminding the audience that a
tale is being performed:

> (1) Unas novas vos VUELH CONTAR que auzi dezir a un joglar ("Castia-
> gilos," 1–2). [I WANT TO TELL you a tale I heard recounted by a
> jongleur.]

> (2) Mas NO-M QUAL DIR, a mon semblan,
> Los gais envits que chascus fai,
> Mais aitan sivals ne DIRAI: . . . [*Flamenca*, 6496ff.]

But it DOESN'T BEHOOVE ME, so I think, to tell about the pleasur-
able moves each one makes. But this much I WILL TELL . . .

I would point out parenthetically that observations made about speech-
event presents are usually also valid for other forms normally associated
with *discours:* futures (DIRAI above is 'future' in relation to the speaker),
imperatives (in (4) below), and notably PC. The OFr. compound past form
is still, in most instances, solidly a perfect, i.e. a past connected to present
time (but see Beck forthcoming), whether to the actual present (speech-
event time) or to a surrogate present established by the use of NP, as in:

> (3) Tut sun aver qu'od sei AD *portét*, / *Tut le* **depart** par Alsis la citét.
> (*Alexis*, 91f.) [All the wealth he HAS *brought* with him, / He **dis-**
> **tributes** it all throughout the city of Alsis.]

In either case PC marks an event as completed at the time of the event
referred to by the present-tense verb and (subjectively) relevant to that
event. Thus (3) might be interpreted 'All the wealth he has brought with
him—and which he has with him now—he distributes throughout the
city. . . '. As a tense of *énonciation*, the OFr. PC typically served as a device
to shift the focus, however briefly, from an 'internal' (context of diegesis)
to an 'external' (context of the act of narration) point of view. This transi-
tional function is illustrated in the formula *se com vous aves oï et entendu*
[as well you have heard],[30] through which the narrator momentarily rein-
states the external world of the performance before continuing on to another episode in the story.

Speech-event presents may also have a *conative* function of under-
scoring the interactive dimension of performance narrative by drawing
listeners into the diegetic universe:

---

30. This formula introduces the prose laisses 1, 6, 10, 12, 18, 20, 28, 36 of *Aucassin*.

(4) Aucassins ala par le forest . . . NE CUIDIES MIE que les ronces et les espines l'esparnaiscent (*Aucassin*, 24: 1–3). [Aucassin wandered through the forest . . . DON'T THINK FOR A MOMENT that he was spared the brambles and the thorns.]

(5) Seigneurs, SACHIEZ de verité que . . . (*Passion des Jongleurs*, 2138). [My lords, KNOW in truth that . . .]

The narrator momentarily steps out of diegetic time to address his listeners directly. Not infrequently these two pragmatic functions are fulfilled simultaneously, e.g. by jongleuresque formulas such as *sachiez, podeiz saveir*,[31] *es vus*, or *oez*, or *entendez*, etc. Oral punctuation, as it were, these brief interjections serve as subliminal reminders to the audience that they are experiencing a narrative performance.[32]

An important consideration regarding presents oriented toward speech-event time is that *they have no referential function with respect to the events of the story*, and for this reason cannot be replaced by pasts. They have a purely pragmatic role in the discourse. Presents oriented toward narrated-event time (NPs), on the other hand, refer by definition to past events, though, as we shall see, they too function pragmatically, as devices for narrative evaluation. But unlike the speech-event present, the NP functions as a historical tense; its temporal reference is always past (hence Kiparsky's claim [n. 11 above] that HP is a deep-structure past). If we substitute P for NP the semantic interpretation remains unchanged; substituting P for a speech-event PR (e.g. in example (2) above) results, on the discourse level, in an infelicitous utterance.

THE CLAUSAL STRUCTURE OF ORAL NARRATIVE

Linguistic decomposition of an oral narrative reveals a number of different types of clauses. **Narrative clauses**—those preceded by a letter in our sample texts—are those which recapitulate past experience in the order in which the events presumably occurred. Each narrative clause describes one event which is understood to follow the event immediately preceding it and to precede the event immediately following it. These events are

31. Östmann (1981) claims that 'you know' [or translation equivalents] functions as a pragmatic particle used when the speaker wants the addressee to accept as mutual knowledge (or at least be cooperative with respect to) the propositional content of the utterance. Formulaic language in general is acknowledged by oral theorists to be a convenient way of signaling "shared knowledge," of which involvement formulas such as 'you know,' etc. are perhaps the most explicit articulation. For traditional genres such as the epic, the propositional content of entire narratives was frequently mutual knowledge.

32. Narrative strategies that have been associated with orality in general grow out of an emphasis on *interpersonal involvement* between speaker/writer and audience, while strategies that have been associated with literacy grow out of focus on content (Tannen 1982b: xv).

separated from one another by "temporal juncture," which is semantically equivalent to the temporal conjunction 'then': *a* happened, then *b*, then *c*, and so forth. Since narrative clauses are temporally ordered, any change in their ordering (displacement across a temporal juncture) alters the inferred sequence of events in the original semantic interpretation. This becomes apparent if one attempts to juggle lettered clauses of the texts in the Appendix. Only *main* clauses are relevant to temporal sequence; subordinate clauses may be moved about to varying degrees without disturbing the temporal order of the semantic interpretation. By reading down the sequence of narrative clauses, (the reader is encouraged to do this) the backbone of a story or "primary sequence" emerges (Labov & Waletzky 1967).

This definition of narrative clauses calls for several remarks which bear on differences between oral and written narrative. Labov and Waletzky define a narrative as "one verbal technique for recapitulating experience, in particular a technique for constructing narrative units which match the temporal sequence of that experience" (13). They emphasize that the sequence of narrative units follows the sequence of experiential units being described. While this may be true in general for natural narrative (leaving aside altogether the epistemological problem alluded to above of segmenting a seamless experiential continuum into a set of discrete evenemential units), it need not hold—and often does not—for "artistic" narrative. Hence the opposition invoked by Genette, Todorov, and others between the "time of the signified" (the order of events as they presumably occurred) and the "time of the signifier" (an author/narrator's disposition of these events in a narrative)—which ultimately goes back to the Formalist opposition fabula vs. plot. While a coincidence between these two temporal orders such as Labov proposes for natural narrative is doubtless more common in oral artistic narratives than in written, or especially cinematic, narratives,[33] even the *chanson de geste*—among the medieval narrative genres conceivably the purest oral form—often departs from the known chronology of events, signaling this departure by a temporal dislocation whereby the time relationship conventionally established by a tense form is at odds with the order of events in the story. A classic example from *Roland:* Ganelon's treason is proleptically alluded to in v. 178 in the PS (*Guenes i vint qui la traïson fist* [Ganelon came, the one who *committed* treason]), though the events constituting the betrayal have yet to be fully played out. In traditional poetry such as the Romance epic, cataphoric references of this type function to split the time frame momentarily between the diegetic world and the situation of performance. Underlying v. 178 is something like "Ganelon came, who—as you know, having heard this story many times before—committed treason" (cf. n.

---

33. Cf. Blanc's remarks apropos, cited above.

30). Where the content of a story is shared knowledge, the narrator will often begin *in medias res* and relate events not in any strict linear sequence (cf. Ong 1981). Even with respect to natural narrative one might not want to insist too strongly on a strict correspondence between the chronology of events in real time and their ordering in the text, although the match is predictably closer than in planned, artistic narrative forms. This caveat in no way undermines the notion of temporal juncture on which our definition of the narrative clause is based. The event boundary (= temporal juncture), like the notion of 'event' itself, is but a heuristic construct devised for the purpose of analyzing narrative.

In contrast to narrative clauses, **restricted clauses** are not temporally ordered in a narrow sense. Rather, they report events which often subsume those of the temporally ordered clauses. They report more extended events and have a temporal scope which is usually restricted to a specific scene or episode. Restricted clauses may therefore be reshuffled or displaced over limited sections of the narrative without changing the inferred chronology of the original semantic interpretation. The restricted clause in *Aucassin*, 1. 30 describes an event viewed not as complete and punctual, but as drawn out over a duration: Aucassin's enemies "went along discussing how they would kill him." This clause could precede any of the narrative clauses *a.–f.* (with necessary adjustments for anaphoric reference) without altering the temporal sequence of the original semantic interpretation. In the Weinrich text, clauses 62, 69, 71–73 report similarly extended or ongoing events: the hitch-hikers "were beginning to give up" (durative), the passing cars "would all stop right away or would turn" (iterative). Cf. also lines 82, 92 and Villehardouin, 2–10. Descriptive in nature, these backgrounded clauses could in every instance be moved over "restricted" sections of their respective texts without altering the original semantic structures.

Two other clause types less directly relevant to our purpose will be mentioned here only briefly. **Coordinate clauses** are those which may be interchanged with one another without disrupting the original sequence of events, e.g. *Aucassin*, j.–k., l.–m. These are generally used for actions reported as going on simultaneously, where no relationship of logical subordination obtains. If subordination is implied, then a change in clause order, *in the absence of a subordinating conjunction* (explicit markers of subordination are frequently ellipsed in oral narrative), will alter the intended meaning.[34]

Finally, there are **free clauses,** which have no fixed relationship to temporal sequence, and can range freely throughout a narrative:

34. If subordinating conjunctions are lacking—whether temporal (when *a, b*), or causal (because *a,* [therefore]*b*), or conditional (if *a,* [then] *b*)—then the order of two clauses must be iconic to the normal antecedent-consequent relationship of the events. This point is developed in Fleischman 1986, forthcoming.

(8) Li vallés fu grans et fors,/ et li cevax so quoi il sist fu remuans
    (*Aucassin*, 35–36). [The lad was big and strong and the horse he sat
    on was spirited.]

These clauses could be moved to any point in the text, their displacement
having no effect on the temporal logic of the story. They in fact appear with
almost identical wording (they are likely formulaic) in the preceding orientation section, vv. 6–9.

THE OVERALL STRUCTURE OF ORAL NARRATIVE

A fully developed narrative will exhibit all or most of the following sections: Abstract, Orientation, Complicating Action—in which the major
events of the story are set forth, Evaluation, Result or Resolution, and
Coda. Each of these components responds to a particular question:

   a. Abstract: what was this about?
   b. Orientation: who, what, when, where?
   c. Complicating Action: then what happened?
   d. Evaluation: so what?
   e. Resolution: what finally happened?
   [f. Coda: relation to present context]

Labov (1972: 370) notes that in principle only complicating action is essential to a narrative. The abstract, orientation, resolution, and evaluation
answer questions that bear on the function of *effective* narration: the first
three to clarify referential functions, evaluation to make explicit why the
story is told—its raison d'être. The coda, found less frequently than any
other narrative element, does not answer, but rather puts off a question: it
signals that questions c. and d. are no longer relevant, providing definitive
closure. In the following paragraphs I will elaborate on each of these elements, beginning with the coda and abstract, which together provide a
frame for the narrative proper, linking it to the context of its *énonciation*.
While abstracts and codas are not always present in conversational performed stories, their importance increases in artistic narratives. In our
medieval texts they typically take the form of narrator prologues and
epilogues, which appear only in absolute text-initial and text-final positions, hence their absence from our sample texts.

   The Coda. It is a device for returning the verbal perspective to the time
of the speech-event. As a rule, the sequence of events described in a narrative does not extend up to present time. By means of a coda the narrator
can bridge the gap between the moment of time at the end of the story and
the present. Examples (9) and (10) are typical conversational narrative
codas:

   (9) . . . and, you know, I'VE *been looking* for one like it ever since.

(10) . . . although I'VE never *seen* the guy since, I'll never forget that look on his face.

The coda's function of connecting past events to the speaker's present explains the frequency of the present perfect—by definition a past with "present relevance" (cf. Harris 1982, Fleischman 1983b), and of other tenses associated with *discours*. Ramon Vidal de Besalu's courtly fabliau of the "Castia-gilos" closes with a coda describing the reaction of King Alfonso VIII of Castile's court to the tale that has just been performed:

> (11) Can lo reys *fenic* sa razo,
> anc non *ac* en la cort baro,
> cavaier, donzel ni donzela,
> sesta ni sest, ni sel ni sela,
> de las novas no.s azautes
> e per bonas non las lauzes
> e que cascus no *fos* cochos
> d'apenre Castia-gilos.[35]

When the king *finished* his speech, there *was* no one in the court—nobleman, knight, page or damsel, this one that one—who was not delighted by the tale and did not praise its excellence, nor anyone who *was* not eager to learn the Castia-gilos.

The Abstract. Narrators often begin by establishing the point of a story or by giving the most salient events in a nutshell:

(12) Let me tell you about the time the roof started leaking right in the middle of our dinner party! (personal data)

(13) Ar auiatz, senher, cals desastre li avenc per sa gilozia ("Castia-gilos," vv. 44f.). [Hear now, gentlemen, what a disaster befell him (Alfonso of Barbastro) on account of his jealousy.][36]

Abstracts can also introduce an *evaluative* judgment on the narrative as a whole, signaling to the listener in advance the narrator's reading of the events of the story. The Schiffrin text begins with just such an evaluative abstract:

(14) Oh it was so crazy
     I remember this.

---

35. This text is particularly interesting from the perspective of narrative structure: the tale itself is set into a multi-level frame which includes its presumed context of performance. Ramon Vidal claims to have heard the tale performed by a *joglar* at the court of Alfonso (see ex. (1) above), and periodically inserts this courtly scenario into the narrative. The coda returns the verbal perspective to the "implied" present of the performing *joglar* rather than to Ramon Vidal's own present. The "Castia-gilos" is doubtless among the most striking documentations of a medieval performed story, in which performance is literally embedded into the text.

36. The multiple embedding of the tale in "Castia-gilos" explains why this abstract appears not in absolute text-initial position, but forty-four verses later, following an orientation section establishing the courtly setting in which the tale will be performed.

Maybe I shouldn't say it now.

It was really a weird thing.

(This reading of the experience is then reconfirmed in the final evaluation section [lines 50–54]).

We may observe that the reference of the abstract tends to encompass that of orientation, complicating action, and evaluation: it not only states what the narrative is about, but also why it is being told. Our three (Old and Modern) French texts, however, do not contain abstracts, but begin directly with orientation.

Orientation. At the outset of a narrative it is necessary to identify the time, place, participants and their activity, and situation in which the events take place. While this can be accomplished in the first few narrative clauses, most narratives begin with an orientation section composed of free and restricted clauses which provide this background information. Notice that the most frequent tenses in orientation are imperfective pasts expressing continuous or habitual action. Thus in English we find a heavy concentration of imperfects (*it was our birthdays*)[37] or past progressives (*we were all going out for lunch*) that sketch the kind of thing that *was going on* before the first narrative event of the story or during the entire episode, or for events collateral to the main narrative events, as in the last verse of (15):

(15) **Ceint** Murglies s'espee a sun costed (narrative event) En Tachebrun, sun destrer, EST *munted* (narrative event [+completed]) L'estreu *tint* sun oncle Guinemer (collateral event [+durative] [Murglie **girds** his sword to his side/ on Tachebrun his steed he IS/HAS *mounted./* His uncle Guinemer *was holding* the stirrup. (*Roland,* 347ff.)

Also pluperfects for explanatory circumstantial material—what *had already happened* to produce the situation in which the events of the story will take place: *on avait décidé d'aller aux Sables-d'Olonne* [we had decided to go to the Sables-d'Olonne] (Weinrich, line 3). This distribution of verbal forms accords nicely with the correlation between backgrounded clauses and imperfective aspect suggested in Hopper 1979a and 1979b. In Modern French we find a similar predominance of imperfects in orientation (see the Weinrich text), whereas in the older language certain of the descriptive functions now the domain of the imperfect were handled by the PS (*tint* in (15) above; cf. Foulet 1919: §§325–26, Faye 1933), which is the predominant tense for orientation in *Aucassin.* (The Villehardouin text shows heavier use of the imperfect.)

In theory all "free" orientation clauses could be placed at the head of a

---

37. The imperfective/perfective distinction is not formally encoded in the English past system (except via the progressive).

narrative, but in practice they tend not to be; orientation is often embedded directly into the complicating action, even into the resolution and evaluation (Weinrich, 106–08, 113–15). Embedded orientation clauses are enclosed in square brackets. While free orientation clauses are in principle movable to any point in the text (cf. *Aucassin*, 5–9), restricted orientation clauses are not (cf. Villehardouin, 12–13, 20, 33, 35, 37, 42–47, 51–54). These last two passages from Villehardouin (42–47, 51–54) also show present-tense forms occurring in orientation clauses. But note that these presents are not NPs; their temporal reference is to *real* present time. With SACHIEZ (45) it is the moment of speech itself, with APELLE (53) a broader span of time which obviously includes the moment of speech. The point then is that presents in orientation will almost always be either general or speech-event presents, never NPs. Functionally these presents are not the same as those appearing in the narrative clauses of complicating action, whose temporal reference is always past, the time of narrated events. The commutation test (substituting a past for a present) confirms the contrast.

An important theoretical issue alluded to earlier underlies the distinction we are making here among the various types of present. As linguists are coming to acknowledge more and more, the 'meanings' of tense-aspect forms—like the meanings of other grammatical elements, and of words themselves—are context dependent. Semantics has become inextricably bound up with pragmatics. A verb form is a *virtuel*, comprising multiple values actualized in different discourse and situation contexts. As we shall see below, in the context of the complicating action of oral narratives the PR acquires a temporal value of [+past], and in certain *états de langue*, also an aspectual value of [+perfective]—features it does not display in other textual environments (e.g. orientation) or in other varieties of discourse (direct speech). Investigators studying the tense usage of the early vernaculars, in particular those who have undertaken frequency counts or similarly slanted statistical analyses, have on the whole given insufficient attention to context, considering as tokens of a single linguistic form—the 'present tense'—these functionally diverse types of present (cf. n. 9).

Complicating Action. The narrative events that make up a story constitute collectively the complicating action. This is as a rule the longest section of a narrative, into which may be embedded both orientation and evaluation, as indicated by the bracketed clauses in our texts. *Narrative events* are reported in narrative clauses (as defined above). The "primary sequence" of a narrative is the ordered set of these events, which are separated from one another by temporal juncture.

It will be observed that the events reported in the lettered (narrative) clauses are complete and punctual: their time reference is past, their aspectual value perfective; the expected verb form is a preterit—expressed by whatever form the language uses as an exponent of this function. In the medieval vernaculars as in English this is the simple past, in modern spoken French the compound formation. In this particular textual environment—narrative clauses of the complicating action—we also find PR alternating with, and referentially (temporally) equivalent to, P. The boldface PRs of our sample texts are all aspectually perfective. Here again the commutation test proves illuminating: these presents could in all instances be replaced by *perfective* pasts without changing the semantic interpretation, but not by *imperfective* pasts. If imperfects are substituted, the events referred to by these verbs cease to be narrative events and become the kind of descriptive or background information normally found in free or restricted clauses but not in narrative clauses.

Summing up our findings to this point, the two tense functions occurring in narrative clauses of the complicating action are preterit and NP, both aspectually perfective, both encoding punctual events with temporal juncture. Restricted clauses, on the other hand, which can be displaced across temporal junctures, do not contain NPs. Since they often describe action occurring simultaneous to the main narrative events, restricted clauses contain backgrounding tenses: imperfective forms expressing continuous, habitual, or iterated, but not punctual action. The expected paradigms are the imperfect, and if available in the language, progressives.

English, unlike French, has explicit progressive forms. The present progressive—which does occur in restricted clauses (cf. Schiffrin 1981: 59f.), though no examples appear in our sample text—functions like a *progressive NP*, depicting action ongoing at the time of the event referred to by the NP,[38] as in:

(16a) I'**m walking** into the house when all of a sudden I **see** this squirrel hanging on a chain from the ceiling! (personal data)

In this example both present forms could be replaced by past equivalents, the one imperfective/continuous, the other perfective/punctual, with no change in referential meaning:

(16b) I *was walking* into the house when all of a sudden I *saw* this squirrel hanging on a chain from the ceiling!

The aspectual meaning conveyed in English by means of the present progressive cannot be expressed morphologically in Modern French, which therefore has no diegetic presents in restricted clauses: this function is carried out by past imperfects (see the Weinrich text). But such was not always the case. As we shall see below, the language of our earliest performance narratives was in this regard analogous to Modern English, albeit without distinct forms for the functions expressed respectively by the

---

38. This is the referential function of the progressive NP. Like its simple counterpart, the progressive form also carries out an evaluative function.

English simple and progressive NPs, for which we will adopt the (functional) labels *"présent moteur"* and *"présent visuel."*[39]

Resolution. The last clause(s) of the complicating action typically contain the resolution of the story. The complication builds up to a certain point, then comes a clause which answers the question "what *finally* happened?" In the Schiffrin text this is given in r. (*And after a while he got out*), in Weinrich in w. (*Alors on est arrivé en même temps que le car* [so we got there the same time as the bus]). The resolutions of our medieval texts offer 'interim' closure, i.e. of individual episodes, which are then followed by other episodes with their own internal structuration. In *Aucassin* this interim resolution comes in clause z., where Count Bougar gives his word not to foment any more trouble. The narrative clauses that follow see him led off to safety. In Villehardouin the resolution of the episode of the tower of Galatha is given in the final clauses (81–83), in which the tower is captured with the Greeks inside. This is followed by a summative statement on prisoners and casualties.

Evaluation. Often the resolution will be set off from the preceding complication by evaluation. Evaluation refers to the means by which the narrator comments on the events of the story and indicates their relative importance to him. One of the most important components in effective narration, evaluation operates to communicate the *point* of the story. Its function is to answer in advance, hence render infelicitous, the withering question "so what?" A narrative that contains orientation, complication, and a result is not a complete narrative; while it may carry out adequately the referential function, it will probably be difficult to follow. A narrative lacking evaluation lacks significance; it has no point. On the level of the text as a whole, evaluation communicates the information: this experience was terrifying, dangerous, wonderful, amusing, weird, crazy; more generally, that is was out of the ordinary, hence worthy of recounting (cf. Labov 1972: 370f.). An effective narrator will make use of evaluation strategies to structure his text so that the point of the story and the events s/he considers noteworthy will come across as such.

Narrators often seek to mark the point at which the complication has reached its peak: the break between complicating action and resolution. This is typically accomplished by introducing a formal evaluation section just before the clause(s) expressing the resolution, as in Schiffrin, 45–48. The type of evaluation found in this passage is what Labov calls *external* evaluation: the narrator exits from the diegetic world—and narrated event

---

39. These terms are taken from Buffin 1925, a somewhat obscure and by now dated, if nonetheless perceptive analysis of tense/aspect in French. Buffin contrasts a present used to express action and movement (our 'narrative events')—the *présent moteur*—with another present used for descriptions and stative situations (of the type found in restricted clauses)—the *présent visuel*. This distinction is purely functional; formally the two are identical.

time—to address an evaluative comment directly to his listeners. Thus at the close of the Hildesheim *St. Alexis,* the saint and his family are at last reunited in heaven, to which the narrator comments:

> (17) Ne vus sai dirre cum lur ledece **est** grande [I cannot tell you how happy they **are**[40]

Apropos of a particularly upsetting military setback Villehardouin comments:

> (18) Et sachiez que ce fu *la plus granz dolors* qui onques avenist en ost. [Know that it was *the greatest misfortune* that ever befell an army.] (Villehardouin, 85)[41]

Such statements to the audience function as pragmatic signboards saying "these are momentous events." Labov has observed external evaluation to be most common among middle-class narrators, who frequently interrupt their stories to offer their listeners interpretative clues.

Not all evaluation, however, has the structural property of suspending the complicating action. Evaluation is often *internal,* embedded directly in the complication through various strategies, not all of which will be discussed here (see Labov 1972: 372ff.).

Internal evaluation may be carried out *lexically* through intensifiers, as in:

> (19) it was *so* crazy . . . it was really a *weird* thing (Schiffrin, 1, 4)

> (20) Einsi partirent *par mal* l'empereres Baudoins de Costantinople et Bonifaces li marchis de Montferrat, et *par malvais conseil* [Thus, hélas, did Baldwin of Constantinople and Boniface, Marquis of Montferrat, depart, victims of unwise counsel] (Villehardouin, §278),

or even through metaphors, as in the description of Aucassin's sudden burst of martial zeal:

> (21) il fait un caple autour de lui *autresi con li senglers quand li cien l'asalent en le forest* [he wreaks slaughter all around him, just like a wild boar when attacked by hounds in the forest] (*Aucassin,* 42–44).

Alternatively, the narrator may report the judgment as something that occurred to him at the moment:

> (22) . . . and just then I realized why you have to wear shoes when you do Chinese cooking! (personal data)

This type of evaluation, common in medieval romances, is conspicuously absent from epics (fc. Grunmann 1975: 205), where other 'internal' strategies seem to be preferred.

---

40. PR is rare in external evaluation (Schiffrin reports no examples in her data). The predominant tense is P.

41. Villehardouin's undisguised bias on the events he narrates typically takes the form of external evaluation, cf. §§ 220, 271, 379, 409 of the Faral edition.

Internal evaluation may also be carried out by presenting commentary in the form of direct statements, by the narrator or, better, by a third party, as in (23) from *Roland:*

(23) Il [Roland] dist al rei: "Ja *mar* crerez Marsilie" [Roland said to the king: "Woe will be to you who believes Marsile] (v. 196).[42]

Similarly in the Schiffrin text, clause m. Having the girl utter this statement is doubtless more dramatic, and less overtly interventional, than had the narrator simply continued: "And I was real scared because I didn't think he knew what he was doing." Aucassin's histrionic "Ha, Dix! . . . sont çou mi anemi mortel . . . " [Oh God! . . . are these my mortal enemies?] (33–34) communicates quite effectively the idea that the individuals in question are out for blood.

An internal evaluation strategy frequent in epic narration is evaluative action: telling what people did rather than what they said. This allows events to speak for themselves, and provides a less obtrusive form of commentary than judgments addressed directly to the listener. It also presupposes that norms for evaluating experience are shared—what is referred to as "empathy".[43] Evaluative action, as Labov points out, typically has the effect of dramatizing a narrative. The prominence of this technique in the *chanson de geste* has been widely observed. Recall the description of Charlemagne that closes the Oxford *Roland:*

(24) **Pluret** des oilz, sa barbe blanche **tiret** [His eyes **weep,** he **strokes** his white beard] (v. 4002).

Two minimal narrative clauses which symbolically encapsulate a major ideological crisis confronting the military-feudal world.

It should now be apparent that narrative clauses themselves may be evaluative, which is where TS comes into play. Evaluation has been defined as that component of narrative that reveals the speaker's attitude toward the events of the story by emphasizing the relative salience of some narrative units as compared with others. One effective stretegy for *foregrounding* events is to report them in the present.[44] Thus it has been

---

42. A *mot clef* of OFr. narrative evaluation, *mar* is the subject of exhaustive analysis by Cerquiglini (1981: Part 2), who characterizes it as "a prescriptive modalisation (*une modalité d'ordre du thétique*), expressing the speaker's negative judgment on the content of his utterance" (173).

43. Wolfson (1982) sees empathy as a precondition for a speaker's breakthrough into performance. The issue of empathetic presuppositions in medieval narrative, which is also a question of genre, is fascinating in its complexity, but beyond the scope of this investigation.

44. It is from this perspective of narrative focus (foregrounding and backgrounding) that Hatcher's analysis approaches our own. Blanc (1964) also interprets TS in terms of narrative focus, drawing a parallel to the alternating tenses of simultaneous sportscasting. Striking as this parallelism may seem at first glance, a rugby match does not have the internal narrative structure of a 'story', nor is a *simulcast* a re-presentation of past experience. Wolfson (1978, 1979) insists that the PR phenomenon found in performed stories operates according to different rules from those of other oral genres, including jokes and sportscasts.

variously argued for conversational narrative that the switch to present tense—and I emphasize that only the NP is at issue here, not general presents nor speech-event presents—*is fundamentally a device for internal evaluation:* it allows the narrator to present events as if they were occurring at the moment of *énonciation*, so that the audience can hear for itself what happened and interpret for itself the significance of those events for the experience.[45] Rather than interpret the events of the story for the listener, the narrator allows events to speak for themselves, relying on the more subtle internal devices, including TS, to foreground individual narrative units. Labov finds internal evaluation particularly prominent among older, highly skilled narrators from traditional working-class backgrounds. *Mutatis mutandis,* this observation may shed light on its prominence among medieval jongleuresque narrators, notably poets of the *chansons de geste.*

I find it puzzling that the phenomenon of internal evaluation has seemed to escape the notice of medieval narratologists. The "immediate" discourse of epic is frequently contrasted to the more self-conscious discourse of romance, in which a narrator actively mediates between a text and its consumers, distancing himself from his *matière* in order to observe and evaluate it with a degree of purported detachment.[46] It is ostensibly from this perspective that Pickens (1979) argues that in the solidly oral genres, in which temporal and esthetic distance are lacking, "there is little room for mature evaluation or for reflection" (169), "'dramatic' immediacy suggests an indifference toward analysis" (182). This argument tacitly equates analysis/evaluation with "commentative text"—what would here be termed *external* evaluation. That evaluation in narrative can also be carried out—and very effectively—in "diegetic" and "mimetic" text (Pickens' categories), i.e. through *internal* strategies, seems to have passed unnoticed.

THE DIEGETIC PRESENT IN MEDIEVAL NARRATIVE

Thus far our analysis of performance narrative has indicated that the variety of present here referred to as the NP occurs in a sharply profiled textual environment—the narrative clauses of complicating action—and functions as a device for internal evaluation. It should now be apparent that this hypothesis supports the traditional view that the present serves to

---

45. Cf. Schiffrin 1981, Silva-Corvalán 1983. Tannen (1982a: 4) suggests further that internal evaluation is an essentially oral strategy, external evaluation a literate strategy, which seems to support Labov's sociolinguistic correlations between class and narrative strategies (see what follows).

46. I explore the problem of narrator involvement in greater depth in Fleischman 1983b: 295–98. Cf. also Jauss 1963: 73ff.

dramatize events and render them more vivid. Yet several investigators have pointed to instances in which the most salient events of a narrative are reported not in PR but in P.[47] However, as Wolfson herself points out, the NP alternation is an *optional* feature of performed stories, which is never actualized in all instances in which it could be. It has an *interactional* function which causes it to be used in some settings and not in others. This alone would undermine the objection that some important events are encoded in P rather than PR.[48]

The hypothesis that the NP functions as an internal evaluation mechanism of performed stories can, I believe, be supported in all the texts to which the label 'performed story' is appropriate. However, the distributional restriction whereby NPs occur exclusively in narrative clauses of complicating action holds only for the later oral texts, in particular those of the thirteenth century. In the Oxford *Roland*, for example, or the eleventh-century *Alexis*, diegetic presents occur also in other clause types and other sections of the narrative.

The simple NP as defined above is aspectually perfective; it substitutes for past forms which represent events as punctual and complete. Blanc (1964) labels this aspect "attainment" and contrasts it to an aspect of "continuance," i.e. action represented as ongoing. A variety of terms have been used in the literature on aspect to refer to this opposition; for convenience Blanc's labels will be retained here. As has been shown above, English has a specific morphological form, the present progressive, to indicate continuous or durative action in present time—what we referred to earlier as the *présent visuel*. Just as the simple NP, or *présent moteur*, substitutes for a past expressing attainment, the progressive NP substitutes for a past expressing continuance, as observed in the examples in (16) above.

French has never had a specific morphological exponent for continuous action in the present.[49] The simple PR of early Old French, as Blanc

---

47. Cf. Kiparsky 1968, Paden 1977, Wolfson 1979, 1982. Wolfson has advanced an alternative hypothesis, namely that TS is a *discourse* device for separating narrative events from one another (the direction of the shift is for her irrelevant). Leaving aside here the problem of what constitutes an 'event,' on which consensus is lacking, neither our own data nor those of Schiffrin or Silva-Corvalán bear this out. However Schiffrin does acknowledge this function for the switch *out of* NP.

48. In comparing multiple versions of a story told by the same speaker, I have observed considerable variation in the use of NP. Comparison of the various MSS of Villehardouin's chronicle is likewise illuminating in this regard: a number of diegetic presents in Faral's text (based mainly on MS O of Group I) appear as preterits in the later MSS of Group II (these PRs are marked by a * in the passage quoted in the Appendix). Comparison of different versions of a *chanson de geste* likewise reveals NP to be an optional strategy, although here each MS may reflect a different performance tradition and quite likely a different jongleur.

49. The *aller (en)* . . . *-ant* construction (cf. *Aucassin*, 30, Villehardouin, 25) is a marked progressive form and has always been of limited use, given that *aller* has retained to a greater or lesser degree its spatial meaning, and has not been bleached to an auxiliary.

points out, expressed both aspects, continuance and attainment (i.e., the opposition was neutralized). Hence we should not be surprised to encounter in the early texts diegetic presents referring not only to punctual events in narrative clauses—*présents moteurs* with aspect of attainment—, but also to events of more extended duration—*présents visuels*—of the type found in restricted clauses. This can be seen in the following passage from *Roland,* accompanied for the purpose of comparison by Goldin's translation:

(25a) *La Chanson de Roland,* ed. F. Whitehead, trans. F. Goldin (vv. 1412–17)

La bataille **est** merveilleuse et pesant;	The battle **is** fearful and full of grief.
Mult bien i **fiert** Oliver e Rollant,	Oliver and Roland **strike** like good men,
Li arcevesques plus de mil colps i **rent,**	the Archbishop, more than a thousand blows.
Li .xii. per **ne s'en targent** nient,	and the 12 peers **do not hang back,** they **strike**,
E li Franceis **fierent** cumunement.	The French **fight** side by side, all as one man.
Moerent paien a millers e a cent.	The pagans **die** by hundreds, by thousands.

In attempting to preserve the tense usage of the original, this translation camouflages an aspectual distinction which could be rendered in English through the simple-progressive opposition. Compare the following revised translation, in which the continuous/durative nature of certain events is rendered explicit by a formally distinct *présent visuel*—the progressive:

(25b) The battle is fearful and full of grief. / Oliver and Roland **strike / are striking**(?) like good men, / the Archibishop, more than a thousand blows. / and the 12 peers **do not hang back,** they strike! / The French **are fighting** side by side, all as one man. / The pagans **are dying** by hundreds, by thousands.

What emerges from this comparison is that the simple NP of *early* Old French is distributionally more flexible than its modern English counterpart, occurring in both narrative and restricted clauses. This is because the functional opposition expressed by the simple-progressive contrast in English is in French neutralized in a single present form. Until now we have been claiming that the NP substitutes only for a preterit, i.e. for a past form with aspect of attainment, and that this form in the languages at issue—except modern spoken French—is the simple past. However the simple past in Old French could also express continuous action and was used, as noted earlier, in certain situations in which the modern language would require an imperfect. Many of the *passé simples* in the orientation clauses of *Aucassin* and Villehardouin would be *imparfaits* in Modern French. The wider functional scope of the diegetic present in early Old French, which was both a *présent visuel* and a *présent moteur,* must relate to the fact that the PS was also functionally broader, since in all instances it is a PS that the NP replaces. At a time when the PS was functionally more flexible, the

NP in its turn displayed greater flexibility. In the course of the thirteenth century, grosso modo, the PS begins to lose ground to the *imparfait*.[50] And at the same time the NP loses its ability to express aspect of continuance, a function which it too yields to the *imparfait* (Buffin 1925: 111, Blanc 1964: 116f.). This gradual narrowing of the functional scope of both PS and NP is reflected in the tense usage of the texts, particularly if we compare the use of NP in twelfth-century *chansons de geste* with that in thirteenth-century texts, whose tense usage in this regard has already come to resemble that of Modern French.

Again, I would emphasize that we are dealing exclusively with narrative transmitted orally. The HP of modern written genres, though presumed to have evolved from the medieval NP, is not subject to the same distributional constraints, nor does it exhibit the switching patterns. The modern HP often involves sequences of PR verbs sustained over narrative and restricted clauses alike[51]—in this regard not unlike the usage of the early performance texts. A comparative overview of tense usage in narrative diegesis in the various *états de langue* here under survey is given in the following table.

Tense Usage in Narrative Diegesis

	Punctual Events (Narrative [Main] Clauses)		Durative/Iterative/ Stative Events (Restricted Clauses)	
	Past Form	Present Substitute	Past Form	Present Substitute
Mod. English convers. narrative	Simple Past	NP (prés. moteur)	Simple Past/ Past Progr.	Progessive NP
Early OFrench performed narrative	PS	NP (prés. moteur)	PS	présent visuel
Late OFrench performed narrative	PS	NP (prés. moteur)	Imparfait PS	Imparfait
Modern French convers. narrative	PC	NP (prés. moteur)	Imparfait	Imparfait
Modern French written narrative	PS	prés. hist.[52]	Imparfait	prés. hist.

50. Buffin (1925: 105) sees Joinville as a major turning point.

51. As Buffin remarks: "Use of the present is found in tales with a popular flavor, and in the epic style. . . . Characteristic of all the aborted seventeenth-century attempts at epic, to greater or lesser degrees, is this cold and stilted present, so different from that of medieval usage, where past tenses would often intervene to break the monotony" (1925: 102).

52. A second alternative to the PS is offered by the *imparfait*. See Saunders 1969, who observes that in modern literary narrative writing the *imparfait* is increasingly adopting a preterit role, neutralizing in many instances the aspectual contrast normally expressed by the PS/Imperfect opposition (161).

CONCLUSIONS

It is appropriate at this point to sum up the main points of our discussion. First, the 'idiosyncratic' tense alternation of medieval vernacular narrative cannot be explained away as simply an archaizing quirk of poetic language, a phenomenon divorced from *parole*. It is to the contrary a technique rooted in spoken language, albeit of a very specific type: oral performed narrative. Tense switching is absent from textual dialogue, as Sandmann has demonstrated, but for the obvious reason that dialogue—itself an internal evaluation strategy—generally consists of disconnected short utterances; it is not sustained, cohesive discourse requiring certain 'traffic signals'. Occasionally diegetic passages will be reported as direct speech, e.g. in monologues, and in such instances the NP can occur (cf. Blanc 1964: 99n, Ollier 1978: 101). Second, the NP alternation is an optional feature of performed stories, one of several strategies through which internal evaluation is carried out. Evaluation is essential to effective narration,[53] and all the more so for professional storytellers whose success—and livelihood!—depended directly on the efficacy of their performances.

I have sought here to refine the traditional "past-more-vivid" interpretation of the diegetic present through examination of the overall structure of oral narrative, with a view toward identifying the textual environments in which particular verb forms occur. Distribution will vary somewhat from one language to another, as well as diachronically over the history of a language. However, as I have attempted to show through comparison with contemporary (French and English) performed stories, certain basic principles governing the structure of oral narrative and the distribution of tense/aspect functions seem to hold across languages, across time, and across genres.[54]

53. Certain theoreticians might argue, to the contrary, that a lack of evaluation would have the effect of multiplying the possible interpretations of the events, thereby enhancing rather than detracting from the experience of the text. However, empiral observation indicates that this is not the way good storytellers tell stories.

54. The genre question is a complex one, which cannot be pursued here. Various investigators (Benveniste, Weinrich, Banfield, Hamburger) have argued that *narrative* (which is generally understood to mean literary narrative) represents a special pragmatic context, and that its grammar deviates in certain respects from that of ordinary language. (For a critique of this view, with particular reference to tense usage, see Bellos 1978.) Yet "narrative" is not a monolithic category, but rather an umbrella for a variety of discourse forms. Thus certain linguistic idiosyncracies identified by Banfield 1982 as distinctive marks of (modern fictional) narrative, features that would be considered deviant in the grammar of ordinary conversation, are similarly impossible in certain genres of performance narrative, which, unlike modern novelistic narratives, *do* conform to a "communication model of language," i.e. one in which a speaker communicates directly with a tangible addressee. The presence of the addressee—perhaps the most important feature distinguishing performance narrative from its written counterpart—has important linguistic and, notably, pragmatic consequences, which should be explored further.

The focus of this investigation is an old philological problem at the crossroads of linguistics and literature. My objective has been to reexamine it in the context of recent theoretical work on textual performance and natural narrative. I believe this approach has implications of consequence not only to philologists and narratologists (strange bedfellows), but to literary medievalists as well: for in recognizing that the past-present alternation is a strategy instrinsic to oral narrative, we move a step closer to a long overdue acknowledgment that the major 'literary monuments' of the vernacular Middle Ages were first and foremost acts of performance— composed, structured, and played out according to conventions demonstrably different from those of the "planned" textual forms most familiar to modern literary analysts. As Richard Bauman observes:

> It is possible to move from artistic texts identified in formal or other terms, to performance, by simply looking at how such texts are rendered in action terms. But this is to proceed backwards, by approaching phenomena whose primary social reality lies in their nature as oral communication in terms of the abstract textual products of the communicative process. [Bauman, 1978: 8]

Once this step has been taken in the differentiation of performance texts from the written/read variety, it may be useful to step back and consider in a larger perspective the status of the basic opposition oral-written. The idea of 'oral narrative' is but a convenient construct, whose artificiality becomes evident when one realizes that *all* reading and *all* speaking of past events suppose, in the reactualization required by the processes of encoding and decoding, the voice of the sender or that of the addressee, re-PRE-SENT-ing in consciousness particular signifieds by their signifiers. Hence all narration, ultimately, is always oral, whether representing "out loud" and instantaneously, or "silently" by mediation through writing and reading.[55]

---

55. These concluding observations were suggested by Jonathan Beck, whose reading of an earlier version of this paper helped clarify many of the ideas contained in it.

APPENDIX OF TEXTS
(For marking conventions, see n. 1)

Text 1: Prose laisse (no. 10) from **Aucassin et Nicolette**, *first half of thirteenth century.*

10. Or Dient et Content

Aucassins *fu armés* sor son ceval,	1	ORIENTATION
si con vos AVES oï et *entendu.*		
Dix! con li *sist* li escus au col		
et li hiaumes u cief et li renge		
de s'espee sor le senestre hance!	5	
Et li vallés *fu* grans et fors		
et biax et gens et bien fornis,		
et li cevaus sor quoi il *sist*		
rades et corans,		
et li vallés l'*ot* bien *adrecié*	10	
par mi la porte		
OR NE QUIDIES VOUS		
qu'il *pensast* n'a bués		
n'a vaces n'a civres prendre,		
ne qu'il *ferist* cevalier.	15	
ne autres lui.		
Nenil nient!		
onques ne l'en *sovint*;		
ains *pensa* tant a Nicolete		
sa douce amie	20	
qu'il *oublia* ses resnes		
et quanques il *dut* faire;		
et li cevax qui *ot senti* les esperons		COMPLICATING
a. l'en *porta* par mi le presse,		ACTION
b. se **se lance** tres entre mi ses anemis;	25	
c. et il **getent** les mains de toutes pars,		
d. si le **prendent**,		
e. si le **dessaisisent** de l'escu et de le lance,		
f. si l'en **mannent** tot estrousement pris,		
et aloient ja porparlant	30	(restr. clause)
de quel mort il feroient morir.		
Et quant Aucassins l'*entendi*:		
g. "Ha! Dix," **fait** il, "douce creature!		
sont çou mi anemi mortel . . ."		
Li vallés *fu* grans et fors,	35	ORIENTATION
et li cevax [so quoi il sist] *fu* remuans;		

h. et il *mist* le main a l'espee,		COMPLICATING
i. si **comence** a ferir		ACTION
a destre et a senestre		
j. et **caupe** hiaumes et naseus	40	(coordinated
et puins et bras		clauses)
k. et **fait** un caple entor lui,		
[autresi con li senglers		[EMBEDDED
quant li cient l'ASALENT en le forest,]		EVALUATION]
l. et qu'il lor **abat** dis cevaliers	45	(coordinated
m. et **navre** set		clauses)
n. et qu'il **se jete**		
tot estroseement de le prese		
o. et qu'il **s'en revient** les galopiax ariere,		
s'espee en sa main.	50	
Li quens Bougars de Valence *oi dire*		ORIENTATION
c'on penderoit Aucassin son anemi,		
si venoit cele part;		
et Aucassins ne le *mescoisi* mie:		
p. il *tint* l'espee en la main,	55	COMPLICATING
q. se le **fiert** par mi le hiaume		ACTION
r. si qu'i li **enbare** el cief.		
Il *fu* si estonés		
s. qu'il *caï* a terre;		
t. et Aucassins **tent** le main,	60	
u. si le **prent**		
v. et l'en **mainne** pris		
par le nasel del hiame		
w. et le **rent** a son pere.		
x. "Pere," **fait** Aucassins,	65	
"ves ci vostre anemi		
qui tant vous agerroié		
et mal fait:		
vint ans ja dure ceste guerre;		
onques ne pot iestre acievee par home." . . .	70	

[In the remainder of the laisse the action is presented largely through direct discourse, introduced consistently by **fait**] . . .

y. "Enondu!" **fait** il		
"je vous afie quanque il vous plaist."		
z. Il li **afie**;		RESOLUTION

aa. et Aucassins le **fait** monter sur un ceval,		
bb. et il **monte** sur un autre,	75	
cc. si le *conduist*		
tant qu'il *fu* a sauveté.		

Text 1: Prose laisse from Aucassin et Nicolette *(ed. Mario Roques)*

Aucassin *was* on his horse, fully armed,
as you have now heard.
God! How [well] his shield *sat* on his neck
  and his helmet on his head
  and his sword-belt on his left hip.
And the lad *was* big and strong,
  handsome and comely, with fine features,
and the horse he *sat* on
  [*was*] swift and spirited.
And the boy had led him
  right through the gate.
Now DON'T GO IMAGINING
he *was* thinking about cattle
  or cows, nor about catching goats,
nor that he *attacked* any knights
  nor others (*attacked*) him.
Perish the thought!
It never *occurred* to him.
Rather his thoughts *were* so much
  with his sweet friend Nicolette
that he *forgot* all about the reins
and everything he *had* to do.

And the horse, who had felt the spurs,
a. *carried* him into the fray.
b. He **throws** himself amidst his enemies,
c. And their hands **are** on him from all sides,
d. they **grab** him,
e. **divest** him of his shield and his lance,
f. **lead** him away, securely captured.
  discussing as they were going along
    how they would kill him.
  And when Aucassin *heard* this,
g. "Oh God!," he **goes** "my sweet one,
    are these my mortal enemies . . . ?"
  The lad *was* big and strong,
  and the horse he *sat* on *was* spirited;
h. And he *placed* his hand on his sword,
i. he **starts** to attack
    left and right,
j. and **slashes** helmets and nose guards,
    wrists and arms,
k. and **wreaks** slaughter all around him,
    just like a wild boar
      when hounds ATTACK it in the forest.

l. And he **slays** ten of their knights,

m. and **wounds** seven,

n. and **throws** himself
   headlong into the fray

o. and then **comes** galloping back,
   sword in hand.
   Count Bougar of Valence *heard*
   that they would hang his enemy Aucassin
   if he came that way.
   and Aucassin *did not fail to spot* him:

p. He *took* his sword in hand,

q. **strikes** through the helmet,

r. **bashes** him in the head.
   He [Bougar] *was* so stunned

s. that he *fell* to the ground.

t. And Aucassin **takes** his hand,
   holds it,

v. and **leads** him off
   by the nose-piece of his helmet,

w. and **surrenders** him to his [A's] father.

x. "Father," **goes** Aucassin,
   "here is your enemy
   who has waged war against you for so long
   and done so much evil:
   this war has been going on for 20 years;
   never could it be ended
   by any man." . . .

y. "In God's name," he **goes**,
   "I promise you anything you like."

z. He **gives** him his word.

aa. and Aucassin **puts** him on a horse,

bb. and he **mounts** another,

cc. he *led* him away

dd. until he *reached* safety.

Text 2: Villehardouin. La Conquête de Constantinople, §§ *155–61.*
Beginning of thirteenth century.

(155)	Li termes *vint* si com *devisez* fu;	1 ORIENTATION
	et li chevalier *furent* es uissiers tuit, avec lor destriers,	
	et *furent* tuit armé,	
	les helmes *laciez* et li cheval *covert* et ensellé;	

	et les autres genz qui n'avoient mie si 5
	    grant mestier en bataille *furent* es
	    granz nés tuit;	

et les galees *furent armees* et *atornees*
totes.

(156)   Et li matins *fu* biels, aprés le solei un poi
levant.

Et l'emperieres Alexis les attendoit a
granz batailles et a granz corroiz de
l'autre part.   10

a. Et on **sone***ª les bozines,   COMPLICATING

et chascune galie *fu* a un uissier *liee* por   ACTION
passer oltre plus delivreement.

Et il ne **demandent*** mie chascuns qui   EVALUATION
doit aler devant;ᵇ

b. mais qui ançois **puet** ançois **arive**.   15

c. Et li chevalier *issirent* des uissiers,

d. et **saillent*** en la mer trosque a la çain-
ture,

[tuit armé, les laciez et les glaives es   [EMBEDDED
mains;   ORIENTATION]

et li bon archier, et li bon serjant, et li
bon arbalestrier,

chascune conpagnie ou endroit ele   20
ariva.

(157)   Et li Greu *firent* mult grant semblant del
retenir.]

Et quant ce *vint* as lances baissier,

e. et li Greu lor **tornent** le dos,

f. si **s'en vont** fuiant

g. et lor **laissent*** le rivage.   25

Et SACHIEZ que onques plus orgueille-   EVALUATION
usement nuls pors ne *fu* pris.

h. Adonc **conmencent*** li marinier a ovrir   COMPLICATING
les portes des uissiers et a giter les   ACTION
pons fors;

i. et on **comence*** les chevax a traire;   30

j. et li chevalier **conmencent** a monter sor
lor chevaus,

k. et les batailles **se conmencent** a rengier
[si com il devoient.]   [EMBEDDED

(158)   l. Li cuens Baudoins de Flandres et de Hen-   EVALUATION]
naut **chevauche***,

[qui l'avan garde faisoit,]   35 [EMBEDDED

a. Starred present-tense forms (*) are NPs which appear as preterits in one or
more of the (presumably later) MSS from Group II. Cf. n. 48.

b. Inasmuch as many negative predications report the absence of an event
(an event that might have, but did not take place), it can be argued that they do
not contitute proper "narrative clauses." They are nonetheless clearly evaluative, and therefore, not surprisingly, contain NPs.

	et les autres batailles aprés chascune	ORIENTATION]
	[si cum eles chevauchier devoient.]	[EMBEDDED
m.	Et *alerent* trosque la ou l'emperere Alex-	EVALUATION]
	is avoit esté logiez.	
	[Et il s'en fu tornez vers Costantinople,	[EMBEDDED
	et *laissa* tenduz trés et paveillons.] 40	ORIENTATION]
n.	Et la *gaignerent* assez nostre gent.	

(159)	De nostres barons *fu* tels li conseils	ORIENTATION
	que il se hebergeroient sor la port devant	
	la tor de Galathas,	
	ou la caiene fermoit qui movoit de Cos-	
	tantinoble;	
	Et SACHIEZ de voir que par cele chaiene 45	
	convenoit entrer qui al port de Cos-	
	tantinople voloit entrer;	
	et bien *virent* nostre baron,	
	se il ne prenoient cele tor et rompoient	
	cele chaiene,	
	que il estoient mort et malbailli.	

o.	Eisi *se hebergierent* la nuit 50	COMPLICATING
	[devant la tor et en la juerie,	ACTION
	que l'en APELLE l'Estanor,	[EMBEDDED
	ou il avoit mult bone ville et mult riche.]	ORIENTATION]
(160) p.	Bien *se fissent* la nuit eschaugaitier;	
	et l'endemain, quant *fu* hore de tierce, 55	
q.	si *firent* une assaillie cil de la tor de	
	Galathas et cil qui de Costantinople	
	lor venoient aïdier en barges.	
r.	Et nostre gent **corent*** as armes.	
s.	La *asembla* Jaches d'Avesnes, et la soe	
	maisnie, a pié; 60	
	[Et SACHIEZ que il *fu* mult *chargiez*]	EVALUATIVE
t.	et *fu feruz* par mi le vis d'un glaive et en	ORIENTATION
	aventure de mort.	
	Et un sien chevaliers *fu montez* a cheval,	COMPLICATING
	[qui avoit nom Nicholes de Janlain,] 65	ACTION
u.	et *secorut* mult bien son seignor,	
	[et le *fist* mult bien,	[EMBEDDED
	si que il en *ot* grant pris.]	EVALUATION]
(161) v.	Et li criz *fu levez* en l'ost;	
w.	et nostre gent **vienent*** de totes pars, 70	
x.	et les *mistrent* enz mult laidement,	
	si que assez i *ot* de mors et de pris.	RESOLUTION
	Si que de tels i *ot* qui ne *guenchirent* mie	
	a la tor,	

y. ainz *alerent* as barges dunt il erent venu;
    et la en *rot* assez de noiez,   75
    et alquant en *eschaperent.*
    Et cels qui *guenchirent* a la tor,
z. cil de l'ost les *tindrent* si prés
    que il ne *porent* la porte fermer.
    Enqui *refu* granz li estors a la porte,   80
aa. et la lor *tolirent* par force,
bb. et les *pristrent* laienz:
    la en i *ot* assez de morz et de pris.

(162)   Einsi *fu* li chastiaus de Galathas *pris*   ABSTRACT
         et li porz *gaignez* de Costantinoble par 85
             force.
         . . . .

Text 2: Villehardouin, The Conquest of Constantinople

(155)   The time (for departure) *arrived* as *had been determined.*   1
         and the knights *were* (assembled) in the transport ships
             with their steeds
         and they *were* all *armed.*
         their helmets *fastened* and their horses *saddled* and
             equipped;
         and the other people, of lesser utility in battle, *were* all in   5
             the large vessels.
         and the galleys *were* fully *armed* and *decked out.*
(156)   And the morning *was* beautiful, just after sunrise.
         And the emperor Alexis was awaiting them on the other   10
             side with many batallions and much equipment.
    a. And the trumpets **sound***ᵃ
         and each galley *was tied* to a transport ship in order to
             make the crossing more easily.
         No one **asks*** who is to go first.ᵇ   15
    b. whoever **can, gets there** first.
    c. And the knights *disembarked* from the transport ships,
    d. and **jump*** right into the sea up to their waists
         [fully armed, helmets fastened, swords in hand;
             and the good archers, and the good officers, and the
                 good crossbowmen,
             each company (disembarked) at the place where it *ar-*
                 rived.   20
(157)   And the Greeks *put up* a great show of resisting.]
         And when it *came time* to lower the lances,
    e. the Greeks **turn** their backs on them,
    f. and **go take** flight.

g. and **leave** the shore to them.   25
And KNOW that never *was* a harbor *conquered* with great-
er pride.
h. Then the sailors **begin** to open the doors of the transport
ships and to thrown down the ramps.
i. and they **start** to bring out the horses.   30
j. and the knights **begin** to mount their horses,
k. and the batallions **begin** to form
[according to plan.]

(158)   l. Count Baldwin of Flanders and Hainaut **rides forth**,
[(the one) who was leading the vanguard,]   35
and the other batallions each in turn.
[as they were instructed.]
m. And they *proceeded* to where the emperor Alexis had
been camping,
[And he had gone back to Constantinople,
and *left* his tents and pavillions in place.]   40
And there our men *collected* a great deal of booty.

(159)   The decision of our nobles *was*
that they would set up camp at the harbor in front of the
tower of Galatha,
where the channel ended, which started at Constantinople;
And KNOW in truth that whoever wished to enter the har-   45
bor of Constantinople had to do so via this channel;
And our nobles *saw* clearly
that if they did not take the tower and block the channel,
then they were as good as dead.
o. Thus they *set up camp* for the night   50
[in front of the tower and in the Jewish quarter,
which IS CALLED Estanor,
where there was an important and wealthy town.]

(160)   p. They *kept* careful *watch* that night;
and the next morning, when the hour of tierce *was* at   55
hand,
q. those from Galatha tower along with those from Constantinople who were coming to help them in barges
made an attack.
r. And our men **run** to take arms.
s. There Jacques d'Avesnes and his men *fought* on foot;   60
[And KNOW that he *was* sorely *pressed*]
t. and *was struck* in the face with a lance and in danger of
dying.
and one of his knights was *mounted* on his horse
[(one) named Nicolas de Jainlain]   65

u. and *came* swiftly *to the aid* of his lord.
[And he *performed* so well
that he *received* great praise [for his service.]

(161)   v. And the cry *went up* among the troops;
    w. and our men **come*** running from all sides,   70
    x. and they *did them in* so thoroughly
       that a great number *were* captured and killed.
       And there were those who *did not go for* the tower
    y. but rather *went for* the barges from which they had come,
       a considerable number *were* drowned,   75
       and some *escaped.*
       And those who *went for* the tower,
    z. our men *held* them so tenaciously
       that they *could* not close the gate.
       There at the gate the battle still *raged,*   80
    aa. and they *took* it (the gate) from them by force,
    bb. and *locked* them *up* inside:
        there *were* many prisoners and casualties.

(162)   Thus *was* the tower of Galatha *taken*
         and the harbor of Constantinople *conquered* by force.   85

Text 3: Conversational Performed Story (from Weinrich 1973: 303f.)

Alors, c'était un soir de congé.   1   ORIENTATION
Deux cheftaines étaient de congé,
alors on avait décidé d'aller aux Sables-
    d'Olonne
et alors on était parti en car.
Et même dans le car on s'était amusé   5
parce qu'on préparait une . . .
on préparait une espèce de veillée,
la fête du directeur était le lendemain, je
    CROIS.
On avait fait une chanson avec des paroles
    adaptées,
on s'était bien amusé.   10
Alors donc on était allé passer la journée
    là-bas,
puis le soir on avait . . . on avait manqué
    le car, oui.
Le car devait partir vers cinq heures,
on s'était pas arrangé pour y être à temps,
on avait manqué le car.   15

a. Alors on **se dit**:   COMPLICATING
   "Il faut absolument rentrer ce soir à la   ACTION
   colonie."

[Evidemment on aurait pu . . .
on aurait pu rester à la colonie de garçons
qui était aux Sables-d'Olonne,   20
mais enfin il fallait rentrer à la colonie,
    quoi.]

                                           [EMBEDDED
                                           ORIENTATION]

b. Alors on *a décidé* de faire du stop.   COMPLICATING
c. On **part** sur la route qui . . .   ACTION
   [qui allait vers la Faute, quoi,]   [EMBEDDED
d. et puis on **essaie** d'arrêter des voitures.   25   ORIENTATION]

   Mais c'EST pas ça: ORIENTATION

   Tantôt elles étaient pleines,
   tantôt c'étaient rien que des messieurs,

                                          COMPLICATING
   alors on n'osait pas trop.   ACTION
   Ou bien alors . . . ou bien c'était alors . . .   30 (restricted clauses)
   ils s'arrêtaient tout de suite,
   [mais ils n'allaient pas à la Faute.]   [EMBEDDED
                                            ORIENTATION]

e. On *a fait* un grand bout à pied,
   on n'arrivait pas à trouver quelqu'un.

   Et puis on était en train de se demander   35   ORIENTATION
     si on continuerait ou non,
   parce qu'on avait déjà fait un bon bout.

f. "Mais si on trouve rien,   COMPLICATING
   il vaut autant rester aux Sables-d'Olonne."   ACTION

g. Enfin, on *s'est obstiné* quand même.   40

   Et puis on avait arrêté une petite fourgon-   ORIENTATION
     nette.

h. Elle **s'arrête,**   COMPLICATING
i. Un monsieur **descend** et nous dit: ACTION
   "Bien! montez derrière."

   Y avait sa femme et puis un tout petit   45   ORIENTATION
     bébé.

j. Alors il nous *a fait* monter derrière;   COMPLICATING
k. il nous *a emmenées* jusqu'à . . .   ACTION
   C'était à peine la moitié du chemin.
l. Mais on *s'est dit:*
   "C'est que . . . c'est pas tout!   50

Mais il faut trouver quelque chose pour
      continuer,"
[parce que c'était en pleine nature.   [EMBEDDED
Y avait absolument rien.]   ORIENTATION]

Alors à la (?),
m. on **se met** à nouveau au croisement des   55
      chemins,
[parce que là y avait deux . . .   [EMBEDDED
deux routes possibles,   ORIENTATION]
une qui allait sur la Faute
et puis une qui allait . . .
je ne SAIS plus, sur une autre direction.]   60
n. Alors on *s'est mis* sur la route de la Faute,
   et puis on attendait.   (restricted clause)

Puis C'EST que là, alors,   ORIENTATION
c'était un petit chemin,
c'était vraiment un petit chemin.   65
La route EST à peine . . .
elle EST . . .
mais elle EST pas très fréquentée.

                                                       COMPLICATING
Alors on commençait à désespérer,   ACTION
                                                       (restricted clause)
o. on **arrête**, on *a arrêté* plusieurs voitures 70
   qui s'arrêtaient toutes . . .   (restricted clause)
      presque toutes tout de suite,
   ou qui tournaient ou alors . . .
p. Enfin y en a une qui s'arrête.

Elle était pleine, mais pleine.   75   ORIENTATION

q. Et puis on . . . Elle **s'arrête**.   COMPLICATING
r. Puis ils nous *ont fait* monter derrière.   ACTION

On avait juste une toute petite place,   ORIENTATION
et on était deux, oui.
Les deux dames avaient déjà trois ou   80
      quatre gosses.
Y avait . . .
ils étaient étendus dans des espèces de lits.
C'était une fourgonnette aussi.
Et puis . . . y avait trois dames,
et puis un . . . un jeune homme;   85
et puis devant y avait deux messieurs:
c'était les maris des dames, je PENSE.

s. Alors on *s'est mis* dans un coin		COMPLICATING ACTION
[pour ne pas tenir trop de place,		[EMBEDDED
parce qu'elles nous faisaient un peu des sales yeux!]	90	ORIENTATION]
Et puis au bout d'un moment alors . . .		
[et elles avaient pas l'air contentes du tout . . .]		[EMBEDDED ORIENTATION]
t. on *a commencé à* lier conversation un peu,		[EMBEDDED
[parce que c'était pas drôle		
de se regarder comme ça.]	95	ORIENTATION]
u. Alors on leur *a parlé* un peu.		
v. Alors **il y** en **a** une qui me **dit**:		
"Je ne vois vraiment pas pourquoi		
mon mari s'est arrêté.		
Eh bien oui. D'habitude, vous savez . . .	100	
Vous avez eu beaucoup de chance qu'il vous prenne."		
C'était une chance parce qu'autrement! . . .		EVALUATION
Et ils habitaient juste à côté de la colonie, ils étaient en vacances à la Faute.		ORIENTATION
w. Alors on *est arrivé* en même temps que le car,	105	RESOLUTION
[c'EST bien simple,		[EMBEDDED
puisque y avait plusieurs équipes		ORIENTATION]
qui étaient venues nous attendre au car,]		
x. on les *a retrouvées* là-bas en même temps que le car.		RESOLUTION (repeated)
C'était une chance parce que vraiment, y avait pas beaucoup d'autos qui passaient pour aller à la Faute.	110	EVALUATION
[Y avait bien dans l'autre direction parce qu'il y A des villes plus importantes dans l'autre côte.]	115	[EMBEDDED ORIENTATION]
Tandis que vers la Faute, y avait pas grand-chose.		

Text 3: Conversational Performed Story (from Weinrich 1973: 303f.)

So, it was a free night.
Two counsellors were away,

so we had decided to go to the Sables d'Olonne,
and so we had taken off on the bus.
And even on the bus we had had a good time   5
because we were planning a . . .
we were planning a kind of get together,
the director's party was the next day, I THINK.
We had made up a song and adapted the words,
we had really had a good time.   10
So we had gone to spend the day there,
then in the evening we had . . . we had missed the bus.
The bus was supposed to leave around five o'clock,
we hadn't made sure we would be there on time,
(and) we had missed the bus.   15

a. So we **say to ourselves**:
    "We absolutely have to get back to camp tonight."
    [Obviously, we could have . . .
    we could have stayed at the boys' camp
    which was at the Sables d'Olonne   20
    but we really did have to get back to (our) camp, you know.]

b. So we decided to hitchhike.
c. We **set out** on the road that . . .
    [that was going to La Faute, you know,]
d. and then we **try** to stop some cars.   25

    But that's not the thing:

    Either they were all full,
    or else there were only men,

    so we weren't trying all that hard.
    Or else . . . uh . . . or else . . . they would. . . .   30
    they would stop right away,
    [but they weren't going to La Faute.]

e. (So) we *walked* a good bit,
    (but) we didn't manage to find anyone.

    And so we were beginning to wonder   35
        whether we should go on or not,
    'cause we had already walked quite a bit.

f. "But if we don't find anything,
        we might as well stay at the Sables d'Olonne."
g. OK, we *kept on going* anyway.   40
    And then we had stopped this little van.

h. It **stops**,
i. This man **gets out** and **says** to us:
   "Alright, get in in back."

There was his wife and a little tiny baby.   45

j. So he *had* us get in the back seat;
k. he *took* us as far as . . .
   It was barely half way.
l. But we *said to ourselves*:
      "But . . . but, that's not the whole way!   50
      We've got to find something for the rest of the way,"
   ['cause it was out in the middle of nowhere.
   There was absolutely nothing there.]

So when we got to (?)
m. we **go stand** at the crossroad again   55
   ['cause there, there were two . . .
   two possible roads,
   one that went to La Faute
   and then one that went to . . .
   I DON'T KNOW, somewhere else.]   60
n. So we *started off* on the road that went to La Faute,
   and we were waiting.

So IT's there that, uh,
it was a pretty small road,
(I mean,) it was really a small road.   65
The road *is* hardly . . .
it's . . .
but hardly anybody TRAVELS on it.

So we were starting to give up,

o. we **stop**, we *stopped* a few cars   70
   which would all stop . . .
      almost all of them right away,
   or would turn, or else . . .
p. Finally, **there's** this one that **stops**.

It was full, I mean really full.   75

q. And so we . . . it **stops**.
r. So they *had* us *get in* in back.

There was hardly any room,
and there were two of us, you know.

The two women had three or four kids.   80
There was . . .
they were stretched out on these, like, beds.
It was a van too.
And then . . . there were these three women,
and then a . . . a young guy;   85
and then in front there were two men:
they were the husbands of the women, I THINK.

s. So we *squeezed into* a corner

    [so as not to take up too much room,
    'cause the women were already giving us kinda dirty looks!]   90
    And so after that . . .
    [and they didn't look very happy (about it) at all . . .]

t. we *started to* make conversation,
    ['cause it was not very much fun to sit there
        looking at each other like that.]   95
u. So we *talked* to them a little.
v. Then the one of them **says** to me:
    "I really don't see why
        my husband stopped (for you).
        I mean it. Usually, you know . . .   100
        You were really very lucky that he picked you up."

We were lucky because otherwise . . .

And they lived right near the camp,
they were on vacation at La Faute.

w. So we *got there* the same time as the bus,   105
    [it's just like that,
    since there were several groups
        that had come to meet us at the bus,]
x. we *met* THEM there
        at the same time as the bus.

It was really luck, 'cause   110
there weren't very many cars going by
    that were going to La Faute.
[There were lots of them going the other way
'cause there ARE bigger towns
    along the other shore.]   115
Whereas toward La Faute, there wasn't really very much.

Text 4: Conversational Performed Story (from Schiffrin 1981: 47f.)

Oh it was so crazy	1	ABSTRACT
I remember this.		
Maybe I shouldn't say it now.		
It was really a weird thing.		
We were at camp	5	ORIENTATION
and we *did* this crazy thing.		
We were all going out for lunch		
it was our birthdays		
and we were C.I.T.'s		
so we were allowed to.	10	

a.	We *borrowed* someone's car		COMPLICATING ACTION
b.	And we *got* blown out.		
c.	And w— so, the car *stalled*		
d.	but we *didn't ca*— we couldn't call		
	[because we were supposed t' be out t' lunch	15	[EMBEDDED ORIENTATION]
	and why were we here?		
	Cause we had moved . . . off the road t' party.		
	So we were in this car		
	in this— an' we were in Allentown		
	it's real dinky	20	
	an' it's like real hick town off o' Allentown.		
	right around there in this factory.]		
e.	We just *pulled* into this lot		
	[it was just in this lot]		[EMBEDDED ORIENTATION]
f.	and all of a sudden the buzzer **sounds**	25	
g.	and all these guys hh **come** hh out		
h.	and we *didn't know* what t' do		
	[cause we were stuck.]		[EMBEDDED ORIENTATION]
i.	So we asked some guy t' come over and help us.		
j.	So he **opens** the car	30	
k.	and everyone **gets** out except me and my girlfriend.		
	[We were in the front		[EMBEDDED ORIENTATION]
	and just didn't feel like getting out]		

l. And all of a sudden all these sparks **start** t'
    fly

m. So the girl **says**,   35
    "Look, do you know what you're doing?
    Because y' know um . . . this is not my
      car
    an' if you don't know what you're doing,
    just don't do anything."

n. And he **says**,   40
    "Yeh, I have t' do it from inside."

o. And all of a sudden he gets in the car.

p. sits down,

q. and **starts** t' turn on the motor.

We thought he was taking off with us   45   EVALUATION
We really thought—h—he was—
[he was like real—with all tatoos and   [EMBEDDED
    smelled—]   ORIENTATION]

an' we thought that was it! hhh

r. But he *got out* after a while.   RESOLUTION

I really thought I was gonna die   50   EVALUATION
or be taken someplace far away.
It was so crazy,
because we couldn't call anybody.
It was really funny.

REFERENCES

I. Texts Cited

Aucassin et Nicolette. Chantefable du XIIIe siècle. Ed. Mario Roques. 2d rev. ed. CFMA. Paris: Champion, 1973.

Villehardouin, *La Conquête de Constantinople.* Ed. Edmond Faral. 2 vols. 2d ed. Paris: Les Belles Lettres, 1961.

Robert de Clari, *La Conquête de Constantinople.* Ed. Philippe Lauer. CFMA. Paris: Champion, 1924.

Ramon Vidal de Besalu, "Castia-gilos," text from Karl Appel, *Provenzalische Chrestomathie.* Leipzig, 1907.

La Chanson de Roland. Ed. F. Whitehead. Oxford: Blackwell, 1970.

The Song of Roland. Trans. Frederick Goldin. New York: Noonan, 1978.

La Passion des jongleurs. Ed. Anne A. Perry. Paris: Beauchesne, 1981.

La Vie de Saint Alexis. Ed. C. Storey. Oxford: Blackwell, 1981.

Flamenca, in *Les Troubadours.* Ed. René Nelli & René Lavaud. Bruges: Desclée de Brouwer, 1960.

II. Studies Consulted

Antoine, G. 1959. *La Coordination en français.* 2 vols. Paris: D'Artrey.

Banfield. Ann. 1982. *Unspeakable Sentences.* Boston: Routledge & Kegan Paul.

Bauman, Richard, ed. 1977. *Verbal Art as Performance.* Rowley, Mass.: Newbury House. (1st printed 1978).

Baüml, Franz. 1977. "The Unmaking of the Hero: Some Critical Implications of the Transition from Oral to Written Epic." In *The Epic in Medieval Society, Aesthetic and Moral Values.* Ed. H. Scholler. Tübingen: n.d. 86–99.

———. 1980. "Varieties and Consequences of Medieval Literacy and Illiteracy." *Speculum* 55: 237–65.

Beck, Jonathan. Forthcoming. "Towards a Theory of Functional Multiplicity of Tense-Aspect Forms in Old French Narrative."

Beer, Jeanette M. A. 1968. *Villehardouin, Epic Historian.* Geneva: Droz.

———. 1981. *Narrative Conventions of Truth in the Middle Ages.* Geneva: Droz.

Bellos, David M. 1978. "The Narrative Absolute Tense." *Language and Style,* 11: 231–37.

Benveniste, Emile. 1959. "Les Relations de temps dans le verbe français." *Bulletin de la Société Linguistique de Paris* 54: 237–50. Repr. in E. B. *Problèmes de linguistique générale.* 1: 69–82 (Paris: Gallimard, 1966).

Blanc, Michel H. A. 1961. "The Use of Narrative Tenses in Thirteenth-Century French Prose." Diss., Univ. of London.

———. 1964. "Time and Tense in Old French Narrative." *Archivum Linguisticum* 16: 2: 96–124.

———. 1965. "Le présent épique dans la *Chanson de Roland.*" *Actes du Xe Congrès International de Linguistique et Philologie Romane* (Strasbourg, 1962). Paris: Klincksieck. 565–78.

Bright, William. 1982. "Poetic Structures in Oral Narrative." In Tannen 1982b. 171–84.

Buffin, J. M. 1925. *Remarques sur le moyens d'expression de la durée et du temps en français.* Paris: PUF.

Bull, William E. 1960. *Time, Tense, and the Verb.* Berkeley & Los Angeles: Univ. of California Press.

Cerquiglini, Bernard. 1981. *La Parole médiévale.* Paris: Editions de Minuit.

Dembowski, Peter F. 1963. *La Chronique de Robert de Clari. Etude de la langue et du style.* Univ. of Toronto Romance Series, 6. Toronto: Univ. of Toronto Press.

Emery, Annie Crosby. 1897. *The Historical Present in Early Latin.* Ellsworth, ME: Hancock.

Faye, Paul-Louis, 1933. "L'Equivalence passé défini-imparfait en ancien français." *The University of Colorado Studies* 20:4: 267–308.

Fleischman, Suzanne. 1982a. *The Future in Thought and Language. Diachronic Evidence from Romance.* Cambridge Studies in Linguistics, 36. Cambridge: Cambridge UP.

———. 1982b. "The Past and the Future: Are They 'Coming' or 'Going'?" *Proceedings of the 8th Annual Meeting of the Berkeley Linguistic Society.* 322–34.

———. 1983a. "From Pragmatics to Grammar: Diachronic Reflexions on the Development of Complex Pasts and Futures in Romance." *Lingua* 60:183–214.

———. 1983b. "On the Representation of History and Fiction in the Middle Ages." *History and Theory* 22:3: 278–310.

———. 1986. "Discourse Functions of Tense-Aspect Oppositions in Narrative: Towards a Theory of Grounding." To appear in *Linguistics* 24:1.

Fotitch, Tatiana. 1950. *The Narrative Tenses in Chrétien de Troyes. A Study in Syntax and Stylistics.* CUASRLL, 38. Washington, D.C.

Foulet, Lucien. 1920. "La Disparition du prétérit." *Romania* 46: 271–313.

———. 1919. *Petite syntaxe de l'ancien français.* 3d ed. repr. 1974 (1st ed. 1928). Paris: Champion.

Grunmann, Minette. "Narrative Voice in the Old French Epic and Romance, Exemplified by *La Chanson de Roland, Galeran de Bretagne,* and *Guillaume de Dole.*" *Romance Philology* 29:2: 201–209.

Grunmann-Gaudet, Minette. 1980. "The Representation of Time in the *Chanson de Roland.*" In *The Nature of Medieval Narrative.* Ed. M. G. G. & Robin F. Jones. Lexington, Ky.: French Forum. 77–98.

Hamburger, Käte. 1973. *The Logic of Literature.* Trans. Marilyn Rose. 2d rev. ed. Bloomington & London: Indiana UP.

Harris, Martin B. 1982. "The 'Past Simple' and the 'Present Perfect' in Romance." In *Studies in the Romance Verb.* Ed. M. B. H. and Nigel Vincent. London: Croom Helm. 42–70.

Hatcher, Anna Granville. 1942. "Tense-Usage in the *Roland.*" *Studies in Philology* 39: 597–624.

Hopper, Paul J. 1979a. "Aspect and Foregrounding in Discourse." *Discourse and Syntax.* Ed. Talmy Givón. *Syntax and Semantics,* 12. New York: Academic Press. 213–41.

———. 1979b. "Some Observations on the Typology of Focus and Aspect in Narrative Language." *Studies in Language* 3: 1: 37–64.

Hymes, Dell 1974. "Breakthrough into Performance." In *Folklore, Performance, and Communication.* Ed. D. Ben Amos & K. Goldstein. The Hague: Mouton.

Jakobson, Roman. 1957. *Shifters, Verbal Categories and the Russian Verb.* Cambridge, Mass.: Harvard Univ. Russian Language Project.

Jauss, Hans Robert. "Chanson de geste et roman courtois." In *Chanson de geste und höfischer Roman.* Heidelberger Kolloquium. Heidelberg. 61–77.

Kiparsky, Paul. 1968. "Tense and Mood in Indo-European Syntax." *Foundations of Language* 4: 30–57.

Kuen, H. 1934. Rev. of W. von Wartburg (1934). *Zeitschrift fur französische Sprache und Literatur* 58: 489–507.

Labov, William. 1972. "The Transformation of Experience in Narrative Syntax." In *Language in the Inner City.* Philadelphia: Univ. of Pennsylvania Press. 354–96.

Labov, William & Joshua Waletzky. 1969. "Narrative Analysis: Oral Versions of Personal Experience." In *Essays on the Verbal and Visual Arts.* Proceedings of the 1966 Annual Spring Meeting of the American Ethnological Society. Ed. June Helm (McNeish). Seattle: Univ. of Washington Press. 12–44.

Ochs, Elinor. 1979. "Planned and Unplanned Discourse." *Discourse and Syntax.* Ed. Talmy Givón. *Syntax and Semantics,* 12. New York: Academic Press. 51–80.

Ollier, Marie Louise. 1978. "Le Présent du récit: temporalité et roman en vers." *Langue Française* 40: 99–112.

Olson, David R. 1977. "From Utterance to Text: The Bias of Language in Speech and Writing." *Harvard Educational Review* 47: 257–81.

Ong, Walter J., S. J. 1981. "Oral Remembering and Narrative Structure." In *Analyzing Discourse: Text and Talk.* Ed. Deborah Tannen. GURT 1981. Washington, D.C.: Georgetown UP. 12–24.

Östmann, Jan-Ola. 1981. *'You Know': A Discourse-Functional Study.* Amsterdam: Benjamins.

Paden, William D., Jr. 1977. "L'Emploi vicaire du présent verbal dans les plus anciens textes narratifs romans." *XIV Congresso internazionale di linguistica e filologia romanze (Napoli, 15–20 aprile 1974).* 4: 545–57. Napoli: Macchiaroli; Amsterdam: Benjamins.

Pickens, Rupert T. 1979. "Historical Consciousness in Old French Narrative." *French Forum* 4: 2 168–84.

Poirion, Daniel. 1978. "Les Paragraphes et le pré-texte de Villehardouin." *Langue Française* 40: 45–59.

Polanyi, Livia. 1982. "Literary Complexity in Everyday Storytelling." In Tannen, ed. 1982b. 155–70.

Ruelle, Pierre. 1976. "Temps grammatical et temps réel dans la *Chanson de Roland.*" *Mélanges de langue et de littérature romanes offerts à Karl Theodor Gossen.* Ed. G. Colón and R. Kopp. 2: 777–92. Berne: Francke; Liège: Marche Romane.

Sandmann, Manfred G. 1953. "Narrative Tenses of the Past in the *Cantar de Mio*

Cid." Studies. . . . Presented to John Orr. Manchester: Manchester UP. 258–81. Repr. (in Fr.) in Sandmann 1973, 123–44.

———. 1957. "Die Tempora der Erzählung im Altfranzösischen." *Vox Romanica* 16: 287–96. Repr. (in French) in Sandmann 1973, 167–74.

———. 1960. "Syntaxe verbale et style épique." *Atti del VIII Congresso Internazionale di Studi Romanzi (1956).* 2: 379–402. Florence. Repr. in Sandmann 1973, 145–65.

———. 1968. Rev. of Stefenelli-Furst (1966) in *Romance Philology* 21: 4: 570–74.

———. 1973. *Expériences et critiques.* Bibl. Française et Romane, série A, 25. Paris: Klincksieck.

Saunders, H. 1969. "The Evolution of French Narrative Tenses." *Forum for Modern Language Studies* 5: 141–61.

Scheub, Harold. 1977. "Body and Image in Oral Narrative Performance." *New Literary History* 8: 3: 345–67.

Schiffrin, Deborah. 1981. "Tense Variation in Narrative." *Language* 57: 45–62.

Schøsler, Lene. 1973. *Les Temps du passé dans 'Aucassin et Nicolette'.* Etudes Romanes de l'Univ. d'Odense. Odense: Odense Universitetsforlag.

Segre, Cesare. 1979 [=1974] "Analysis of Tale, Narrative Logic, and Time." In *Structures and Time.* Trans. John Meddemann (orig. title *Le Strutture e il Tempo*) Chicago: Univ. of Chicago Press. 1–64.

Silva-Corvalán, Carmen. 1983. "Tense and Aspect in Oral Spanish Narrative: Context and Meaning." *Language* 59: 4 760–80.

Stefenelli-Furst, F. 1966. *Die Tempora der Vergangenheit in der Chanson de Geste.* Weiner Romanistische Arbeiten, 5. Wien-Stuttgart: Willhelm Braunmuller.

Sternberg, Meir. 1978. *Expositional Modes and Temporal Ordering in Fiction.* Baltimore: Johns Hopkins UP.

Stewart, Joan Hinde. 1977. "Some Aspects of Verb Usage in *Aucassin et Nicolette.*" *French Review* 50: 429–36.

Stock, Brian. *The Implications of Literacy, Written Language and Models of Interpretation in the Eleventh and Twelfth Centuries.* Princeton: Princeton UP.

Sutherland, D. R. 1939. "On the Use of Tenses in Old and Middle French." In *Mélanges M. K. Pope.* Manchester: Manchester UP.

Tannen, Deborah, ed. 1981. *Analyzing Discourse: Text and Talk.* GURT 1981. Washington, D.C.: Georgetown UP.

———. 1982a. "Oral and Literate Strategies in Spoken and Written Narratives." *Language* 58: 1: 1–21.

———, ed. 1982b. *Spoken and Written Language. Exploring Orality and Literacy.* Norwood, NJ: Ablex.

Uitti, Karl D. 1973. *Story, Myth and Celebration.* Princeton: Princeton UP.

Wartburg, Walther von. 1971 [1st ed. 1937]. *Evolution et structure de la langue française.* 10th ed. Berne: Francke.

Weinrich, Harald. 1973 [=1964] *Le Temps.* Trans. M. Lacoste. Paris: Seuil.

White, Hayden. 1980. "The Value of Narrativity in the Representation of Reality." *Critical Inquiry* 7: 5–27.

Wolfson, Nessa. 1978. "Features of Performed Narrative: the Conversational Historical Present." *Language in Society* 7: 215–37.

———. 1979. "The Conversational Historical Present Alternation." *Language* 55: 1: 168–82.

———. 1982. *The Conversational Historical Present in American English Narrative.* Topics in Sociolinguistics, 1. Dordrecht: Reidel; Cinnamson, NJ: Foris.

Worthington, Martha Garrett. 1966. "The Compound Past Tense in Old French Narrative Poems." *Romance Philology* 19: 397–417.

Zumthor, Paul. 1979. "Pour une poétique de la voix." *Poétique* 40: 514–24.

———. 1983. *Introduction à la poésie orale.* Paris: Seuil.

———. 1984. *La Poésie et la voix dans la civilisation médiévale.* Essais et Conférences, Collège de France. Paris: PUF.

Contributors

R. HOWARD BLOCH is Professor of French at the University of California, Berkeley. He is the author of *Medieval French Literature and Law* (1977) and *Etymologies and Genealogies: A Literary Anthropology of the French Middle Ages* (1983). He has recently completed a study of the Old French *fabliau.*

KEVIN BROWNLEE, Associate Professor of French and Italian at Dartmouth College, specializes in Medieval French and Dante studies. He is the author of *Poetic Identity in Guillaume de Machaut* (1984) and co-editor of *Romance: Generic Transformation from Chrétien de Troyes to Cervantes* (1985). He is currently completing a book on discourse and authority in Jean de Meun.

BERNARD CERQUIGLINI is Professor of Medieval French Language and Literature at the University of Paris VIII. His book *La Parole médiévale* appeared in 1981. He is currently Directeur des écoles au ministère de l'éducation nationale.

SUZANNE FLEISCHMAN is Associate Professor of French at the University of California, Berkeley. She is the author of *Cultural and Linguistic Factors in Word Formation* (1976) and *The Future in Thought and Language: Diachronic Evidence from Romance* (1982).

CYNTHIA HOFFMAN is a graduate student in the French Department at Yale University.

ALEXANDRE LEUPIN is Associate Professor of French at Louisiana State University. His book *Le Graal et la littérature* appeared in 1984. He is currently working on a study of the poetic corpus of Adam de la Halle.

JOHN D. LYONS is Professor of French and Italian at Dartmouth College. He is coeditor of *Mimesis: From Mirror to Method, Augustine to Descartes* (1982) and his most recent book is *The Listening Voice: An Essay on the Rhetoric of Saint-Amant* (1982). He is currently working on a study of exemplarity in French and Italian Renaissance and seventeenth-century literature.

PEGGY McCRACKEN is a graduate student in the French Department at Yale University.

MARGARET MINER is a graduate student in the French Department at Yale University.

STEPHEN G. NICHOLS, Professor of Romance Languages at the University of Pennsylvania, is coeditor of *Mimesis: From Mirror to Method, Augustine to Descartes* (1982). His most recent book, *Romanesque Signs: Early Medieval Narrative and Iconography*, appeared in 1983. He is currently completing a book on visionary discourse in the middle ages.

DAVID PELIZZARI is a graduate student in the English Department at Yale University.

NANCY F. REGALADO is Professor of French at New York University and has published *Poetic Patterns in Rutebeuf: A Study of Noncourtly Poetic Modes of the Thirteenth Century* (1970). She has recently completed a book entitled *Reading Villon's "Testament"*.

BRIAN STOCK is a Fellow of the Pontifical Institute of Mediaeval Studies, Toronto. He is the author of *Myth and Science in the Twelfth Century: A Study of Bernard Silvester* (1972) and *The Implications of Literacy: Written Language and Models of Interpretation in the Eleventh and Twelfth Centuries* (1983).

EUGENE VANCE is a Professor in the Department of Modern Languages and Classics at Emory University, where he teaches medieval French literature and literary theory. His book *Marvelous Signals: Poetics and Sign Theory in the Middle Ages* is due out shortly.

MICHEL ZINK is Professor of Medieval French Literature at the University of Toulouse-Le Mirail. Among his many books are *La Prédication en langue romane avant 1300* (1976), *Roman rose et rose rouge: Le "Roman de la rose ou de Guillaume de Dole"* (1979), and, most recently, *La Subjectivité littéraire. Autour du siècle de Saint Louis* (1985).

The following issues are available through Yale University Press, Customer Service Department, 92A Yale Station, New Haven, CT 06520.

63 The Pedagogical Imperative:
   Teaching as a Literary Genre
   (1982) $12.95
64 Montaigne: Essays in Reading
   (1983) $12.95
65 The Language of Difference:
   Writing in QUEBEC(ois)
   (1983) $12.95
66 The Anxiety of Anticipation
   (1984) $12.95

67 Concepts of Closure
   (1984) $12.95
68 Sartre after Sartre
   (1985) $12.95
69 The Lesson of Paul de Man
   (1985) $12.95
70 Images of Power:
   Medieval History/Discourse/Literature
   (1986) $12.95
71 Forthcoming Issue
   (1986) $12.95

Special subscription rates are available on a calendar year basis (2 issues per year):

Individual subscriptions $22.00
Institutional subscriptions $25.90

ORDER FORM   Yale University Press, 92A Yale Station, New Haven, CT 06520

Please enter my subscription for the calendar year
☐ **1985** (Nos. 68 and 69)   ☐ **1986** (Nos. 70 and 71)

I would like to purchase the following individual issues:

_____

_____

For individual issues, please add postage and handling:
Single issue, United States $1.00
Each additional issue $.50
Connecticut residents please add sales tax of 7½%.

Single issue, foreign countries $1.50
Each additional issue $.75

Payment of $_____ is enclosed (including sales tax if applicable).
Mastercard no. _____
4-digit bank no. _____ Expiration date _____
VISA no. _____ Expiration date _____
Signature _____
SHIP TO: _____
_____
_____

See the next page for ordering issues 1–59 and 61–62. **Yale French Studies** is also available through Xerox University Microfilms, 300 North Zeeb Road, Ann Arbor, MI 48106.

The following issues are still available through the Yale French Studies Office, 315 William L. Harkness Hall, Yale University, New Haven, Conn. 06520.

Add for postage & handling

Single issue, United States $1.00

Single issue, foreign countries $1.50
Each additional issue $.50

Each additional issue $.75

YALE FRENCH STUDIES 315 William L. Harkness Hall, Yale University, New Haven, Connecticut 06520

A check made payable to YFS is enclosed. Please send me the following issue(s):

Issue no.	Title	Price
	Postage & handling	
	Total	

Name _____

Number/Street _____

City _____ State _____ Zip _____

The following issues are now available through Kraus Reprint Company, Route 100, Millwood, N.Y. 10546.

36 37 Structuralism has been reprinted by Doubleday as an Anchor Book.
55/56 Literature and Psychoanalysis has been reprinted by Johns Hopkins University Press, and can be ordered through Customer Service, Johns Hopkins University Press, Baltimore, MD 21218.

The Old French Fabliaux

Charles Muscatine

Distinguished medievalist Charles Muscatine here provides the first general introduction in English to the Old French fabliaux — comic and often bawdy poems which were not only literary predecessors of the humorous narratives of Boccaccio and Chaucer but which also reveal centrally important aspects of medieval culture and sensibility.

"Muscatine conducts his investigation with grace as well as intellectual rigor."
—Roy J. Pearcy $21.50

Pleasures of the Belle Epoque

Entertainment and Festivity in Turn-of-the-Century France
Charles Rearick

An engaging and beautiful tour of the France of Toulouse-Lautrec and Jules Cheret and its "places of pleasure" — the Follies-Bergère, Bastille Day celebrations, bicycle races, early cinema, world fairs — recreating them through words, photographs, and art of the period.

"Lively and original." —John Gross, *The New York Times*   70 b/w + 8 color illus.
$29.95

Confessions of a Concierge

Madame Lucie's History of Twentieth-Century France
Bonnie G. Smith

"A sidewalk-level view of eighty years of French history . . . sometimes familiar, sometimes surprising, and always interesting." —Phoebe-Lou Adams, *The Atlantic Monthly*

"Deeply engaging. . . . It will be hard ever to hear the word 'concierge' without thinking of Madame Lucie." —Christopher Lehmann-Haupt, *The New York Times*
$14.95

Romanesque Signs

Early Medieval Narrative and Iconography
Stephen G. Nichols

A study of eleventh-century narrative and iconography, specifically the Charlemagne canon as the basis for a medieval tradition interweaving art, architecture, literature, theology, and history.

"Intelligent, well researched, rich in insights, and instructive throughout. . . . Nichols has much that is important and new to say about romanesque art."
—Norris J. Lacy, *French Review* $10.95

Rodin's *Thinker* and the Dilemmas of Modern Public Sculpture

Albert Elsen

In this first serious study of Rodin's *Thinker*, Albert Elsen discusses this universally known sculpture as a work of art, tracing the history of its creation, its meanings, and its critical reception. His handsomely illustrated book also includes a lively section of advertisements and caricatures, showing how *The Thinker* has been used and abused for commercial and political ends.   75 illus. $10.95 paper

Yale University Press
Dept. YFS
92A Yale Station
New Haven, CT 06520